New Orleans Dockworkers

SUNY Series in
American Labor History

Robert Asher and
Charles Stephenson, Editors

New Orleans Dockworkers: Race, Labor, and Unionism, 1892–1923

Daniel Rosenberg

State University of New York Press

Published by
State University of New York Press, Albany

© 1988   State University of New York

For information, address State University of New York
Press, State University Plaza, Albany, N.Y., 12246

Library of Congress Cataloging in Publication Data

Rosenberg, Daniel, 1953-
    New Orleans dockworkers.

    (SUNY series in American labor history)
    Bibliography: p.
    Includes index.
    1. Stevedores—Louisiana—New Orleans—History.
2. Trade-unions—Stevedores—Louisiana—New Orleans—
History.   3. Strikes and lockouts—Stevedores—
Louisiana—New Orleans—History.   4. New Orleans (La.)—
Race relations.   I. Title.   II. Series.
HD8039.L82U664   1988   31.7'61387164'0976335   87-10156
ISBN 0-88706-649-6
ISBN 0-88706-650-X (pbk.)

TO NORA

Contents

Acknowledgments

Over the years during which this study has been prepared, I have accumulated debts of gratitude, of which mention here can do only partial justice. I have benefitted in the first place from the advice and guidance of Professors Eric Foner and Michael Wreszin. Able and skilled scholars who furnished honest, helpful criticism throughout, they extended solidarity when technical, practical, and human obstacles appeared along the path. I have had the advantage of perceptive and supportive editors: Robert Asher and Charles Stephenson. And I am particularly beholden to several historians whose counsel was invaluable: Dr. Herbert Aptheker, Dr. Philip S. Foner, Dr. Ronald L. Lewis, and Charles B. Rousseve.

Gracious assistance in research came from many quarters: Gisela Lozada and the staff at Special Collections, Louisiana State University Libraries; the staff of the Wisconsin State Historical Society; the staff of the Rosenberg Memorial Library in Galveston; the staff of the Louisiana Division of the New Orleans Public Library; the staff of the Tamiment Institute at New York University's Bobst Library; the staff of the Amistad Research Center in New Orleans; Rose Lambert of the Louisiana State Museum in New Orleans; the staff of the Louisiana Division at Tulane's Howard-Tilton Library; the staff of the Earl K. Long Library at the University of New Orleans; the staff of the Butler Library at Columbia University; Dr. Charles Nolan of the New Orleans Archidiocese; Father Robert Stahl of Notre Dame Seminary in New Orleans; the staff of the Research Division, New York Public Library; the staff of the Schomburg Center in New York; Dr. Helga Feder of the Library at the City University Graduate Center; and John Vandereedt of the Civil Archives Division at the National Archives.

My parents and brothers gave sustenance and counsel through every page and dimension of this project. My cousin, Joe Diamond, drew the cover illustrations of dockworkers E. S. Swan, Thomas Harrison (from photos in the *New Orleans Daily Picayune*, September 6, 1904), and James E. Porter (from a *Daily Picayune* photo, September 4, 1906). The Mercadel and Bellin families, and the very dear Vita Barsky did much to see this work through. When strange clouds obscured the horizon, I was able to rely on the encouragement of my longtime friend, Dr. Rudy Fichtenbaum. And I have above all drawn strength from my wife Nora, my closest ally: for her love and support, I am deeply grateful.

To all who contributed to this project, who made this book in a sense a joint creation, I again express my gratitude.

Introduction

For the first time in his political life, Martin Behrman, the Mayor of New Orleans, was truly worried. Only days before, he had been instrumental in apparently ending a strike of dockworkers that had shaken the city to its foundations in this month of October 1907. He had counted then on finally compensating for three weeks of little sleep, of agonizing consternation over commerce lost and ruined. His own settlement scheme had been in the spirit of his well-known flexibility and diplomacy: let four employers and four dockworkers constitute a committee to investigate port conditions and make recommendations.

An enlightened big-city boss, the New York-born Behrman was also a confirmed white supremacist. But he was quite familiar with the unusual status of race relations on the docks that had prevailed for nearly ten years — the "half-and-half" concept — so it was not strange for him to have proposed that two of the four workers in the committee be Black. That was how the unions operated now on the levee. Half-and-half had become the standard, and, despite his inner animus, Behrman accepted it as a *fait accompli*.

But the levee's business community — the steamship firms and their agents — had declared negotiations with Blacks impossible. It was anathema. If four *white* workers were named, the investigation could proceed: but the participation of Blacks threatened "to pull down the barriers which bar them from equity in all things with the superior race."

The city could not bear resumption of the strike. Much trade had already been diverted to other ports; the rat-infested wharves stank more than usual from tons of backed-up rotting fruit, sugar, and other cargo. Hundreds of thousands of cotton bales on the levee still awaited shipment. New Orleans was in crisis.

That Thursday afternoon of October 31, Behrman reached a decision. He would ask, insist, that the dockworkers withdraw the two Black nominees. He would present the current emergency in blunt terms. He would convince the unions that "levee peace" now demanded abandoning the half-and-half principle by which their great strike had been conducted and under which dock unionism had been organized for an extended period.

He contacted the unions and drove that night to Screwmen's Hall. Inside, on the second floor, 36 whites and 36 Blacks, the representatives of some 11,000 dock unionists, awaited his arrival. Behrman alighted and greeted the two union

1

men guarding the door: one white, the other Black. He entered the hall and was ushered upstairs by two other sentries, also white and Black.

The Dock and Cotton Council, before which he now appeared, comprised all the organizations of port workers: screwmen, longshoremen, yardmen, teamsters, scalemen. The council had led the general dock strike. Behrman nodded to white screwman James Byrnes, the presiding officer, and to Black cotton yardman C. P. Beck seated next to Byrnes at the front of the hall. Looking around, the mayor saw others that he knew: among the whites, longshoreman Chris Scully, longtime proponent of Black-white cooperation Rufus Ruiz, and screwmen's leader Thomas Harrison, whose recent bitter attacks on commercial interests had horrified Behrman, his fellow leading Democrat. Among the Blacks, ex-slaves James Porter and E. S. Swan were present; so, too, were the Socialist-leaning Alonzo Ellis and Joseph Coats and the militant anti-disfranchisement leader I. G. Wynn. All these men, their unions, and their constituents had lived and breathed half-and-half.

The Dock and Cotton Council had met often during the strike. It now listened to Behrman as to one it had come to know well, and to respect, for the mayor had tended to oppose the open-shop aspirations of employers. Behrman took the stand and explained the situation in detail. He minced no words. Although the strike was over, commerce remained at a virtual standstill. *You* must take the initiative, he told the workmen; *you* must break the impasse by sending a white-only delegation to meet with employers, as the latter would have nothing to do with a white-Black union team.

In any case, he went on, the half-and-half, Black-white setup was a bad idea in general. "This community" opposed Black participation in deliberations of such importance, he told the 72 assembled dockworkers. The unions would "display bad judgement should they insist on colored men being on the committee." Behrman felt that Blacks could surely find "some white men in whose hands they might entrust their case." He spoke for an hour and concluded with a final reminder of "the sentiment of the community on a question of this kind." The mayor left the hall, descending the stairs to the lobby where he awaited the council's vote. Although the day was not especially warm, Behrman was sweating. The white and Black sentries at the door watched him calmly.

Upstairs, council president Byrnes called on Black and white speakers in alternating sequence, as was the custom under half-and-half. One after another repudiated Behrman's appeal. Every white delegate opposed the withdrawal of the Black nominees. The council voted to uphold the originally proposed interracial delegation and sent Chris Scully and Alonzo Ellis downstairs to inform Mayor Behrman.

The Mayor was stunned. Had his efforts been wasted? Didn't labor appreciate the logic of the moment? He argued with Ellis and Scully. Finally, he left the hall. Frustrated, Behrman told the press: "I tried to make these people understand . . . I told them very plainly what the sentiment of this community is as to having colored men figure so prominently in public matters."

But they didn't listen to him.[1]

During the early twentieth century, New Orleans dockworkers turned a deaf ear to this type of appeal on more than one occasion. In fact, Black and white levee workers and their unions seemed unable to grasp certain prevailing assumptions of the period.

Much has been written of the uniqueness of New Orleans. Like its parent colony and state, the city counted French and Spanish traders among its early settlers. "To supply the labor needs of the colony," slavery had been established, but it assumed its own form. In its Spanish-French roots, the history of Crescent City interracial contact offers parallels with experiences of colonial settlement and labor in South America and the Caribbean, and holds significance in the study of comparative systems of slavery. The spreading colonial city seemed to develop in confusion, its European population for decades consisting mainly of men, its slaves increasing through colonial times to a majority by the time of the Louisiana Purchase in 1803. Catholic moral and legal codification, the acceptance of the slave as a human being with a soul, indeed produced a special set of relations in the aforementioned regions and in New Orleans. Indeed, New Orleans contrasted with most areas of the American South. Hence, a recent study of postbellum race relations in Southern cities was not in error in excluding New Orleans from it survey, because the city's "pattern of race relations was likely to be atypical."[2]

But the evidence adduced by scholars of slavery in the Americas cautions against posing too strict a dichotomy between "North European" — British-American — race relations on the one hand and the relations which developed in Iberio-Mediterranean (Spanish, Portuguese, and French) settlements on the other. The colonial and antebellum status quo made heavy demands on Blacks in Louisiana, free and slave. Slave codes, before and after Louisiana entered the United States, restricted slave movement, ownership of goods, opportunities to assemble. They prescribed measures of discipline no more chic than those propounded elsewhere in the South, including the cropping of ears and branding the arms of captured fugitives.

Numerous studies inspire questions about the apparent tendency of slaveholders in the Caribbean and South America, themselves Caucasians often of olive skin, to get along better with Africans and Afro-Americans than did the lighter-hued Northern Europeans, seemingly as a result of the closer physical resemblance or shorter "somatic distance" they perceived between Blacks and themselves. Data indicating persistent problems with slavery, including resistance and disciplinary responses of harsh character, in eighteenth-century French-ruled Martinique, Guadeloupe, and Saint-Domingue inspire recon-sideration of the ameliorative trend of French Catholic slavery, at the very least of the depth of that trend. Likewise, records of frequent brutal treatment of slaves in Brazil belie allegations of Portuguese-Spanish — generically Catholic — respect for the slave's humanity and spirit. Church intervention indeed yielded certain protections and perhaps "better" conditions, but in no wise prevented the evolution over time of white supremacist strictures and concepts in the areas of Iberio-Mediterranean slavery. By the mid-nineteenth century, Cuban white supremacy, for example, was well developed in thought and policy, strengthened no dcubt by those whites seeking annexation by the United States in cooperation with the pro-slavery U. S. filibusterers who made their head-quarters in New Orleans.[3]

Evidence also evokes questions about assumptions that North Europeans as a group — the British — held preconceived (perhaps "somatically" more distant) race perceptions at the seedtime of slavery. Scholars find reason to believe that race relations may not at first have been hostile, that certain groups of North Europeans in the colonial period — indentured servants, for example — may indeed have been slow to accept white supremacist concepts. At the inception, race relations in South Carolina did not exhibit the tensions of the wider "somatic" gap between Africans and English settlers; frontier farmers, writes Peter H. Wood, in effect "shared" with their slaves "a common under-taking as members of an interracial family unit." The expansion and needs of the plantation economy and the increase in white immigration contributed to the deterioration of race relations in the colony.

In Colonial Virginia, miscegenation between slaves and white indentured servants occurred despite the prejudices of upper-class planters accustomed to free access to Black women. Indeed, white wealthy planters sought to instill " an attitude of race superiority" in the poor whites to prevent their cooperating with slaves; servants and slaves nevertheless evolved a whole network of cooperative relationships on their own. A historian detected that newly arrived white servants "must have lacked much of the 'natural race prejudice' that is attributed to the governing aristocrat." Indeed, they "had not learned to hold the attitude toward the Negro that had been developed among the older set-tlers." They were moreover despised by the "master class": "there must have been strong feelings that developed class relations with the Negro."

Lower-class, white-Black cooperation in colonial Virginia — where, as elsewhere in British America, the first bondsmen were white — including complicity in rebellion, notes Edmund Morgan, went far toward inducing a purposeful effort by authorities "to separate dangerous free whites from dangerous slave blacks by a screen of racial contempt," through active propaga-tion of policies and ideas constituting racism. Indeed, Morgan's work, as that of others, gives good reason to reconsider historical assumptions of innate preconceived notions of white supremacy among white settlers from England: Race perceptions were not uniform, and race relations evolved over time, through circumstance, through the development of political, economic, and cultural relations.[4]

Therefore, in examining the evolution of race relations, it cannot be easily supposed that one system of slavery, racial subordination, and race relations was "better" or "easier" than another, or that notions of white supremacy came more readily to the settlers in the one than in the other, or that all levels of white society accepted or interpreted white supremacy in the same way. In the study of New Orleans and of its labor movement, one must be particularly careful on this score. Significantly, the astute scholar of the city's past, John Blassingame, emphasizes the term "complex" in estimating its race relations. Thus, he warns, one must be "extremely careful in drawing generalizations." Subordination there was, and always; segregation was endemic and did not disappear. Perennially, the city was a center of the slave trade, its auction block strategic in the region; glorying in the city's uniqueness and charm, its leading spokesmen would lose little time (after the city and Louisiana joined the Union in 1803) in nevertheless associating the city with the South as such and with Southern slavery.

But manumission and miscegenation early on, due indeed to a different Spanish-French Catholic approach to and experience with slavery (perhaps derived, at least in part, from the essentially feudal trappings of the mother societies, in contrast with the more directly materialistic flavor in British settlement and slavery) led in fact to the growth of a free Black population, often skilled, educated, and respected, and unquestionably "freer" than its counterparts in other parts of the South. A certain tradition of interracial intimacy, licit and illicit, developed; some integration managed to endure until the end of the nineteenth century. Crescent City whites in antebellum days, writes John Blassingame, manifested "far less abhorrence for blacks than did their brothers in the North and far less than their rhetoric often implied." New Orleans race relations, he notes, embraced "a very complex and varied pattern of complete, partial, or occasional integration and intimacy in several areas." Still, he terms the free Black Creole a "quasicitizen," "neither bound nor free," who "bore much of the responsibilities of citizenship with few of its privileges."[5]

Crescent City free Blacks, before the Civil War, were able to push for and achieve certain opportunities. But these ebbed at first relatively and then dramatically after the city became part of the United States. "Free" they were indeed, for no one owned them, they might earn wages, pursue professions, own property, buy and sell, sue and be sued, join organizations, and establish churches. But they could not leave the city without permission, form a benevolent society or hold a ball without official sanction, attend a horserace, own a store where liquor was sold, or walk the streets without a permit. Blacks alone, free included, were put to death upon conviction for arson or for raping a white woman. By the 1850s, free Creoles were to find local treatment so abusive that many emigrated to Haiti. Recognition of their advantages must be tempered with appreciation of their humiliations. Free Creoles even so may well have enjoyed more "freedom" than their free brethren elsewhere: but although they were unfettered, they were yet confined. Like other free Blacks, but perhaps with greater frustration, the freemen of New Orleans "straddled one of hell's elusive boundaries."[6] The complexity of race relations afforded opportunity to a degree, the potential to move up the ladder to a point, while obstacles and possibilities of setback were omnipresent. And, of course, for the slaves, "opportunities" were even more narrowly delineated. Multilayered and mutlifold, New Orleans's unique set of antebellum race relations placed Blacks in a variety of subordinate positions rooted in slavery and suffused with white supremacy.

Humiliating, exploitive limits surrounded the freedom of free Blacks, infusing even that most fabled expression of interracial association: the quadroon ball, drawing white bluebloods after free Black women in a system of prostitution winked at and patronized by gentlemen of standing. Still, local free Blacks built a strong community. They emerged as protagonists of greater opportunity and of slavery's abolition. They played a vital role during the Civil War and labored on the freedmen's behalf on many fronts during the Reconstruction Era. Postbellum history is replete with battles for education, access to public places, and a battery of organized and spontaneous endeavors involving both the freedmen and the Creole community. Exceptionally well organized, the Black Creoles helped create an atmosphere of assertive struggle in which actual victories were scored; if Crescent City Blacks made important encroachments on white supremacist exclusion and subordination after slavery, they indeed owed much to that historically unique set of relations under which a Creole, free community had originated, organized, and flexed muscle, despite the pressures.

Black achievements under Reconstruction, writes Blassingame, stitched an "almost unbelievably complex pattern" in local race relations. Interracial contact persisted in many areas, including the arena of male-female relations. Now, however, greater numbers of the white men involved were lower class and foreign-born. Blassingame's indication that immigrants possessed "less antipathy to blacks than native-born whites, especially Anglo-Saxons," is worth noting in its resemblance to the apparent failure of newly arrived indentured servants to accept white supremacist expectations in colonial days. Insofar as recent immigrants might have been slower to grasp the norms of white supremacy, it is important to note that the white work force on the late nineteenth century docks was in fact multinational, including many first and second generation Irish, German, Portuguese, and Italian workers.

That New Orleans was a cosmopolitan city may have contributed to a loosening of racial strictures, particularly on the docks where whites of many nationalities and Afro-American men were thrown together by the thousands every day, more than in other parts of the city, more than in other industries. Perhaps first and second generation Americans were "not so sensitive about color," reluctant to assimilate "themselves into the culture of white Southerners": a "hindrance to white solidarity." It has been found in this regard that European immigrants in Birmingham, Alabama's turn-of-the-century iron and steel mills "did not share traditional Southern habits and patterns of thought" with regard to Blacks; there, too, solidarity evolved.

The city, of course, was not the only port where a multinational work force labored on the levee; there were others, including the Great Lakes ports where cosmopolitan work forces worked on separate ships or in separate gangs by nationality — unlike New Orleans dockworkers at the time — during the early twentieth century.[7] But in New Orleans, certain other factors served to promote solidarity. Foreign seamen visited the Crescent City often; many were trade unionists with their own traditions of struggle and solidarity which may have impressed local dockworkers. Still another European-derived element might well have blended into the local dimensions of levee unionism: casuality and seasonality of dock labor made necessary in New Orleans the invocation of a European custom: the exchange of cards between different unions. Seasonality truly devastated those levee trades entirely dependent upon cotton: the yard-men and the screwmen. Even though seasonality affected all levee trades, the dockworkers who handled cotton exclusively became more desperate in the off season, consequently seeking other, union-sanctioned, employment.

Residential proximity of white and Black, a leftover from slavery, continued long after emancipation in New Orleans. Taken with the custom of interracial contact and the city's legacy of Black struggles and gains, this pattern may have contributed to a favorable context for the growth of interracial cooperation in the labor movement after the Civil War. Such cooperation, which arose in other Southern cities at certain moments, persisted remarkably in the South's chief port, where radical trends and militant unions sprouted, the foreign-born joined Afro-Americans on the docks and in the communities, and years of common experiences helped inspire approaches to working class solidarity.

Still, in treating labor, as in all areas concerning local race relations, one recalls the essential "complexity." While the Crescent City witnessed a coming together of white and Black working men after the Civil War, and though its history doubtless made this a more conceivable occurrence than elsewhere, there was little in its fabled and complex tradition that encouraged joint action by the white and Black components of the laboring class. Through experiences, local labor, dock labor initially, developed its own tradition of solidarity. Surely the historical legacy constituted a more sympathetic backdrop. But working-class solidarity was entirely different from the older forms of "contact" between the races; and although its actual operation would exhibit features of inequality, its logical persistence on the docks suggests that white and Black levee men developed and felt a common interest as workers and union members. And this, despite all hitches, limitations, and contrary prevailing winds, flew in the face of the new, no less than the older, forms and precepts of white supremacy.

The late nineteenth and early twentieth centuries were part of the "nadir," the low point in American race relations, during which segregation — a longtime Southern practice — became entrenched and acquired legal teeth. Southern society entered the nadir against the backdrop of emergent imperialism with attendant ideologies and policies. Industrial expansion and broader investment in the South accompanied and required the intensification of segregation: the steamship and railroad agents employing and seeking to racially split dock labor in the early twentieth century represented industrial and commercial giants. Intertwining, these currents held sway in power and thought. Chauvinism and theories of racial superiority proliferated and legitimized the intensification of segregation practices that had been prevalent, but not necessarily official since the end of slavery.[8]

The discriminatory practices that expanded after the Reconstruction Era had lacked legal sanction: for some time, interracial contact was not uncommon. In Louisiana, Blacks retained certain rights well into the 1890s, including the right to serve on juries. Even though segregated streetcars came into general use in New Orleans during the 1880s, Blacks and whites nevertheless often rode together. In short, as C. Vann Woodward points out, the South's "era of stiff conformity and fanatical rigidity . . . had not yet closed off all contact between the races, driven the Negroes from all public forums, silenced all white dissenters, put a stop to all rational discussion and exchange of views, and precluded all variety and experiment in types of interracial associations."[9]

To counter Republican resurgence in the early 1890s and Populist efforts later on (both waves involving Blacks and lower-class whites), the Southern elite brought about what J. Morgan Kousser terms a "reactionary revolution." Streamlining and deepening efforts to consolidate "white solidarity," Democratic party principals combined legal and illegal means to ensure segregation and disfranchise many hundreds of thousands of voters. Indeed, the cooperation of Blacks and lower-class whites had given strength to Republican, Populist, Fusion, and Independent movements whose white participants, notes Kousser, had "submerged the racism which they, as white Southerners, must have felt." C. Vann Woodward suggests, in fact, that the "brief Populist upheaval of the nineties," may well have witnessed "a greater comity of mind and harmony of political purpose" between Blacks and whites than at any other point in Southern history.

The steps taken by the elite in the late nineteenth and early twentieth centuries transformed segregation from a not quite universal pattern into lawful suppression, exclusion of Blacks and many whites from politics, and the aggressively pursued subordination of Blacks. By 1910, Kousser comments, the post-Reconstruction Era tendencies toward segregation, Democratic hegemony, and upper-class white authority, "were hardened into fundamental legal postulates of the society. To put it differently, folkways became stateways, with all the psychological power of legality and the social power of enforceability behind them." No longer might Blacks find redress in legal decree. The laws now sanctioned inequality.[10]

Some of the literature on Southern labor in the late nineteenth century suggests that the institutionalization of Jim Crow tolled the bell for an important trend of interracial cooperation that had developed during and after the Reconstruction. The period before the reactionary revolution had indeed witnessed expressions of white-Black labor solidarity. Recent studies show, in one scholar's words, that the post-Reconstruction South was "less 'solid' " than historians once assumed. The Knights of Labor in the South — for instance in Louisiana's sugar parishes — had often functioned on the basis of Black-white cooperation, despite concerted opposition from state and local government. White and Black trade unionists in New Orleans had coalesced politically in the 1880s. New Orleans workers carried out a massive, united general strike in 1892 and cooperated interracially over a ten-year span after 1880.[11]

But some historians have alleged that this trend came to an end in the nadir with the definitive establishment of Jim Crow in the late nineteenth and early twentieth centuries. Melton A. McLaurin contends that the erosion of solidarity in the Knights of Labor under white supremacist, antiunion pressures reflected the "inablility of whites to grasp the truth that their long-term economic interests were identical to those of Blacks." According to David Paul Bennetts, white unionists' racism in the mid-and late 1890s in New Orleans drove Black longshoremen out of and away from trade unionism, "in the direction of Booker T. Washington and his pro-employer, anti-union policies."[12]

Closely related is the assumption that lower-class whites constituted the motivating constituency of segregation and exclusion of Blacks from the broader avenues of Southern life. This view avers that wealthy, conservative whites and oppressed Blacks joined in a self- and mutually protective "understanding" against white labor. Blacks, several scholars have held, developed an "affinity for the conservative whites." They became "employer-oriented."[13]

In fact, interracial labor cooperation persisted as a significant "minor theme" in the early twentieth century. Although segregation and exclusion prevailed — and in fact were the main policy of organized labor — exceptions to the rule appeared. The experiences of Black and white dockworkers in early twentieth century New Orleans formed part of a trend that defied prevailing notions and conditions.

Among longshoremen, miners, timber workers, iron workers, and others, interracial cooperation emerged and withstood the divisive pressures of the wealthy conservatives with whom Blacks had allegedly concluded an "understanding." Herbert Gutman found much evidence of interracial unionism in the United Mine Workers at the turn of the century in both the North and South. James R. Green has shown how Louisiana's white and Black timber workers formed militant, integrated organizations on the eve of World War I. W. E. B. DuBois wrote of Black-white cooperation among workers in Jacksonville, Atlanta, Danville, Savannah, Richmond, Athens, New Orleans, Augusta, Winston-Salem, and Memphis, involving bricklayers, cigarmakers, masons, carpenters, painters, and longshoremen. At the turn of the century, whites and Blacks, including thousands of European immigrants, established an interracial trade unionism in Birmingham, organized the unorganized, elected whites and Blacks to leadership, and for a time successfully resisted violent attacks and race-baiting. Here, notes Paul Worthman, were whites who "did not share traditional Southern habits and patterns of thought." They were "less moved by appeals to white solidarity" and "not only supported organiza- tion of black laborers, but also encouraged such organization."[14]

In the port of New Orleans, whose lifesblood was supplied by the cotton trade, dockworkers developed a pattern of race relations that likewise contrasted with prevailing norms. Dock unionists insisted that the exactions of work and exploitation made necessary and engendered white-Black cooperation. They explained that the faster pace and heavier work load increasingly sought by employers left levee men no choice but to "amalgamate" interracially to better control the work. From racially divisive hiring practices to public advocacy of levee segregation, employers manifested a most consistent and remarkable will to keep white and Black workers at each others' throats. Their views were those of the contemporary Louisiana elite so well epitomized by historian William Ivey Hair: "The most rabid Negrophobes in the state were as consistently vehement in defense of upper class privileges."[15] Nor did Crescent City employers hesitate to state the benefits to themselves of a divided levee labor movement: greater productivity, weaker unions, and commercial "parity," at long last, with such segregated open-shop ports as Galveston and Savannah.

Through it all, half-and-half endured. While the fight over "parity" and union power intensified, management stepped up racially divisive appeals, pro- mises, and warnings. These bore no fruit. The races, as a white longshoreman stated in September 1907, remained "together for mutual protection, deter- mined to see that they get justice," ready to resist all attempts to "make trouble" between them.[16]

Out of the bitter contention on the levee in the early twentieth century grew a labor movement strong enough and sufficiently cohesive to wage and win a mammoth general dock strike in 1907, defeating the open-shop efforts of employers. Historians have accorded special significance to that strike. It was "the most massive struggle of the period," with "Black-white unity explicitly and decisively asserted";[17] it was "one of the most stirring manifestations of labor solidarity in American history."[18] A contemporary daily termed it "probably unique," and added, "Its chief lesson is the value of solidarity."[19]

In an earlier period, the pioneering historian Roger Shugg observed, "race prejudice . . . filled the void of class hatred."[20] And so it was generally in the labor movement in the early twentieth century. But what happened when interracial solidarity triumphed over "race prejudice?" By what process, through what experiences, did this evolve? And what then became of the "void of class hatred?"

This book investigates the conditions which made possible a remarkable instance of Black-white solidarity, and contributes to the study of lower-class interracial cooperation during an especially difficult period in race relations. The first chapter explores the national and local context of race relations and organized labor. This is followed by an examination of the character of longshore work in New Orleans; the evolution and nature of levee unionism; and the activities, concerns, and attitudes of dockworkers and their organizations. The third chapter traces the origins and development of the half-and-half concept and practice on the docks between 1900 and 1906. The fourth chapter describes the labor upsurge during the spring and summer of 1907, culminating in the formation of a new, dockworker-led, labor council espousing industrial unionism. The next chapter probes the causes and conduct of the 1907 general dock strike, and the efforts by employers to defeat it. The final chapter discusses the investigation of, and attack upon, half-and-half by the Port Investigation Commission after the 1907 strike; changes in the work force, rules, and technology after 1910; and the decline of interracial cooperation on the levee. The experience of New Orleans dockworkers constitutes a chapter in Jim Crow's "strange career."

Chapter One

Race, Labor, and Unionism

> . . . If the colored man continues to lend himself to the work of
> tearing down what the white man has built up, a race hatred far
> worse than any ever known will result. Caucasian civilization will
> serve notice that its uplifting process is not to be interfered with
> in any way.
>
> Samuel Gompers, 1905[1]

New Orleans dockworkers developed interracial solidarity under difficult conditions in the early twentieth century. Race relations had reached its lowest point. New Orleans was, for the most part, a segregated city, and the segregation was in fact deepening. The great majority of Black dockworkers, like Black Orleanians generally, could not vote. White supremacy prevailed in politics and in labor, too.

The American Federation of Labor's sanctioning of segregation in the labor movement at the turn of the century had its reflection in New Orleans. Two racially distinct central labor councils operated. In most trades, and on the docks as well, local unions were generally segregated.

Despite the sociopolitical climate and the policy of organized labor, a vigorous dockworkers' movement arose in the early twentieth century. It brought together levee laborers of both races, including whites who often supported white supremacist politics and Blacks who protested the hardships of segregation. The dockworkers who crossed the color bar in New Orleans were part of the real world of that segregated city. The obstacles they faced were as genuine as the experiences that led them to interracial unionism.

Labor and the Nadir in New Orleans

"One is tempted," wrote historian Rayford Logan of the late nineteenth century, "to refer to this quarter of a century as 'The Dark Ages of Recent

American History'." This was the nadir of American race relations: the high point for lynching and the systematic promotion of white supremacy and segregation, bringing about "the descent of the Negro to the lowest and lowliest position that he has occupied since emancipation."[2]

Historians agree that the last decade of the nineteenth century signaled the entrenchment of white supremacy. By then, a historian submits, "even the most sympathetic Southerners accepted the idea of innate racial differences, and the inferiority of the Negro." Moreover, the trend was national: " . . . Public opinion in the North had come to feel that Negroes were an inferior race, unfitted for the franchise, and that white domination was justified."

In science, medicine, literature, and the press, white supremacist theories found favor. "Negro ruffian," "Black fiend," "Black brute," "colored cannibal," and other such terms filled many a Northern and Southern headline. The major, established press presented Blacks in the poorest light. Among the worst, according to Rayford Logan, was the *Picayune*, the first paper to call for the "white primary": it justified lynching in the 1890s. (As shall be shown, the *Picayune* often quoted Blacks in "dialect.") Turn-of-the-century Congressional debates became a virtual forum for white supremacist vituperation.[3]

During the late nineteenth century, concurrent with the rise of imperialism and industrial growth, a "New South" had taken shape, sparked by intensified investment and industrialization. Port commerce expanded, particularly in Gulf cities of Mobile, Galveston, and New Orleans. The Democratic party, liberated now for some time from Reconstruction rule, became the political vehicle for this powerful trend.

The effort to build, maintain, and politically ensure the New South evoked opposition at points throughout the late nineteenth century, particularly from Blacks and lower-class whites. Occasionally uniting, as in the Populist movement, they scored significant political victories. In many cases, they developed independent, Republican, Fusion, or other anti-Democratic forms.

Clearly, this trend threatened Democratic hegemony and all it represented. The party's leaders and wealthy elite thus developed a many-sided approach to eroding and eliminating opposition. Measures to disfranchise Blacks and poor whites appeared in all forms, from physical intimidation to poll taxes to new state constitutions; in many cases, the new constitutions marked the culmination, rather than the beginning, of suffrage restriction.

Although segregation had long obtained in the South, and had in fact further deepened after the Civil War, it remained more as custom than as law until the late nineteenth century. Legal, aggressively pursued segregation and subordination of Blacks awaited the adoption of the elitist approach embodied in disfranchisement.

White supremacy, consciously advanced and enforced, became a crucial means to disfranchisement. The disfranchisers, C. Vann Woodward notes, supported their efforts "with white supremacy propaganda in which race hatred, suspicion, and jealousy were whipped up to a dangerous pitch."[4]

Lynchings exploded through the South. Blacks constituted an ever higher proportion of the attacked; by 1910, they were 90% of the victims. On the floor of the Senate, Ben Tillman of South Carolina declared in 1900:

> We have done our level best; we have scratched our heads to find out how we could eliminate them [Negroes]. We stuffed ballot boxes. We shot them [Negroes]. We are not ashamed of it.[5]

In major cities — Raleigh, Nashville, Atlanta, Montgomery, and Richmond — housing, schools, jobs, juries, police, hospitals, and prisons were segregated. "Separate but equal" educations were obtained in Southern urban schools *before* the Supreme Court sanctioned the concept, and conditions were not equal.

The institutionalization of white supremacy, however, did require national sanction to answer the protests engendered by the South's segregation of street-cars, public places, theaters, and schools. The *Plessy v. Ferguson* decision of 1896, writes Otto Olson, met this need. Denying that racial separation implied inequality, the decision rather affirmed that the races were equal but different. "With a view to the promotion of their comfort and the preservation of the public peace and good order," the Supreme Court went on record in support of "the established usages, customs and traditions of the people," in other words, segregation. The states could then move vigorously ahead with segregation. In Olson's view, the decision rested on both the white supremacy surge and the lack of sustained, effective pressure against segregation. But *Plessy v. Ferguson* was not forced upon the Court by "hayseed" Populists and the lower classes. Instead,

> one suspects that the aristocratic predilections of the justices inclined them toward racial as well as class distinctions, and that they moved toward segrega-tion as a policy that fulfilled the needs or calmed the fears of a conservative elite.

Capping a series of blows at equality, *Plessy v. Ferguson* upheld the states comprehensively and established a general doctrine.[6]

The National Labor Movement

The years just after the 1890s depression were, in one historian's words, "uniquely favorable for trade unionism," and the labor movement grew quickly. AFL membership averaged 1.3 million between 1900 and 1910, peaking at 1.7

million in 1904. One-half million workers belonged to unions outside the AFL.[7]

Despite the more tolerant approach of employers to unionism, the growth of organized labor, and the general prosperity during and after the Spanish-American War, workers register minimal gains in living standards. Real wages of industrial workers declined. Corporate mergers produced stronger firms more capable of resisting the labor movement. Indeed, the rising number of strikes engendered an open-shop drive. Industrial giants, writes David Brody, "had not counted on a painful period of trial and error, on what seemed to them violations of agreements, on strikes and rank-and-file militancy."

The drive for the open shop contributed heavily to a slump in organized labor after 1904. Employer associations broke agreements and contracts, formed "antiboycott" groups, blacklisted unionists, disseminated antiunion material, and mounted legal attacks against unions. The open-shop drive, with attendant strikebreaking and prosecutions, travelled throughout the country and visited New Orleans.[8]

Although the AFL's long-held craft outlook had always deemphasized labor's practical interdependence, it had initially encouraged Black-white cooperation. In this, it followed an approach adopted by the Knights of Labor in the 1870s and 1880s. The Knights had organized tens of thousands of Southern Black workers. Even though local Assemblies were usually segregated, state and district Assemblies were more often integrated. A historian notes: "The Knights encountered their most violent opposition from white planters and large farmers, who saw the organization of Blacks as a threat to their labor supply."

White supremacy took its toll on the Knights. The charge of "Black domination" influenced growing numbers of whites and drove them out of the order. Melton A. McLaurin observes that the allegation was groundless: Integrated Assemblies were, in fact, run by whites. But, "The conclusion that white members refused to accept a breach of the South's racial etiquette is inescapable." Still, the Knights regularly affirmed the identity of lower-class Black and white interests.[9]

Evidence confirms Samuel Gomper's early desire to organize Black workers, if possible, in the same union locals as whites. In 1893, the AFL resolved to "reaffirm" that "the working people must organize irrespective of creed, color, sex, nationality or politics." An early membership pledge swore candidates "never to discriminate against a fellow worker on account of color, creed or nationality."[10]

But the craft outlook and white supremacy increasingly interfered with the stated policy as time went on. The dominant unions in the AFL preferred to organize the skilled, few of whom were Blacks. Under pressure from craft unions to reduce job competition during the 1893 depression, and influenced by the intensifying white supremacy, the AFL began admitting white-only unions. In 1900, the AFL sanctioned segregated locals and central councils, not as one of several ways of organizing Blacks, or as the last resort, but as the only way.

By the early twentieth century, Gompers considered Black and Asian workers a threat to "Caucasian civilization," describing Black strikebreakers as "hordes of ignorant blacks . . . possessing but few of those attributes we have learned to revere and love . . . huge, strapping fellows, ignorant and vicious, whose predominant trait was animalism." One could not expect "that with all their traditions, mental, moral, and social, and the fact that they are only 50 years removed from slavery, the negro can understand the fundamental philosophy of human right."[11]

Segregated New Orleans

With a population of 300,000 in 1900, New Orleans was the nation's second leading port. It provided all the facilities of a major business and labor center: several hundred miles of paved streets and street railways, a good number of hospitals, 24 hotels, 200 churches, 7 theatres.[12]

New Orleans dockworkers labored in a city based on commerce and primary processing. Cotton oil factories, rice cleaning mills, sugar refineries, and foundry and cooperage firms serving the molasses and sugar trades: these were the adjuncts of port trade.

During the period, Southern ports garnered a growing share of the nation's commerce. New York, 90 times the size of Galveston, had only 11 times the Texas city's port commerce in 1903. Mobile and Savannah showed tremendous rates of growth. The *Picayune* editorialized: " . . . The wonderful resources of the South will enable it to take the lead and to hold it for a long time to come." The New Orleans Cotton Exchange recorded a record trade in 1903: "At no time since its inauguration in February 1871, has the institution been as prosperous." On Christmas Eve 1904, the port set a new record, "clearing" 15 steamships destined for European, Central American, and other United States ports. Into these ships, New Orleans dockworkers had stowed more than 27,000 cotton bales, 304,000 barrels of corn, 58,000 sacks of cotton and cotton seed cake and meal, 8,000 barrels of cotton seed oil, 5,593 barrels and 44,388 sacks of sugar, and 6,349 barrels of molasses, in addition to rice, meat, lumber, and flour. The *Picayune* celebrated:

> No industry or set of industries affords employment to more people than the shipping, and it is because New Orleans is such a good shipping port that it has retained its supremacy in the cotton trade.[13]

The city's population included many nationalities: Italian, German, Jewish, Irish, Black. The New Orleans Irish, "transformed into urban workers by an ocean journey," predominated among the white dockworkers. Many Germans also worked on the docks, in the growing garment and brewery industries, and as skilled craftsmen: watchmakers, shoemakers, stone masons, bakers, and bookbinders. The brewery industry also drew many dockworkers during the port's off-season, generally the spring and summer months.[14]

In 1900, 80,000 Blacks lived in New Orleans. Between 1880 and 1910, Blacks constituted 27% of the city's population. Dock labor occupied thousands of Black workers, most of whom lived uptown, southwest of Canal Street. Descendants of the free people of color, Black Creoles, lived downtown, northeast of Canal Street. Their living standards suffered in the nadir, but they retained preeminence in certain skilled trades as late as 1910, unlike skilled Black craftsmen in most Southern cities. By 1910, Blacks comprised most of the carpenters and bricklayers. In New Orleans industry, W. E. B. Du Bois commented, "the Negro is very largely the master."

Although segregation affected both, social distinctions remained between Creole and non-Creole Blacks. Violinist Paul Dominguez remembered:

> You see, we Downtown people, we try to be intelligent. Everybody learn a trade, like my daddy was a cigarmaker and so was I . . . . We try to bar jail. Uptown, cross Canal yonder, they *used* to jail . . . . There's a vast difference here in this town. Uptown folk all ruffians, cut up in the face and live on the river. All they know is — get out on the levee and truck cotton — be longshoremen, screwmen. And me, I ain't never been on the river *a day in my life*.[15]

The commercially successful Crescent City, heavily reliant on dock labor, was racially segregated in 1900. Equal access to schools, public transportation, and public places had actually never been realized before the 1890s. Nevertheless, the Jim Crow streetcars of the 1880s possessed no legal mandate: "Negroes were not forced to use them and whites sometimes rode in them." Blacks and whites could and did intermarry. Construction worker-musician Johnny St. Cyr recalled that his cousin had married a white woman during the 1890s; but after 1902, "it got so bad around here it made a fellow want to go North if he had a chance." Still, before the 1890s, Blacks had not suffered the restrictions of deliberately applied segregation laws.

A historian writes, "After 1900, the rate at which Louisiana enacted segregation statutes increased notably." Intermarriage, transportation, education, saloons, housing, and mental hospitals all fell before the legal segregative power of the state of Louisiana by 1912. Black-white association in sports competition came to an end. In the mid-1890s, the New Orleans Archdiocese established St. Katherine's Church — for Blacks only.[16]

Despite the laws, many thousands of Blacks and whites lived in the same neighborhoods. Evidence indicates a persistence in 1900 of the housing patterns of an earlier period: in many communities, white and Black lived next door, across the street, down the block, or near each other. Even though all-white and all-Black areas existed, the persistence of Black-white proximity in many wards distinguished the city's housing from that of other major Southern cities. Elsewhere, Black populations were generally concentrated in separate areas apart from whites by the turn of the century: Blacks lived outside the city limits, in shanties and shacks.

This was not the case in early twentieth century New Orleans, but recurrent or continuous proximity did not necessarily produce friendships or harmony. On several occasions, whites protested "interminable 'ragtime' selections" by "discordant" brass bands at neighborhood picnics attended by Blacks. White petitioners protested the "execrable" music at next door lawn parties in one uptown neighborhood. But interracial lawn parties, featuring the same "execrable" music and "interminable ragtime," also took place, attended in the main by Irish and Black dockworkers (usually on Monday nights).

Whites and Blacks may have walked to work in the same direction, perhaps even together, left work together, seen each other on days off, and their children may have played together. And, at the same time, whites and Blacks (particularly dockworkers) came into contact on the job.[17]

Nevertheless, segregation proceeded apace in the early twentieth century. Separation of white and Black on streetcars became standard and was enforced. Whenever the white section of a streetcar filled up, the separating screen was moved back to make room for more whites.

School segregation received amplification in biology from the state Supreme Court in 1910. Not only were "white" and "colored" to attend separate schools, but "colored" was shown to embrace various quotients of "negro blood": "negroes," "who are distinguished by crisped or curly hair, flat noses and protruding lips"; "griffs," who were "the issue" of "mulattoes" and "negroes"; and "quadroons," who were "distinctly whiter" than mulattoes, were all barred from white schools. Black education took place in crumbling buildings or in new facilities established in the "Red Light" district after whites pressured the City Council to erect "colored schools" at a distance from their homes.[18]

The Black death rate in 1900 was 42.2 deaths per 1,000; the white death rate 23.8. The respective rates in 1890 had been 36.61 and 25.41. The Board of Health attributed the rising Black mortality rate to tuberculosis and alcohol, "the greatest scourges of that race." Typhoid, smallpox, diptheria, and scarlet fever took both white and Black lives by the hundreds in 1906 and 1907.[19]

Pursuing science in 1907, the Board of Health injected chemicals used in molasses processing into nine Black convicts to determine whether these substances were harmful. The Black weekly *Southwestern Christian Advocate* commented bitterly that the test assumed that "Negroes were a public utility to be used at every convenience. What would the country do without the convenient Negro, anyway?"

Blacks seeking civil service jobs found the door closed. Preparatory courses for civil service exams excluded Blacks after 1908: The major paper charged that the exams in any case led Blacks to false assumptions of advancement. The police force, which still hired Blacks at the turn of the century, ultimately barred Blacks. A 1901 City Council debate charged that Black policemen were as "impertinent as they were good for nothing," and the shooting of a white bartender by Black officers in 1906 gave further impetus to the effort to exclude them.

After the appointment of E. S. Whitaker as Police Inspector in 1905, relations between Blacks and the police further deteriorated. Whitaker, whose antiunion views would emerge during the 1907 levee strike, brought intense white supremacist opinions to his job. After a white boy whipped a Black girl in March 1907, a white policeman told the boy's mother to keep him "off the sidewalk" because Blacks had "as much feelings" as whites; Whitaker censured the officer. He declared the policeman's conduct intolerable: speaking in an "ugly tone" to the white woman in supporting the charge of the Black girl and her father, the officer had inspired an atmosphere of equality. Blacks had the same legal rights as whites, Whitaker conceded, "but police officers should not accept such complaints from them becuase it only made them impertinent." And he ordered the whipped girl's father, "an impertinent negro," arrested.[20]

While interracial cooperation unfolded on the docks, the major local paper increasingly propagated white supremacy. The *Picayune* countered the famous address of the Niagara Movement in 1906 — a declaration that claimed for Blacks "every single right that belongs to a freeborn American" — by calling for the deportation of "some millions of these people" to the North and to "the tropical regions of America."

Only this could solve that most serious of white-Black problems, in the *Picayune*'s view: "frightful crimes of assault upon [white] women"; pending dispersion, only "popular justice" sufficed to answer such crimes. Because bureaucracy inhibited legal procedures, "the enraged and disappointed people" could not be blamed for consequent lynchings. Besides, the Niagara leaders were "a lot of negro dreamers and agitators for complete political and social equality." Equality was impossible, editorialized the *Picayune* in January 1906 (and throughout the decade):

If the negro had been intellectually, morally and spiritually the equal of the
white man, he would long ago have demonstrated the fact, but from the beginning of recorded history, first in the Old World and later in the New, the whites
and negroes have been working together or engaged in the struggle for
supremacy, and the negroes, whether as freemen or slaves, have always
succumbed to the unalterable and invincible laws which have placed the whites
in full control and domination.[21]

Politics and Labor

Substandard health care, higher mortality, inferior education, exclusion
from public places, segregated transportation, and, fundamentally, disfranchisement, created unequal living conditions for Black Orleanians. The state's
1898 constitutional convention, capping a series of suffrage restriction measures,
ensured the status quo and Democratic hegemony. Indeed, although other matters came up in that convention, they were "of minor importance when compared to that one which overshadows all . . . ." "We know that this convention has been called together by the people of the State to eliminate from the
electorate the mass of corrupt and illiterate voters who during the last quarter
of a century degraded our politics."

The state's Black registration dropped from 127,923 in 1890 to 5,320. Fewer
than 2,000 Black Louisianians registered in 1908; less than 1,000 in 1924. In
New Orleans, 600 Blacks were eligible to vote between 1903 and 1904. Premised
on elitism, disfranchisement also excluded tens of thousands of whites from
the polls. Between 1897 and 1900, the state's white registration fell from 164,088
to 125,437; it dropped to 91,716 in 1904.[22]

On the crest of white supremacy and disfranchisement, leading Democrats
formed the Choctaw Club in New Orleans in the 1890s. Drawing merchants,
bankers, manufacturers, skilled workers, and professional politicians, the club
aimed at institutionalizing one-party rule in the city. Several key members
attended the 1898 constitutional convention. The Choctaw Club's historian
stressed that the club represented business interests.[23]

Among the Democratic elite, several men figured prominently in the
levee's interracial configuration during the early twentieth century. Their
eminence, particularly in the business world, suggests something of the drama
of the clash between management and political officials on one side, and a
cooperative white-Black dockworkers' movement on the other. Levee disputes
involved the city's very lifeline and always drew in the political leaders. A survey
of several such men suggests the depth of their white supremacist commitment
and the intensity of their antagonism to interracial solidarity.

Lawyer-businessman E. B. Kruttschnidt (who died in 1906), for example,
chaired the 1898 disfranchisement convention and led the state's Democratic

party, which relied on white union support in several local wards. Nephew of Confederate influential Judah Benjamin, he participated in the famous White League coup against the state's Reconstruction government in 1874. He was on the board of directors of the Equitable Life Assurance Society, which was tied to the Harriman and Morgan fortunes.[24]

Paul Capdevielle, who served as mayor from 1899 to 1904 and took part in many negotiations with white and Black dockworkers, was a Confederate veteran, scion of a wealthy family. He was president of the Merchants Insurance Company of New Orleans.[25]

Robert E. Lee (1863–1916) was a machinist who served eight terms as head of the white Central Trades and Labor Council, while he served in the state Senate. A delegate to the 1898 constitutional convention, he was a sincere craft unionist who avoided all but minimal contact with Black workers. Employer of ten men in his own machine shop, he was state Commissioner of Labor from 1904 to 1908.[26]

Adolph Ricks headed the New Orleans Brewing Association, whose employer-members hired many dockworkers during the commercial off season. His Association's antiunion stance precipitated a city-wide, dockworker-led labor upheaval on the eve of the 1907 general levee strike. Elected to the City Council in 1895, Ricks was president of the Metropolitan Bank.[27]

The most remarkable Democratic leader in the early twentieth century was Martin Behrman (1864–1926), mayor from 1904 to 1920 and 1925 to 1926. Successfully fighting off reform challenges in all but one election campaign, Behrman was for one-quarter century the dominant figure in New Orleans machine politics; he broke the retirement imposed by defeat by returning to City Hall in 1925, remaining in office until his death the following year.

New York-born, brought to New Orleans at an early age, orphaned at 12, Behrman worked in a grocery after high school. He became wealthy as a wholesaler and later as an official for Edison Electric. A protege of E. B. Kruttschnidt and a delegate to the 1898 convention, he held a battery of local and state posts before becoming mayor: member of the School Board, clerk of the City Council, assessor of the Fifth District, president of the Board of Assessors, and State Auditor.

An outstanding politician, Berhman worked hard to obtain and keep labor's respect. Thoroughly pro-business, willing to do whatever necessary to promote the cotton trade, he accepted trade unionism as a fact of life. Central Trades and Labor Council head Pat Welsh acknowledged in 1906 Behrman's "deep interest . . . for the needs of the laboring people," his readiness "at all times . . . to ameliorate their condition in life and promote them socially and intellectually." In turn, Berhman told the Council in 1908, "It is not necessary for me to tell you that I am a believer in organized labor. I do not think you could be successful unless you organized."

He held clear-cut views on race. Growing up during the Reconstruction Era, "I saw the fact that the negroes were able to vote was at the bottom of a great deal of trouble." At the 1898 constitutional convention, "we promised the people to put the negroes out of politics and to keep him out." Interracial cooperation was not realistic: "Naturally, white men will not get along with negroes as they will with other men. It is not to be expected."

Work-sharing agreements between white and Black dockworkers only became possible after Blacks were politically suppressed. Cooperation between unequals then resulted. Disfranchisement put Black advancement into a different, nonthreatening context. The Black-white division of levee jobs and union posts on the half-and-half basis "could not have been made when negroes had votes."

Behrman preferred gradual, supervised change in society. He abhorred local Socialist Covington Hall (an "extreme radical") and others who tried to make "big changes all of a sudden"; they did not see that the "capitalistic system" was human nature.[28]

Interracial levee cooperation was entered into by white union locals whose leaders were often heavily involved in the activities of the Democratic party. These men ignored the exta-levee demands for political rights made by their Black trade union partners. Democratic involvement of certain dockworkers' leaders also brought them into contact with leading politicians, cotton merchants, and shipping agents. In bringing labor's vote to the Democrats, they worked closely with the Central Trades and Labor Council and its president, Robert E. Lee. But as disputes with management intensified on the levee in the early 1900s and especially in 1907, the adherence of white unionists to interracial cooperation threatened relationships with political white supremacy.

Still, when white union leaders discussed labor's political role, they omitted Blacks from the picture. During the early twentieth century, organized white labor formed political associations to run workers for office or support representatives of workers' interests. The labor-backed *Union Advocate*'s claim that "there's good stuff in the working rank to hold any job quite fair from the street sweeper to janitor and the [*sic*] way up to mayor" was widely shared. Thirty white union presidents, including the Longshoremen's Harry Keegan, joined to form a Workingmen's Protective League in early 1903. Cotton yardmen's leader Fred Grosz served as president. Laboring men, stated the *Union Advocate*, had determined to assert themselves "shoulder to shoulder politically" by backing workers and others "who have shown their friendship and sympathy for organized labor." The paper urged white workers to vote selectively and to take full advantage of the "white Democratic primaries" that "public outcry" had brought about.[29]

"So far as can be learned, however, the colored brother has not been discussed by the League as yet," commented the *Picayune* soon after the organization's birth. The *Picayune* warned of the consequences if the League were to include Blacks: labor's political clout would be dangerously enhanced, while the races would "be brought into such intimate relations that it is impossible to predict what may result."[30]

But the Workingmen's Protective League made no overtures to Blacks, nor did the independent political campaigns of several dockers who challenged the Choctaw Club machine. Black union leaders felt their organizations should have been invited to take part, pointing out that workers had a common interest and that some Afro-American workers — though indeed few — could still vote. So integral were they to local organized labor, stated one Black dock leader, that no labor party that excluded Blacks could hope to succeed: "Is this political labor movement going to disfranchise the colored labor unions?"[31]

When the Workingmen's Protective League, the Union Labor League, and the Democratic Labor League (tied to the Choctaw Club) ran or endorsed candidates, they made special appeals to white labor's interests. Serving in the campaigns of leading Democrats, key levee unionists often found levee employers sitting beside them in the election committees. Among the most active supporters of publisher Robert Ewing's (a delegate to the 1898 constitutional convention) bid for ward leader in 1903 was screwman Thomas Harrison.[32]

Running for leader of the first ward in 1903, white screwmen's president Robert Trainor challenged the Choctaw Club candidate. Backed by the Union Labor League (successor to the Workingman's Protective League), on whose executive committee sat longshoremen's leader Rufus Ruiz and other dock unionists, he conducted an active campaign. But Trainor fell victim to the discriminatory petition requirements for independent candidates, a matter he later pursued in court.[33]

Although most white levee union leaders generally supported Choctaw Club nominees, they split in 1904 over the mayoral candidacy of Martin Berhman. Several endorsed him, but others protested the "despotic pressures" of the party hierarchy in engineering his nomination by backing the breakaway "Home Rulers." Cotton yardman Fred Grosz ran for Commissioner of Public works on the Home Rulers's ticket. During the campaign, dock unionists in either camp exchanged charges of betraying the interests of workers.[34]

An anti-Choctaw Club trend in the white Central Trades and Labor Council in 1905 succeeded in getting through a resolution ousting council delegates who either held political office or were not working at their trades. A Home Rulers member in the council was its chief proponent. Targets included council delegates Thomas Harrison (Screwmen), James Hughes (Longshoremen), and Robert E. Lee (Machinists), all of whom worked in local government. The resolution squeezed through, but the Screwmen and the Longshoremen vowed to quit the council if the measure took effect. Soon after, the resolution was rescinded.[35]

Organized white labor renewed its appeal for workers to run and support sympathetic candidates at several points during the decade. It announced support in 1907 for any man "who is fair to the worker": " . . . His affiliations make no difference." In 1908, Thomas Harrison ran for Tax Collector. That autumn, the local *United Labor Journal* declared: "The avowed enemy of trades unionism is not fit to hold public office."

Throughout the decade, however, the whites' appeal to class interests in politics never extended to Black trade unionists.[36] Something of the conflicting tendencies among white levee union leaders may be gleaned from an examination of several such men. For many of the very same backers — and sometime candidates — of the local Democrats were steadfast proponents of white-Black unity on the docks. They distinguished between Black political rights, which they neglected or did not support, and fighting together with Blacks for labor's rights. But in uniting with Black dockworkers, they stepped on the toes of Democrats of the upper strata.

White longshoreman Rufus Ruiz had collaborated in drafting one of the levee's initial half-and-half agreements for equal division of work between the white and Black longshoremen's locals. He joined the union in 1882 at age 17. He went on to become an early president of the Central Trades and Labor Council and a commissioned AFL organizer. For his support of industrial unionism, he lost his commission in 1907. Later that year, he helped to found the interracial United Labor Council.[37]

Christopher Scully, president of the white longshoremen from 1905 until his death in 1910, was a "firm, determined and conservative man," in the words of the *Picayune.* Labor editor Oscar Ameringer remembered Scully as "a redheaded Irishman in every sense of the word, . . . with a good dash of Irish wit coupled with an uncontrollable temper and an ingrown hatred of bosses, irrespective of race, nationality, religion and state of moral turpitude."

Scully's labor experience included the levee race riots of 1894, when jobseeking white dockworkers attacked Black dockworkers, killing several. By the early 1900s, when he became prominent in Tenth Ward Democratic politics and local labor cooperatives, he was an active leader of joint Black-white levee union councils and negotiating teams. Both white and Black longshoremen stopped work at noon on the day of his funeral.[38]

White screwman Thomas Harrison, born in 1869, went to work in a cracker factory at age 13. At 15, he began levee work as a longshoreman and a screwman; by 1900, he was the Screwmen's delegate to the Central Trades and Labor Council. Two years earlier, however, he had been named Chief Clerk to the First City Criminal Court; thus, after 1898 did not earn a living as a screwman. A leading Democrat in the Tenth Ward, he held a number of civic appointments. He was the state's first Labor Commissioner, from 1900 to 1904.

Harrison remained a union member. He held the post of secretary in the white screwmen's local for many years. His support for the industrial form of organization — not only on the docks, but throughout the city — made his name poison to longtime colleagues in the white Central Trades and Labor Council, like the above-mentioned Robert E. Lee. He played a significant part in the breakaway, interracial United Labor Council formed in 1907, and was its president. Harrison believed that labor's right to advance was a "divine creation" that "cannot be withheld." Organized labor strove to "accomplish this right" and moreover, to bring about

> the real coming of the golden age, when the acrimony of strife shall have been chastened and softened; when the laborer, worthy of his hire, shall reap his full reward; when mutual rights and obligations shall be engendered and fostered; when capital and labor shall reciprocally accord to each other its just quantum of merit, and there shall exist, in truth, a common brotherhood among all mankind.

Ultimately, Harrison became president of the white screwmen's local. He held that post through the early 1920s, until levee employers achieved the open shop.[39]

Screwman Thomas Gannon worked in the breweries when trade slacked off on the levee. A screwmen's leader in the early 1900s and president of the white local in 1904, by 1907 he had become a beer driver and was no longer working on the docks. As president of Brewery Workers' Local 215 — beer drivers — he resisted the AFL-backed attempt by the Teamsters to convert Local 215 into a Teamsters local along craft lines. With Thomas Harrison, Gannon led the exodus of sympathizing white unions out of the white Central Trades and Labor Council and into the interracial United Labor Council. His ties to the local Democrats were more tenuous: Gannon drew close to the Industrial Workers of the World (IWW).[40]

These men were industrial unionists who adhered to white-Black solidarity against the open-shop drive in the city's most decisive industry. Political allegiances often placed them cheek-by-jowl with their employers. Yet, in important ways their consistent collaboration with Blacks set them against the city's political and economic elite. They defied that basic tenet of segregation which held that white and Black workers had no interests in common.

Opposition to Segregation

Black resistance to segregation began after the Civil War, growing with the enactment and enforcement of laws and practices following the Reconstruction Era. By the 1890s, a Citizen's Committee (mostly Black) and a newspaper (the *Daily Crusader*) were already established in the city to promote antisegregation efforts. Composed mainly of Black Creoles, the committee fought the earliest statutes segregating New Orleans streetcars (1892) and protested the founding of segregated St. Katherine's Church (1895). In June 1892, it chose to challenge segregation on railroads by assigning Homere Plessy to sit in the white-only section of a railway car. After the trial, Plessy was found guilty of violating the Separate Car Act of 1890. The Supreme Court upheld his conviction in 1896. The commmittee disbanded, but not before prosecuting other cases, including one involving housing discrimination.

Several unions and working-class organizations supported the Citizen's Committee. Fraternal organizations contributed money, as did the bricklayers' and cigarmakers' unions. Cigarmakers president Ramon Pages, "a Spaniard," told an 1893 meeting:

> . . . [T]he sun did not divide off a portion of its rays for one class and a portion for the other, a part for the whites and a part for the blacks; but shone equally for everybody. All that grew on the earth and live in the seas were equally the property of all mankind, as all were provided with the same organs, had the same necessities and required the same nourishment and sustenance.[41]

Protest against segregation continued in the early twentieth century. The *Christian Advocate* reflected the deep resentment of Blacks at the wave of insults and indignities. Insisting on "justice," it assailed "so-called leaders [who] are willing to make any concession, they say, 'for the sake of peace'." When a Black minister vocally defended disfranchisement in May 1906, the *Christian Advocate* denounced him as "the good Negro sort who tips his hat and grins in order to court favor," a representative of the "antebellum spirit who makes a little curtsy and says 'yes sir, boss' to everything." A "new Negro" was emerging, the paper stated in 1907, who refused to "maintain any servile or truckling relation" and was ready to "think and act, and to determine his own incoming and outgoing."

The *Christian Advocate* insisted on restoring the right to vote: 'The unit of power in the American government is the ballot, and this the Negro must have." Denial of the franchise and the rise in lynching might indeed lead one "to question whether he lives in a civilized country":

> To live in a country that boasts of its greatness, glories in the bravery of its army and navy, proclaims its high civilization and just laws, to live under a flag whose mission it is to bring liberty to the world, and yet to know that one's life is constantly in danger sets the mind all a-going at the inconsistency of it all.

And thus, "the Negro becomes an unenviable citizen . . . of our great republic. A republic did we say? Hardly. A democratic government? Not by any means: it is a government of one class for the suppression of another class."[42]

New Orleans was one of several cities witnessing protests against streetcar segregation in the late nineteenth and early twentieth centuries. Blacks could neither sit nor stand in front; even in the rear compartment to which they were confined (behind a screen), they were obligated to surrender their seats to whites if all seats became filled in front. The *Christian Advocate* expressed outrage at such "shameful, unjust treatment."

Blacks occasionally refused to sit in the back or give up their seats to whites. Thus, Elizabeth Roach insisted in February 1904 on her right to sit in front, ignored the conductor's order to move, and defied threats of arrest by a policeman: . . . "[E]ven this did not cause the woman to move." She was convicted under the Separate Car Act of 1890.[43]

Black Orleanians considered a boycott of substandard schools in March 1907. The *Christian Advocate* wondered: "Are the Negroes not a part of the city's population? Have they no rights?"

This insistence on rights ran through the Black press: the *Christian Advocate,* the *Republican Liberator* (organ of the Black screwmen's and longshoremen's locals), the *Southern Republican.* While the *Christian Advocate* also praised Booker T. Washington ("a leader more in sympathy with his people's struggles than any other man that's in the fore front") and certain aspects of his philosophy ("agriculture is the backbone of our prosperity"), publisher Reverend Robert E. Jones commended the Niagara Movement, deemed its 1906 Address "worthy of study," and won W. E. B. Du Bois's esteem.[44]

Assertion of rights took other forms. A small Black group followed the separatist teachings of Bishop Henry M. Turner and sold the magazine of his movement, *Voice of Missions.* When Turner-follower Robert Charles was harassed by police in July 1900, he responded by shooting one, precipitating a large-scale race riot. "Men were beat up on streetcars, and transportation had absolutely quit," Jelly Roll Morton remembered. Hundreds of Blacks were assaulted; Charles killed 27 whites before he was apprehended. His captors shot him 34 times. Thirty-eight years later, Morton described the notorious Charles as a "fine fella," and recalled that after the riot a "Robert Charles song" had become popular among Blacks. But "this song was crushed," said Morton: "It was a trouble-breeder."[45]

Though neither homogeneous nor the only tendency, opposition to the imposition of Jim Crow was a consistent element in New Orleans life. To be sure, Booker T. Washington's program influenced many, including some opponents of segregation. Indeed, the powerfully backed Washington had visited the city in 1899 under longshoremen's auspices, had addressed the union members and had met the mayor. His 1902 return visit, under different auspices, received wide press coverage. At a mass meeting, chaired by Democratic leader E. B. Kruttschnidt, Washington cogently outlined his program and urged Blacks to vigorously pursue the "common occupations" or "there will come into the South a race of foreigners which will replace us." He suggested: "We cannot begin at the top, we must begin at the bottom, and gradually grow up through these common industries that are about our doors to higher and more important positions."

Still, noted the *Crisis* some time later, currents of resistance to inequality and abuse persisted in New Orleans, "notwithstanding everything that has been done to have the colored people believe that they are natural hewers of wood and drawers of water."[46]

The Equal Rights League

Many Black dockworkers shared the sentiments and swam with the currents of opposition to the steady erosion of their conditions. In 1904, they founded an organization to ensure that Black political interests would still, or again, be represented and defended by the local Republican party. Given the disfranchisement of most Blacks, they hoped that pressure would help retain at least a modicum of political participation, in particular the right of Afro-Americans to play a role in the Republican party. This very right met severe challenge in the early twentieth century from the white supremacist Republican tendency known as "Lily-whiteism," a trend discussed by C. Vann Woodward, Louis Harlan, and Paul Casdorph, among others.

The Equal Rights League, whose key officers were all Black dock union leaders, came into being in early 1904 for the express purpose of combatting Lily-whiteism. Those who hammered out half-and-half and cooperation agreements with white dockworkers in the heat of intensifying levee controversy were all here. Also involving many clergymen, the League pressed for an interracial Louisiana delegation to the 1904 Republican convention in Chicago. The "Lily's" held a state meeting in May endorsing white supremacy, opposed "white monopoly," and selected one Black party member to be in the state delegation to the national convention.[47]

But the Equal Rights League's condemnation of the Lily's was unsparing. A mass meeting in February, with cotton yardman I. G. Wynn and longshoreman James E. Porter presiding, denounced silence as acquiescence and claimed equal rights for Blacks under the United States Constitution. Speakers urged a more aggressive fight for political participation. Screwman A. J. Ellis orated "with volubility and a vehemence that showed his deep earnestness," demanding political rights for Blacks. Indicting the Lily-white's efforts to involve Blacks, the meeting resolved to brand and consider all colored men who permit themselves to be used as delegates in the Convention of the Lily Whites . . . or stands as a delegate to the National Convention from said State Convention, a traitor to the race; and all who are so low and despicable to subscribe their own humiliation and political degradation, we call upon all honorable colored men to ostracize them and treat them with contempt, if they can be so base, either from the promise of menial service or by virtue of holding office of high or low degree, at this time to be induced to compromise away the rights of his race. Such should be held up to view as cowards, poltroons and time servants, unfit for the association and unentitled to the respect and confidence of the men and women of the race who place principle above self.[48]

In later months, the Equal Rights League (alternately titled the Colored Men's Association of Louisiana) strove to establish a base in every New Orleans ward. After the Lily-whites affirmed white supremacy at their May convention, the league published an appeal to Northern Blacks "advising them to join the regular Republicans in their fight against the Lily Whites." Ultimately, the national convention seated delegations of both the Lily's and the Regulars from Louisiana. But the convention later accredited only the latter delegation. The Equal Rights League was jubilant. Blacks greeted the development at mass meetings throughout the city: some whites also attended. League president I. G. Wynn proposed a state convention of Black Republicans for the near future.[49]

Although league activities slowed, dockworkers continued to speak out against Lily-whiteism. I. G. Wynn addressed a 1905 gathering on Emancipation Day, at Central Congregational Church. Later that year, screwmen A. J. Ellis and L. J. Obert spoke at a festival that included political rights among its themes.[50]

The treatment accorded Blacks by the Republican party became a consistent topic in the *Republican Liberator,* concurrently the official organ of the Black screwmen's and longshoremen's unions. Its motto in 1905 was "Justice to all irrespective to Race or Condition"; in 1908 "God's field of humanity our Concern, Therefore We Mean and Shall Labor For All, Irrespective to Race or Condition." Pledging to prosecute "the fight against Lily-whiteism at the South" and to expose "the brighting evils in our midst," the paper warned of the capitulation of the regular Republicans to the Lily's, and urged pressure to guarantee a strong Black presence at the party's 1908 national convention. Cooperation with the Lily's for the sake of party unity was unthinkable: "Oh! No! gentlemen, no 'harmony,' at the further cost to the party, our cause and liberties. These are not on the alter."

The paper found Theodore Roosevelt and William Howard Taft too sympathetic to the Southern Democrats and hoped "the very air would breathe that 'Anti-Taft' be written in positive and unmistakable terms." Blacks would not support those who sacrificed their interests; they would "not permit themselves like dum-driven cattle, [to be] delivered as usual, and again, for slaughter."[51]

Representing thousands of dockworkers, the leading Black unionists condemned the curtailment of Black political rights. They also participated actively in the half-and-half process of interracial trade unionism. They considered white-Black solidarity a necessity. A survey indicates that they were dedicated unionists, activists on several planes.

Longshoreman James E. Porter had been a slave. Born in Mississippi in the mid-1850s, he was brought to New Orleans while still very young. By the time he attained age 30, Porter was a union leader on the levee. In the 1890s, his organizing efforts brought an AFL organizer's commission. He helped develop an early work-sharing arrangement with the whites. He was a leader in the Black city central — the Central Labor Union (CLU) — and in the Black longshoremen's local during the early twentieth century. He was a vice-president of the national longshore union for several years. He also became prominent in the Equal Rights League. The *Picayune* wrote of him in 1903: "He probably holds more offices in different associations and societies than any other colored man in New Orleans."[52]

Screwman A. J. Ellis was a major force in the levee unions. By 1900, when he was 50, he had spent more than 20 years in the local labor movement. But his trade union experience, recalled labor editor Oscar Ameringer, extended beyond the docks:

> Ellis stood no more than five feet-five and weighed about a hundred and ten. In his youth he had been a jockey and in that capacity had seen much of the world. When he had become too heavy for jockeying, . . . he secured a job on one of the boats of the Hamburg-American line . . . . Later he became a member of the German Seamen, the reddest of the German unions, had acquired a fair smattering of German, and more than a fair understanding of the *Communist Manifesto*.

With James E. Porter and others, Ellis played an active part in the Equal Rights League. In civil rights and labor meetings, his "very strong voice and cast iron lungs" made him a superb speaker. According to Ellis, his steady support for Black-white labor cooperation cost him his job on the docks: he suspected a blacklist. By the end of the first decade of the twentieth century, Ellis no longer worked on the levee. He became a watchman; evidence suggests he also worked as a sleeping car porter.[53]

E. S. Swan, president of the Black longshoremen during most of the period, was born into slavery in Virginia. In 1863, he escaped and joined the Union Army. Age 19 by the end of the Civil War, he moved to New Orleans and became a dockworker.

Swan won the election as president in the early 1890s and served eight years. During the 1894–1895 race riots over levee jobs, Swan was accused of having allowed employers to violate Black-white work-sharing arrangements by solely hiring Blacks. Nearly ten years later, many white and Black longshoremen still distrusted him, despite his 25 years in the union. Characterized by the major daily papers as "conservative," Swan, though less prominently than James E. Porter and A. J. Ellis, participated in the Equal Rights League. During the levee disputes of the early twentieth century, he belonged to several joint white-Black councils and advocated interracial solidarity. He represented his local in the industrial-unionist United Labor Council, the militant white-Black central that arose on the eve of the 1907 levee strike.[54]

Cotton yardman I. G. Wynn was president of the Equal Rights League. For most of the early twentieth century, he headed the CLU and was prominent in several interracial levee committees. Throughout the period, he led the Black local of the cotton yardmen. He was a delegate to several AFL conventions. He was a leader of the Israel Lodge, Grand United Order of Odd Fellows for many years.

The Mississippi-born Wynn campaigned indefatigably against the Lily-white Republican trend. He wrote resolutions, spoke at meetings, addressed churches and other organizations, and published materials.[55]

In supporting labor solidarity, Black as well as white leaders of dock unionism represented the evolution of a far from simple or automatic process involving more than 10,000 workers of both races. New Orleans dockworkers brought a tradition of unionism and cooperation into the twentieth century. Organized labor as a whole had reached its dramatic peak in a mammoth 1892 general strike. An examination of the period of that effort reveals a series of significant experiences affecting dock unions and the labor movement.

During New Orlean's commercial ascent in the nadir, the dockworkers played an important part on the labor scene. Before the Civil War, the typographical and screwmen's unions had been the city's only labor organizations, but after the war many others emerged. Twenty unions (among them the segregated locals of screwmen, longshoremen, and cotton yardmen) operated by 1880. Formed in 1881, the Central Trades and Labor Assembly drew delegates from both white and Black organizations; the Assembly's 30 unions represented between 15,000 and 20,000 members by 1894. Black unions, in most cases parallel to white organizations, functioned in nonlevee trades as well: cigarmakers, waiters, coopers. Powerful white unions, the Screwmen for example, sponsored weaker ones, providing support in strikes. In the last quarter on the nineteenth century, Black and white unions in the same trades occasionally cooperated, meeting and taking joint action.[56]

Several segregated Knights of Labor assemblies carried on activity in the 1880s. Of 12 assemblies in 1887, at least six were Black; one of these comprised more than 600 members. David Paul Bennetts observes, however, that the Knights were "never more than a supplementary organization in New Orleans."[57] Instead, the Central Trades and Labor Assembly became the greater vehicle of cooperation and joint action. Its vice president was Black. Although it existed for fewer than ten years (growing quickly from 5,000 members in 1881 to 20,000 at mid-decade and declining just as quickly to 5,000 in 1888 before dissolving), the Assembly and several of its constituent unions realized a degree of solidarity between white and Black workers.[57]

This was an important achievement in a city whose postwar racial trend pushed heavily in the other direction. One of the most violent attacks on Blacks in the postbellum South had occurred in the city in 1867: official reports listed 35 Blacks dead and 127 wounded. The racial violence that dotted the New Orleans longshore during the nadir sandwiched moments of relative coopera-tion. Thus, Black and white dockers struck together in 1865, 1880, 1883, and 1887, while initiating work-sharing arrangements to be described later.[59] But whenever commerce declined, competition for jobs became fierce and took racial forms on the docks; race riots broke out at several points in the late nine-teenth century. Joy L. Jackson notes: " . . . [I]n times of economic panic and depression, racial antipathy tended to flare up." In such periods, Crescent City shippers did not hesitate to use divisions to their own advantage, making wholesale shifts in levee hiring to keep wages down. Continues Jackson: "Usually employment went to the Negroes, whose standard of living allowed them to accept less than white workers." Clashes between white and Black dockers after the 1872 Panic led the unions to consider a preventative medicine against divi-sion. This eventually assumed the form of what Roger W. Shugg termed "interesting expedients":

> In trades like those of the cotton trades [cotton handlers on the levee], where freedmen threatened the integrity of wages, they were organized into affiliated organizations by the screwmen and yardmen, and bound to fill a certain but smaller proportion of jobs at no less than the white man's wage. Eventually, the skilled Negro came to share this work almost equally with whites, and the standard of living of both races was mutually protected.[60]

The Cotton Men's Executive Council — a federation of cotton handling dock unions — became an important vessel for implementing such arrange-ments. Founded in 1880, it embraced the majority of longshore locals, white and Black, and encouraged mutual support during job actions. When the unions' contract proposals were rejected by employers in 1881, the council organizations struck, more or less unitedly; several Black locals, however, returned to work, complaining of being denied a fair share of employment and an equal voice in the council. Physical attacks on the members of these locals then followed, but a strike-related death restored an overall cooperative spirit. When a Black striker fell to a strikebreaker's bullet, some 2,000 whites and Blacks marched in his funeral procession; white screwmen were among the pallbearers.

The council was the first organization "to officially unite black and white unions in a strike effort." The strike victory did much to enhance organized labor's strength in the 1880s. And the council's interracial example likewise promoted an understanding between white and Black labor under increasingly difficult social and political circumstances.[61]

The Cotton Men's Executive Council was a forerunner of a piviotal force in the present study, the Dock and Cotton Council (founded 1901). By 1886, the former included 72 delegates from 12 organizations, of which two actually represented employers, apparently admitted to encourage the closed shop: the boss draymen (employers of teamsters) and the cotton press owners. The council would split over the presence of the employers' groups; later that year, it reorganized without the cotton press owners.

Nevertheless, problems in the council, as in white-Black labor ties generally, reappeared. Sensing an ineqality in decisionmaking and in locating reliable employment within council arrangements, underemployed and jobless Black dockworkers broke with the council in 1886 to pursue available nonunion work. The controversy led union and nonunion men to fight each other on the levee. White and Black cotton yardmen exchanged gunfire.

At the same time, the parent council split again, but not along racial lines. The Black unions that had left the council now joined with the white screwmen to form a rival umbrella body, while other Black locals and the white longshoremen maintained the "Old Council." Here too, Black-white counterparts — longshoremen, in this instance — confronted each other in combat as union or nonunion, according to the council to which they adhered.[62]

Yet again, the solidarity spirit revived. An interracial work-sharing accord of sorts had been initiated by the longshoremen in 1885; though disrupted in 1886, it was extended later that year to include equal division of work between the races. Generally, it followed a similar pact between the yardmen's locals, also in 1886, which stated clearly: "Each press shall employ . . . half and half of the Cotton Yardmen Nos. 1 and 2." These were the first of what came to be known as half-and-half agreements.[63]

Strengthened by solidarity experiences, however checkered, and favored with the pertinent example of several levee trades, organized labor entered the 1890s "ready . . . to expand the traditional definition of free labor." In November 1892, the labor movement conducted a massive general strike to make the Crescent City a closed shop, challenging management's customary "power to hire and fire without let or hindrance."[64] New Orleans labor reached its nineteenth century zenith.

Solidarity infused the prestrike months and the walkout itself. The white and Black longshoremen reaffirmed their half-and-half understanding in March, despite management opposition.[65] A streetcar drivers' strike in May evoked wide sympathy for their closed-shop demand. When Mayor John Fitzpatrick broke the arbitrators' deadlock by deciding in the drivers' favor, the closed-shop sentiment grew generally among the unions. The Board of Labor Union Presidents, created to assist the streetcar drivers, became the Workingmen's Amalgamated Council in August. Representing 30,000 workers in 49 unions by September, its president was printer James Leonard, a prominent figure then and later in local unionism; one officer was Black, a screwman.[66]

The October strike of the Scalemen, the Packers, and the all-Black Teamsters followed these developments, evoking the sympathy that drew the Workingmen's Amalgamated Council into a general strike. These three unions came together as the Triple Alliance to demand the ten-hour day, higher wages, overtime pay, and the closed shop. The Board of Trade expressed willingness to negotiate, but only with the two white unions, the scalemen and the packers. These organizations stuck with the Teamsters, however, and the Triple Alliance held fast.

As the Triple Alliance unions walked out, they encountered special pressures. Strikebreakers were recruited. Confrontations broke out; strikers and their families attacked strikebreaking teamsters, destroyed the wagons ("drays"), cut harnesses, and set free the horses. A major newspaper decried the strike's interracial character and appealed to white supremacy: "The very worst feature, indeed, in the whole case seems to be that the white element of the labor organizations appear to be under the domination of Senegambian influence, or that they are at least lending themselves as willing tools to carry out Senegambian schemes."[67]

With the Triple Alliance under fire, the Workingmen's Amalgamated Council appointed a Committee of Five, including some dockworkers — Black longshoreman James E. Porter among them — to negotiate for the Alliance with the Board of Trade. As the ensuing talks plodded, labor's mood took a decided turn toward a strike by all unions in the city, in support of both the Triple Alliance and of the particular closed shop, wage, and hour demands of each trade. The November 4 declaration of the Committee of Five came as no surprise:

> The gauntlet has been thrown down by the employers that the laboring men have no rights that they are bound to respect and in our opinion the loss of this battle will affect each and every union man in the city, and after trying

every honorable means to attain an equitable and just settlement, we find
no means open but to issue this call to all union men to stop work and to
assist with their presence and open support . . . and how to the merchants
and all others interested that the labor unions are united.[68]

Therefore, 30,000 workers walked off their jobs on November 8. "Our town
is upside down," cotton yardman-AFL organizer John Callaghan wrote Samuel
Gompers: "Every one [sic] in town are [sic] on a strike . . . There is [sic] no
newspapers to be printed. No gas or electric light in the city. No wagons, no
carpenters, painters or in fact any business doing." The strike, continued
Callaghan would make history: "If we win we have the best union city in the
country if we lose we have none."[69]

The strikers' diversity was impressive. Unskilled dockworkers, shoe clerks,
factory workers, and musicians all seemed determined to stay out until all
demands were met. But there were exceptions: the cotton handling unions on
the levee — screwmen, longshoremen, yardmen — remained at work, refusing
to break newly negotiated contracts. Four men in labor's Committee of Five
themselves came from unions that were not striking. In fact, no union with
a contract had stopped work. The recently victorious streetcar drivers did not
join the strike. Clothing, hat, shoe, utility, and musicians' organizations —
"associations from the lower middle class occupations" — constituted the
walkout's backbone.[70]

Employers apparently found the public ear receptive to antiunionism, so
soon after the highly publicized labor battles at Homestead, Pennsylvania, and
Coal Creek, Tennessee. Roger Shugg reasoned that employers welcomed the
strike as a chance to destroy unions, purposefully prolonging negotiations to
parry the main demand: the closed shop. Management united its forces and
wielded the greater power, drawing upon superior resources and support from
major businessmen around the country. They prepared the railroad transport
of thousands of strikebreakers from points east, west, and north. Frustrated
by Mayor Fitzpatrick's refusal to use the police to protect nonunion labor, the
Board of Trade appealed to Governor Murphy Foster to restore order with the
state militia. The governor thereupon ordered a ban on street gatherings,
warning of his readiness to call in the militia. With martial law pending, the
strike was called off after three days. Attorney William S. Parkerson, who would
play a major part in investigating interracial levee unionism 15 years later,
mediated a pact giving the Triple Alliance the ten-hour day, higher wages, and
overtime pay; the closed shop was denied.[71]

That the Committee of Five had retreated before the massed force of
management and government was apparently a conviction among many rank-
and-file workers; moreover, the unions of four committeemen had continued
working. The strike was not well planned, coordinated, or arranged with such

key forces as the screwmen's, longshoremen's and streetcar drivers' unions. David Paul Bennetts suggests that the strike's "negative impact on the labor movement can scarcely be exaggerated." Nevertheless, wrote Roger Shugg, the strike was labor's "high water mark in the South," demonstrating that Crescent City unionism "was remarkable not only for its early origin, strength and persistence after the Civil War, but also for its racial accommodations . . . " AFL president Gompers termed the effort a "very bright ray of hope for the future of organized labor":

> Never in the history of the world was such an exhibition, where all the prejudices existing against the black man, when the white wage-earners . . . would sacrifice their means of livelihood to defend and protect their colored fellow workers. With one fell swoop the economic barrier of color was broken down.

But, flushed with the vindication of their right to hire and fire freely, employers immediately blacklisted strike leaders and activists. More importantly, they moved to punish the labor organizations by filing suit under the Sherman Anti-Trust Act, the first antilabor use of that law. Brought in Federal Circuit Court two days after the strike, the suit charged 44 unions with conspiracy in restraint of trade. Labor leader John Callaghan exclaimed, "If they convict us all the town will go to __ __ __ __ and a man will have to beg for work and starve when he gets it." After the Court granted a preliminary injunction against the unions, the Workingmen's Amalgamated Council appealed and won postponement of the case, which subsequently was thrown out of court.[72]

The spirit of solidarity drowned in the 1893 depression. The crisis struck hard at New Orleans's commerce. Between 1893 and 1894, Joy J. Jackson indicates, "exports decreased over $1,300,000 and imports over $9,400,000 . . . Grain shipments to the city were severely curtailed and the lack of demand for luxury items cut deep into the port's foreign trade." The cotton trade suffered. It became cheaper for shippers to have bales compressed at interior ports, then simply taken through the city to the ships. Cotton handlers, including screwmen, teamsters, yardmen, and longshoremen were, in Jackson's words, "the natural victims" in this situation. The panic, comments David Paul Bennetts, destroyed solidarity: "Both races became more concerned in each other's jobs than they were in their goodwill."[73]

Therefore, the moment was ripe for the revival of the racial hostility that had traditionally accompanied economic slumps on the Crescent City waterfront. Under state, regional, and national circumstances of advancing Jim Crow, New Orleans shippers stimulated, utilized, and promoted divisions to cut wages and undermine unions. Given the particular strains of the panic on longshore work, dockworkers competed for every job. But the Black screwmen had been bound since 1875 by an accord with the white local: the Black local had restricted the number of its working members at any one time to 100; in return, the whites supported their right to equal pay. This agreement remained in effect until the 1893 depression. Then it was that the Cotton Men's Executive Council, the dock federation, heard changes against Black screwmen by their white counterparts. The Black locals — there were two in 1893 — were accused of expanding their job opportunities (contrary to agreement) by accepting work below union scale. These locals admitted the violation, but only one returned to the fold; the second upheld its actions and was promptly expelled from the council.

Recognizing the chance to lower wages, a major shipper switched entirely to Black labor in 1894; precisely then did the Black screwmen still in the council insist upon a more equitable division of jobs with the white local, which demurred. Torn by dissension, the Cotton Men's Executive Council dissolved in October 1894. And by late October, Black Screwmen's Local No. 2 had followed Black Screwmen's Local No. 1 to jobs offered at lower pay.

Joined by sympathetic white longshoremen, white screwmen quit work and walked off the piers. On the night of October 26, between 150 and 200 whites, armed and masked, raided the ships stowed by Blacks; they threw 96 jackscrews — the screwmen's tools — into the Mississippi River. The following afternoon, armed whites attacked Blacks working on the ships. Again tools were thrown overboard. Storage sheds were torched. Although the white screwmen's local quickly denounced (and issued its statement in English, French, and German) "any acts of individuals . . . which can only tend to bring this association into disrepute," whites burned wharves and destroyed cotton at dockside.[74]

Charging that white longshore foremen had been contravening half-and-half work divisions by hiring six whites for every Black, the Black longshoremen's local meanwhile concluded that only by accepting jobs at 40¢ per hour — instead of 50¢ — might Blacks equalize employment opportunities. David Paul Bennetts observes: "Employers all along the levee began hiring Negroes at the reduced rate and jubilantly predicted that the only course left open to the white workers was to lower their charges." By December 1894, wages for all workers had indeed been lowered to 40¢. On December 19, every white worker in the port quit the levee in protest. And although the Black and white longshoremen's locals met the very next day to affirm mutual fidelity to half-and-half, wages remained down and employers continued to hire Blacks at lower rates, counting on their "uncertainty of finding work at the union rate alongside whites who would betray them if necessary."

The depression continued to ravage dockworkers. Violence flared again in March 1895. Whites attacked, shot, and killed a number of working Black dockers. Governor Murphy Foster called in the militia to disperse crowds and protect commerce. Gunfire subdued the white workers. Interracial cooperation and dock unionism were the main casualties.[75]

A new labor council emerged, the United Labor Council, expressing opposition to strikes. The labor movement of the late 1890s was weak in comparison with that of the previous 15 years. The surviving Black and white dock locals remained at odds. To one observer, by 1900 the white levee unions seemed that they would never again oppose "the social mores of the community" by cooperating with Black dockworkers.[76]

But the Crescent City labor movement experienced a significant revival in the early twentieth century. Separate Black and white central labor councils were formed. Union membership grew, the councils expanded. The new centrals included the major white and Black dock locals.

James Leonard, AFL regional organizer, spearheaded the white Central Trades and Labor Council. The first meeting, convened by Leonard, in October 1899, elected longshoreman James Hughes president; the next meeting chose longshoreman Rufus Ruiz chairman of the By-Laws Committee.

After the screwmen's local joined in late 1899, the council usually met at Screwmen's Hall. Ruiz played an increasingly prominent role in the early 1900s. He became president in 1901. Screwman Thomas Harrison was another important dock leader in the council in the early years. Robert E. Lee, the machinist who attended the 1898 constitutional convention and later was elected to the state Senate, became the council delegate from his union at the end of 1900.[77]

Having adopted the policy of issuing charters separately to white and Black centrals in 1900, the AFL paved the way for a Black central trades body in New Orleans. Longshore veteran James E. Porter, a Black man, took the initiative in writing Samuel Gompers for help in establishing a council for Black unions. Gompers urged him to consult first with the white Central Trades and Labor Council to obtain its authorization.

The white council dissented, however. Despite Gompers's mandate, James Leonard felt a Black council might cause harm if formed too soon. Leonard pleaded for postponement to avoid potential "conflict" that might result "if the proper precautions are not taken."

"My people are very anxious for the organization of the Council," wrote Porter to Gompers, after some time had passed. Further delays inspired Porter to stress again to the AFL president, "My members are very impatient." Porter disputed Gompers's advice to the effect "that there is no use kicking against the pricks and we cannot overcome prejudice in a day. I did not understand that there is prejudice where the wages and interests are the same, and can only be held by concert[ed] action."

Ultimately, the white council relented. Its resolution of approval, however, suggested discord, for only after "a most heated discussion" had the Blacks been "given the right, if it pleases Pres. Gompers, to organize" a central body. Even so, the white central stated in the same breath its refusal "to have anything to do with the colored man."[78]

Thus, a Black Central Trades and Labor Council came into being in 1900. It soon changed its name: the white central pointed out to Gompers "the similarity of the titles of the White and Colored Centrals," and asked that "a distinction be made." On the AFL's advice, the Black council became the Central Labor Union (CLU). Total membership of the two bodies between 1900 and 1910 period averaged 30,000 to 40,000; 12,000 to 15,000 participants marched in the respective Labor Day parades organized by the councils.[79]

New Orleans dockworkers, active in the two centrals and in their own unions, often served as delegates to AFL conventions. Segregated in "one special section of the hall" at the AFL's 1902 convention were James E. Porter and cotton yardman I. G. Wynn (along with other Black delegates). No white dockers from New Orleans attended in 1902, 1903, or 1904, but as the sole CLU delegate in 1904, Porter was censured for the CLU's boycott of a white supremacist labor paper, the *United Labor Journal*. Porter also attended the 1906 AFL convention.

Two New Orleans dockworkers, both screwmen, attended the AFL's 1905 meeting in Pittsburgh: L. J. Obert of the CLU and Thomas Harrison, representing the International Longshoremen's Association. Attending the 1906 convention, Harrison voted against the revocation of the charter of the stubbornly industrial-unionist, Socialist-led Brewery Workers' organization. The controversy over the brewers' policies had ramifications in New Orleans the following year.[85]

The International Longshoremen's Association (ILA) was among the few AFL affiliates freely admitting Black workers and electing Blacks to leadership. In the Crescent City, it had a large membership of whites and Blacks — in separate locals. The union encouraged consultation, at the very least, between the locals. The ILA recorded interesting developments in New Orleans. These included, a Black dockworker informed W. E. B. Du Bois in 1902, higher pay, joint meetings, and "unity of action."

Virtually all New Orleans dock unions participated in ILA conventions. The 1901 convention elected James Porter ninth national vice president. A year later, President Daniel Keefe commended Porter for his "untiring" work and "the wonderful progress made in New Orleans and vicinity." New Orleans Black longshoremen, Keefe declared, were "thoroughly trade unionists," who made "every possible effort to have every man at their calling become members of the local."

When Black and white screwmen in 1903 resisted a heavier work load — a substantial increase in the number of cotton bales to be stowed daily into the ships — Keefe nominated Porter to represent him as arbiter. Even though the employers had consented to labor's proposal to call in Keefe, they could not tolerate Porter. The ILA national leadership delegated "full power in the matter" to Porter, but the Cotton Exchange avowed "that he could not serve as arbiter in matters where whites were concerned." Indeed, "such a thing could

not be done in this city." He "would not be acceptable under any circumstances."

Keefe's reiteration of his choice of Porter infuriated the businessmen: They
wondered whether Keefe grasped the "obvious reasons" that Porter was
undesirable. Although the screwmen's locals backed Porter, Keefe ultimately
withdrew his name, admitting the nomination was a mistake. But Porter was
"fair, straight-forward and honest," and Keefe regretted his rejection.[81]

Porter won reelection as an ILA vice president in 1903. He won by acclama-
tion, notwithstanding intensive prior lobbying by New Orleans's white
screwmen's delegates to fill that vice presidency with one of their own: Thomas
Harrison's bid fell short.

Despite the vice-presidency contention, the white screwmen from New
Orleans did seek to strengthen labor solidarity at the 1903 convention. Thomas
Harrison authored a resolution expressing the concerns of local dockworkers.
Employer efforts to increase the workload always featured citations of the faster
work, lower wages, and better attitudes of Galveston's dockworkers as an example
for New Orleans levee men. Harrison called upon the ILA to support a uniform
wage scale for the screwmen of the two ports to prevent undermining of conditions in one city or the other.

Crescent City screwmen dissented from President Keefe's disavowal of
sympathetic strikes. Coming from a city where levee labor was especially seasonal
and irregular, they vigorously opposed a resolution (which was defeated) bar-
ring members from belonging to more than one ILA trade local:

> . . . [W]e realized that it would be the means of depriving some of the
> members of this [Screwmen's] Association from gaining a livelihood, or else
> it would compel them to scab on union labor, either one of which conditions
> this Association could not and will not stand for.
>
> The New Orleans dockworkers resisted a craft approach within the ILA, with
> all its different trade components: yardmen, screwmen, longshoremen, coal
> wheelers. They felt that conditions made cooperation along industrial lines
> essential.[82]

Despite the development of white-Black cooperation among the dock
unions in the city centrals, the central bodies themselves did not often collaborate. The Black CLU made several attempts at joint action, but only rarely
did the white council respond.

Both organizations backed a hard-fought coopers' strike in 1901 and sanctioned boycotts of nonunion firms. Both councils endorsed a massive strike for
the closed shop in the building trades in 1904. They turned out their members
for a huge rally sponsored by the striking unions in April of that year. Seating
arrangements in the hall defied convention, noted the *Picayune,* with " 'the

colored brother' scattered about . . . and sitting among the whites as though the Fifteenth Amendment were observed to the very letter."[83]

The Labor Day marches of the two centrals were separate throughout the period. The white council turned down a request from the Black central for a joint march in 1902. The two councils held separate parades again in 1903, but not before the Central Trades and Labor Council tried to get the Black central to march *behind* it and the Building Trades Alliance in one big parade. Stronger than and organized before the Building Trades Alliance, the CLU demurred, refusing to become a "rear guard." An angry spokesman declared: "We thought we were entitled to second place, anyway."

The *Republican Liberator,* the Black levee paper, carried on the argument for joint parades. The labor movement, it stated, "must have the presence of the colored laborer and workman." Every advance for Black workers had benefitted whites: the emancipation of the slaves, for example, had rid white workers of the "Masters and his 'Niggers' competition" in the skilled crafts, "whereas now, it is an open field, so to speak."[84]

In 1906, the CLU proposed to the Central Trades and Labor Council an agreement to help "adjust any troubles that might spring up between the white and colored workmen." No formal accord resulted, but in July 1907 the councils held their first-ever joint meeting. The CLU suggested that they work together to support the striking local brewery workers, whose industrially organized national union had only recently been excluded from the AFL. "After some trouble" over the CLU overture, the white council agreed to the meeting. The centrals appointed delegations: the CLU sent one composed entirely of dockworkers. (By that time, as will be indicated, no dock locals remained in the white central). But the two councils were irretrievably at odds in the brewery dispute, and failed to reach agreement.[85]

Solidarity among dockworkers evolved in the inhospitable conditions of the nadir, in a segregated city run by a Democratic political machine, against a background of contrary AFL policies, in the face of an open-shop drive. The hostile reaction of cotton merchants in a 1903 dispute to the very suggestion of meeting with Black longshoreman James E. Porter spoke volumes: "Such a thing could not be done in this city." As will be demonstrated, this was not the only thing that "could not be done": interracial solidarity was officially anathema.

The nadir's proscriptions drastically curtailed or made more difficult the development of cooperation between white and Black. Interaction in many areas had persisted before the 1890s, but by the turn of the century, segregation and disfranchisement had become dogma and law, consciously promoted by the political-economic protagonists of the New South. New Orleans labor operated in this context, reflecting the propagation of and resistance to prevailing white supremacy. Dockworkers created a powerful movement, bringing forth distinctive, skilled leaders; but the path to interracial trade union solidarity was strewn with political, legal, ideological, and physical obstructions.

Chapter Two

Work and Organizations

Of the cotton trade, we may premise . . . that it is the mainstay of the city's commerce and prosperity.

Louisiana Chamber of Commerce, 1894

Under ordinary circumstances the shipowner is exonerated from damage by sweat . . . .

Charles Hillcoat, Master Mariner, 1919

It shall be the duty of every member of this Association, in order to more effectually, perpetuate the bonds of Unity and Brotherhood; to aid each other, both in the Association and in their intercourse at large, so far as shall be in their power to do so; and any member who shall injure or attempt to injure a brother member shall be considered as violating the bonds of brotherhood, and on conviction thereof, shall be fined, suspended or expelled as a majority may determine.

By-Laws, Screwmen's Benevolent Association, 1877[1]

Trade in cotton meant everything to the New Orleans economy. Sugar, tobacco, coffee, fruit, grain, and lumber also passed through the port, into the hands of dockworkers, and onto the massive steamships, but it was cotton that made New Orleans the nation's second port. Like commerce in most of the products, the cotton trade was naturally a seasonal business, reaching its zenith in the fall and winter months. Although the port remained open all year, far less work was found during the off-season. Dock labor was therefore inconsistent and irregular. Even during the busy season, dockworkers often outnumbered jobs: the "shaping-up" hiring system left many walking from pier to pier or waiting on the levee for word of incoming ships. Unemployment constantly threatened and struck the labor force: It was a chronic annual condition.

This chapter examines the character of the work and organizations of dock laborers: screwmen, teamsters, yardmen, longshoremen, freight handlers. Along original task or craft lines, these men organized unions; generally each of the unions formed segregated white and Black locals. The diverse dock functions did not overlap, but were contiguous. The tasks of one group followed directly from and led directly to those of others, and thus could not stand autonomously. Dockers maximized job opportunities by joining several dock unions: an Old World custom of exchanging unions cards became a New Orleans tradition.

Contiguity and interdependence combined with the insecurity of dock work to foster the developing cooperation which fueled a powerful dock unionism. The unions bred a moral code of integrity and solidarity consonant with the commandments of the locally circulated "Labor's Decalogue," particularly, "Thou shalt not take thy neighbor's job." When shipping and railroad corporations sought to raise labor's productivity by increasing the work load, dock unions took self-protective action by strengthening interracial solidarity. The struggle to control the work load erupted in a convulsive levee war on the New Orleans riverfront. Productivity became the levee's bone of contention, the centerpiece of the local open-shop drive, the crucial issue bitterly fought out in lockouts, stoppages, and the 1907 general strike.

The Levee

The port constituted the workshop of the Crescent City. Ten thousand men labored along its 15 miles of riverfront and six miles of wharves. By 1900, New Orleans led all world markets in the trade of cotton, sugar, rice, bananas, and cotton seed. Commerce guided manufacture: sugar refining, cotton compressing, tobacco and cigarmaking, lumber, and cotton seed oil production became prominent in the city's small industrial base. Breweries, foundries, shoe factories, confectionaries, and clothing factories took shape in the city before 1900, but the main commercial products served as the basis of manufacture.[2]

New Orleans lay upon swampland. Only the levees (natural and later man-made) were more than 15 feet above sea level: most of the city sat below, or within five feet of, sea level. Enlarged by glacial melting at the end of the Ice Age, the Mississippi River extended its delta, depositing large amounts of sand, silt, clay, boulders, gravel, and cobblestones throughout Louisiana. At the point where the river reached the crescent of the future city, however, only the smaller particles — sand, silt, and semicompactible clay — were left. The area's underlying bedrock became a receptable for both the looser, less dense particles and "a large bulk of soupy organic matter which results from the decomposition of swamp and marsh vegetation." A cross section of the delta would resemble "a shallow clay saucer filled with layer upon layer of warm jello."

Upon raised sections of riverbank New Orleans arose, subject at all times to floods caused by heavy subtropical rains. Throughout its history the city sought to resist the penalties of its location. By 1900, technological advances made building a system of constructed levees along the city's waterfront to offset floods and facilitate drainage possible.[3]

In 1900, the man-made levees were vast confluences of dirt and silt pushed and arranged in low hills behind the wharves. Dusty in dry weather, oozing in the humid periods, the levees desperately needed paving.[4]

Dockworkers labored in the mud, in the heat of a city strewn with open sewers and backyard toilets, whose contents were taken to dumps by the Black drivers of appropriately named "aggravatin' wagons." Vermin proliferated on the docks. An old longshore worker from the early 1900s recalled huge roaches: "Big red flying ones and it really hurt when they bit you." Rats infested the sheds used for temporary storage of flour, rice, wheat, and banana cargoes.[5]

The Industry

Attempting to improve dock conditions in the nation's second leading port, the state legislature had established in 1896 the Board of Commissioners of the Port of New Orleans. Known as the Dock Board, its mandate included the power to build and lease new wharves and sheds. During its first ten years, the board limped along on a meager allocation. It could not rehabilitate deteriorating and filthy wharves or correct other conditions of labor shipping. Only in 1908, after the general strike and massive pressure, was a full investigation launched into the Dock Board's powers to improve the port. Afterward, the sale of bonds was to prove the essential source of Board funds. In the meantime, several steamship lines advanced interest-free loans to the Dock Board and were thus exempted from wharfage charges. The Harrison and Leyland Lines did this in 1903. The Leyland, Harrison, United Fruit Company, and Southern Pacific Lines would all gain from dock improvements. They depended on New Orleans for a great portion of their business.[6]

These lines, and all others using the port — 14 in all in 1901 — appointed "agents" to represent them in New Orleans. As the port developed during the nineteenth century, the agents formed an employers' association: the Conference of Steamship Agents. They were the employers of levee labor.

The Harrison Line, owned by a wealthy British family, began using the port in 1877. Its representative in New Orleans from the 1880s to the 1930s was family member Alfred Le Blanc; the Line's main United States office was, in fact, in the Crescent City, and Le Blanc served as its U. S. General Agent. In 1903, Argentina appointed him vice-consul at its local consulate. Having married into the family of a prominent local cotton merchant, Le Blanc founded an insurance company in the city and became vice president of the Bank of New Orleans. His "very gracious deeds" for the city included substantial philanthropy. A leading personality in New Orleans business circles, Le Blanc played host in 1904 to the Harrison Line's own Frederick J. Harrison, amidst great fanfare.[7]

The British Leyland Steamship Line's New Orleans agent in the early 1900s was M. J. Sanders, a New Orleans native. Leyland's New Orleans business was second only to its commerce in New York. Sanders was president of the Progressive Union, a businessmen's club, from 1904 to 1906. In the latter year, he formed the City Bank and Trust company, with himself as president. He won election to several terms as head of the Joint Conference of the Cotton, Sugar and Rice, Coal, and other Exchanges. M. J. Sanders and Alfred Le Blanc were major spokesmen for the shipping lines in general, particularly on labor matters. In 1905, Sanders was convinced that New Orleans's commercial success was ensured. "Had there been no 'reconstruction period'," Sanders suggested, the boom in port commerce would have been that much greater; but surely the city now would make up for lost time.[8]

Two major railroads owned docks in and/or sent steamships to New Orleans. The Southern Pacific, largest in the nation, and the Illinois Central both belonged to the Harriman system of railroads. The Illinois Central controlled the massive Stuyvesant Docks. The Southern Pacific used the Morgan terminals across the river in Algiers (once an independent town and a part of New Orleans since 1870), named for the formerly independent Morgan railroad line linking New Orleans with points northwest. The Morgan line came under the control of the Southern Pacific in 1885.[9]

The Illinois Central's Stuyvesant terminal was the point where freight trains discharged cotton from out-of-state and Louisiana plantations. The railroad built tracks close to the riverfront. Those who unloaded the trains at dockside were called "freight handlers"; longshoremen then transferred the cargo to the screwmen for stowing aboard ship.

The Morgan dockworkers employed by the Southern Pacific, and also known as freight handlers, did much more than the handlers of the Illinois Central. They actually loaded and unloaded ships, and even stowed cotton; back across the river only longshoremen and screwmen did that work.

Clearly, however, the railroad and steamship lines interacted in the transfer of cotton from plantation to foreign port. The workers employed by shippers and railroads also interacted.

The steamship companies hired dockworkers through contractors called "stevedores." In New Orleans, longshoreman and stevedore were not synonymous; the latter was part of management. Several stevedoring firms achieved prominence in the late nineteenth and early twentieth centuries, particularly John B. Honor, Ltd., and the William J. Kearney Company. Honor was a coal merchant and a member of the Coal Exchange. Kearney inherited his firm from his grandfather in 1892. Vocal, assertive men, Honor and Kearney became major figures in the local shipping industry. Stevedores had their own trade association; with the steamship agents they combined to form a Joint Conference.[10]

Labor

Dock labor was seasonal. Its regularity hinged on the growth and availability of staples, especially cotton, destined for transport through the port. Work was heavy in winter, slack in summer.

Census reports indicate that many dockworkers were unemployed four or more months in a year. Often they looked for other work in the off-season; many belonged to unions in other occupations. The census shows that many dockworkers' wives worked as domestics. The holding of membership cards in more than one dock union facilitated employment when the work in some dock trades was busier than in others. Obituaries and accounts of men who were dockworkers between 1900 and 1910 reveal the versatility necessitated by seasonality. For dockworkers were also postal workers, cotton yardmen were court clerks, screwmen became watchmen and pile drivers, longshoremen worked in breweries, and teamsters were musicians.[11]

With the shipping season's unofficial start on September 1, port labor became the occupation of some 10,000 men: screwmen, teamsters, longshoremen, yardmen, freight handlers, yardmen, and others. The racial and trades composition of this basically closed-shop work force was often confused in contemporary accounts. Estimates of membership varied widely. The *Picayune* reported 6,000 organized dockworkers in April 1903, but 9,000 in May; the *Union Advocate* reported 10,000 members in May.

The *Picayune* and the *New Orleans Daily News* (the latter was pro-labor) placed total membership at 10,000 in October 1907 and gave the following specifics in key dock trades: 1,800 screwmen (1,000 Black), 3,500 longshoremen (2,100 Black), 1,200 cotton yardmen (700 Black), 300 coal wheelers (all Black), and 200 teamsters (all Black). At the same time, the less trustworthy *New Orleans Daily Item* reported three times as many coal wheelers and twice as many teamsters but fewer longshoremen. In 1908, a white screwmen's leader gave figures of 600 white screwmen and 1,200 Blacks, commensurate with most estimates in 1907. A Black longshoremen, however, stated there were only 900 Black longshoremen in March 1908, less than one-half the number estimated in late 1907. (The figures in all cases were of union membership). But scholars Sterling Spero and Abram Harris found the work force "about evenly divided" between white and Black on the eve of World War I.

Seasonality, unemployment, and layoffs played havoc with union membership. In addition, superficial press coverage may have had something to do with the differing estimates. All signs, however, point to an increase over time in the proportion of Blacks to the whole in the early twentieth century. If Blacks were not a clear majority, they were at least one-half of the workers in the key dock trades.[12]

The busy season created work for others along the levee, too: "roustabouts," for example, consisting solely of Black men.

Roustabouts generally performed all types of unskilled labor. They usually worked aboard the smaller vessels headed up the river instead of out to sea. Jelly Roll Morton, a contemporary dockworker-musician, called their work the hardest on the levee. Roustabouts had no union:

> Weren't treated like other fellows. Had a captain over them with a ship or lash in their hands. I had never seen them whipped, but I had often heard they whipped them to keep them going. They would carry on their backs all kinds of things, big boxes of lard. Carried this stuff up the gangplanks. Looked like a man couldn't carry so much. Singing and moving to rhythm of songs as much as they could . . . . Roustabouts would never dream of striking on river boats. They were just like in slavery.

They did odd jobs on the levee, supplementing the tasks of other, more skilled, dockworkers. White men, a steamboat owner told the United States Industrial Commission in 1901, could "not stand the work" performed by roustabouts. Roustabouts were said to be immoral, indulging in "crap games," frequenting "barrel houses," taking up with the "commonest kind of women." Travelling on the steamboats they had loaded to upriver ports where they were to unload, roustabouts were likely "to dodge work when a landing is to be made, so they will hide among the freight and sleep there or even beneath the boilers, where a white man would roast."[13]

Roustabouts were ancillary to the main dock labor and to the port's chief function as a center for global commerce. The cotton teamsters, all Black, on the other hand, were a larger component of the essential work process of exporting cotton. Their work differed from that of "round freight" teamsters who handled sugar and rice. Reporting early to the stables owned by their employers (the boss "draymen"), cotton teamsters fed and groomed the mules and prepared the wagons ("floats" or "drays") for work. By 7:00 a.m., they were on their way either to the docks or to the cotton yards to pick up pressed cotton bales now ready for transfer onto the ships. For more than one teamster, the 7:00 a.m. starting time meant leaving the house long before dawn to prepare the mules and wagons. One cotton teamster who supplemented his income with a job at night, remembered how it had been for him around 1908:

You'd leave 5:00 a.m. and catch the streetcar to the stables. There you'd pick up your mule team at 6:00 a.m. and start out for the docks to pick up load at 7:00 a.m. Once you got your team hooked up and started toward the docks, you could sleep because your mules would follow the wagon in front. Sometimes you had a helper; he'd drive the wagon where you were going and you'd sleep. He'd wake you up to load or deliver.

In the main, teamsters shuttled between the cotton yards and the docks. Traveling to the cotton yards, cotton teamsters picked up where cotton yardmen left off, their respective tasks adjoined. One group's disputes affected the other. When the teamsters refused (in 1904) orders to begin the workday at 6:30 a.m., or resisted (in 1905) cancellation of their regular lunch hour, the larger, more powerful Black and white cotton yardmen's organizations stopped work and joined negotiations.[14]

Cotton yardmen, Black and white, embraced several labor categories:

the yardmen who unloaded the cotton in the yards and brought it to the warehouse and the cotton press; the cotton classers who classified the cotton according to its quality; the scalehands who put the cotton on the scales and took it off after weighing; the weighers and reweighers who did the actual weighing; the pressmen who operated the cotton press . . . .

Yardmen's contracts covered all or most of these workers. (Scalemen, who weighed rice and coffee — not cotton — had their own small organization, all Black). Men known as "cotton factors" owned the yards and the presses; like the steamship agents and the stevedores, they had formed a trade association.

Here in the yards, cotton was pressed as compactly as possible. So compact were the bales (stacked in the yards until the cotton teamsters came to transfer them to dockside), that if one fell on a worker, certain injury would result. Thus, for example, leading cotton yardman Fred Grosz suffered a broken leg in 1904.

Cotton export stipulated no greater priority than the density and uniformity of cotton bales, to guarantee the stowage of as many as possible. The aim, a contemporary expert wrote, was " to fill all spaces" in the holds of the ships to ensure the "maximum revenue." Each bale pressed in New Orleans, approximately 470 to 500 pounds and 30 cubic feet was, in fact, stowed aboard ship in a space hardly larger than the bale.[15] The stowing of the yardmen's finished product, baled cotton, ultimately rested with men who traditionally used their hands and a jackscrew to squeeze the bales into these spaces: the screwmen.

Longshoremen

Cotton could not be stowed by screwmen, however, until it was placed in their hands by the longshoremen. Longshoremen took the cotton brought to the pier (from either the cotton yards or the dockside tracks) and transferred it, one bale at a time, onto rope-attached slings at the side of the ship. A small engine on the ship, driven by steam in the ship's own boilers, propelled the up-and-down and side-to-side movements of the ropes. One longshoreman hooked the bale-filled sling to the ropes. Another guided it toward the hatch. A third operated the engine, or "winch." He turned on the steam to tighten the sling around the bale. The sling lifted off the pier, and was guided over the hatch and into the ship's hold.

The winchman could feel when the sling was low enough in the hold to be unloaded by the screwmen below, but sometimes the ropes were premarked. The hold decks were nine feet below the hatch. The screwmen in the holds, working in gangs, swung the descending bale in the direction it was to be stowed, and yelled to the winchman to lower it to the deck when it was over the proper place. The winch operator then withdrew the ropes up to the deck where they were caught by a longshoreman called a "whip-runner," and readied for another load. To expedite the procedure, two winches commonly operated at the same time. The winches were generally part of the ship's equipment.[16]

Longshoremen wore gloves or hand-straps to protect their knuckles. The rope controlling vertical movements of the sling was called the "whip." When swingly freely, it was powerful enough to knock a man overboard or through the hatch to the hold below. Moving slings, with 500-pound bales attached, also presented dangers. If the bale hit a man or the sling broke, then injury was certain and death possible. After ropes broke over longshoreman Edward Ryan one September afternoon in 1905, a falling bale of grass killed him. Screwmen, working below and around the hatches, also fell victim to the hazards. Thomas Waterman went to the hospital after a cotton bale knocked him into the hold in October 1903. Black screwman George Lewis suffered severe head injuries in a similar accident several months later, while Richard Murray and Serefino Rodriquez were struck by a collapsing sling filled with timber one day in August 1904. Murray died.[17]

Black and white longshoremen, several thousand strong in the early 1900s, were the largest group of dockworkers. Like the screwmen, they worked in gangs and were hired through the shape-up system. Foremen (who were commonly the first men hired by the contracting stevedores) generally chose the same men for each gang. Foremen were union members: Rule XV of the Black and white longshoremen's joint agreement fined foremen for blacklisting a job-seeking union member or for refusing to hire union men when they were available.

Longshoremen and screwmen reported to the pier early each morning en masse, and were picked if a ship was ready for loading or unloading. But when the gangs were picked, many jobseekers remained. They went over to the other piers in search of work or waited for incoming ships. A longshoreman was lucky if he knew a foreman as well as early Black jazz musician Pops Foster did in 1908:

> Joe Sullivan was the union leader for the longshoremen, and he had all the best musucians working on longshore work. That's what I did most of the time I wasn't playing. Joe lived out in the Irish Channel and would throw lawn parties on Monday nights. He's ask the guys who worked for him to come out and play . . . Joe took care of us and if a good boat was coming in, he'd send word around for the guys to come to work. If a ship needed tying up, it took about ten minutes and you got paid for a half a day at forty cents an hour.

Longshoremen encountered prolonged periods of unemployment. During the busier fall and winter months a longshoreman or screwman might spend hours or days looking for work (and work was practically nonexistent during the off season). A longshoreman told the United States Industrial Relations Commission in 1914 that his work "does not have the most exhilirating effect." A union organizer described how a longshoreman

> may be called at 9 o'clock, or he may be called at 9:30 or 10 or up to 11, and sometimes a half hour, and he has got to be always waiting, and it is pretty laborious work, . . . and if he is a drinking man he is liable to go to a saloon, and that has caused the downgrade of our men, having to lay around and frequent saloons . . . [18]

Longshoremen in New Orleans did more than transfer cotton to the screwmen. They also worked in the holds of ships, skillfully stowing goods that fell outside the traditional parameter of screwmen's work: grain, fruit, sugar, bananas, coffee, and lumber. This division of work dated well back into the ninetheenth century. "I have been a longshoreman since 1872," Black union leader John B. Williams remarked in 1903. "It was in 1872 that the division of work was made and agreed that the Screwmen should handle cotton and tobacco. The Longshoremen stow all other kinds of freight."

In 1889, screwmen and longshoremen further agreed that unloading of cargo was the province of longshoremen: screwmen were only to "break out" the freight, longshoremen then took over. But the freight handlers across the river at the Algiers's Morgan docks (owned by the Southern Pacific) did both longshoremen's and screwmen's work, and this too was apparently traditional, attributable perhaps to Algiers's former separation from the city proper. Further, the longshoremen who stowed coal formed their own organization; coal loading became the sphere of coal wheelers, several hundred in number and all Black.

Longshoremen's work gangs consisted of four men on each side of a hatch in the early 1900s, or "eight-to-a-hatch." In 1903, steamship agents declared that eight-to-a-hatch were too many for the available work and ordered a reduction to four-to-a-hatch, or two on each side. The unions protested the "disposition" of some employers "to work a man to death," "to so reduce the working force on ships that it has become almost impossible for any man to stand a day's work on ships loading or unloading." Breaks for a drink of water "or for any other necessary cause" required a man "to either hire another in his place, or the work will have to cease until his return, and in many instances the man is discharged upon his return." Because "self-preservation is the first law of nature," the longshoremen promised to resist a work pace seemingly designed, said one, to work out "the heartstrings of the men." But they were to lose this time. Neverthless, struggles over the size of work gangs persisted. Steamship agents warned anxious civic leaders in 1906 that they would not yield "their right to the employment of men and the determination of the number of men that were competent to do a certain amount of work."[19]

Longshoremen's work demanded readiness to go up or down the river to work on ships docked at nearby Chalmette, Gretna, or Westwego. Contention frequently arose over the time it took to travel to these piers by tugboat and the number of hours constituting a full day's work in these cases, for the men likened this labor to night or overtime work.

Disputes also emerged when steamship agents sought to assign or encourage longshoremen to do screwmen's work — cotton and tobacco loading — at the (lower) longshoremen's wage. Agents sought to implement the 1903 contract clause requiring longshoremen "to do such work as is required of them" in precisely that way. But labor succeeded in reaffirming the traditional work divisions. Still, controversy continued.[20]

Screwmen

The most skilled workers among the levee's interacting components were the screwmen. Using jackscrews and their own manual dexterity to push cotton bales into tight spaces in the holds, the longshoremen possessing this skill formed their own organization first and apart from those of other dockworkers. The white and Black screwmen's local, founded in 1850 and 1875 respectively, became the strongest dock organizations. The skill of stowing cotton was all-important in New Orleans. Former screwmen Jelly Roll Morton recalled years later: "These were permanent people. Made tremendous salaries. Around $18 a day, and that is way back."

"Permanent" perhaps, but they worked seasonally too, and they also had to labor in other fields, on and off the docks. They were hired in a shape-up.

Furthermore, an occasional foreman or stevedore might let it be known that men who bribed them would definitely be chosen to work. In 1908, Black screwman A. J. Ellis charged that agents and stevedores acted as moneylenders, forcing men to borrow and repay at high interest or risk firing or blacklisting.

Yet screwmen gained a degree of a prestige, and their organizations a strength that other dockworkers lacked. "Through all these years," the local *Union Advocate* observed in 1903, "to be known as a screwman was to receive recognition as to character and responsibility." The union

> gained and maintained prominence during all its career as the champion of oppressed labor, and with a devotion [to] its purposes worthy of all praise, it entered the lists as a sponsor for younger and weaker unions whenever championship and defense was necessary.[21]

Screwmen's work hinged on the compactness of the cotton bales. It required skill to stow a ship fully and evenly. Screwman Thomas Gannon remembered: "Sometimes we thought she'd bust before she reached Europe." Damage to cargo resulted when the loads became unbalanced; moreover, uneven loading or overloading posed dangers to the vessel. In New Orleans, gangs of five screwmen (including a foreman), racially segregated in different hatches until 1902, dragged or rolled each bale to its proper space. They wore protection on their hands. Stacking bales in tiers, screwmen propped an expanding jackscrew between an upright post and a board placed against the cotton, turned the screw until fully tightened, finally releasing this screw with the added counterpressure of other screws and a dolly. The loose bits of wood material — "dunnage" — generally distributed around and about the cotton as protection and insulation, were also thus secured. This time-consuming, highly skilled operation persisted into the 1920s. Nonetheless, screwmen stowed increasingly by hand, not by jackscrew, in the early twentieth century, as cotton presses improved, and the steamship companies enlarged the cargo capacities of vessels. Steamship agents contended in 1902 that the enhanced cargo space had made cotton screwing obsolete.[22]

Even though the men resorted to jackscrews in many cases, they stowed most cotton by hand in the early twentieth century. Hand stowing required tilting two bales on edge against each other and pressing down, forcing them into place. The method became known as "marrying-it-in," and the bales thus "married" as "kissing bales." Some ships required only hand stowing, others both screwing and hand stowing in different holds, while a few still needed cotton screwing exclusively. When steamship agents suggested in 1903 that the ships were large enough to make the screwmen's skill unnecessary and that men in the hold ought to increase the number of hand-stowed bales, a screwman answered that stowing by hand was itself not easy: "Everything seems easy when somebody else is doing it."

That ship-enlarging technology had made jackscrews and even skillful hand stowing basically obsolete was a major argument of employers in the first years of the new century. They disputed the need for a separate category of workers to stow cotton. They insisted that the rate of hand stowing be increased. A steamship agent warned in 1902 that "the days of the screwmen are fast passing away . . . and they should be thankful that they are alive at all."

But workers resisted the suggestion that they were obsolete, that their labor slowed business. The chairman of the joint Black-white screwmen's committee in 1902 "thanked" employers for allowing workers "to live in the country" where steamship agents "rake in the profits while the laboring man barely gets an existence." Indeed, he went on, if cotton screwing impaired commerce, "how is it then, that the companies can continue to build these monster ships and keep sending them out? They seem to pay."[23]

The debate raged in 1902 and 1903. How much should the screwmen stow? Who had the right to decide? Screwmen maintained that the faster the hand stowing, the more dangerous the work. They charged the employers had been pressuring them at a pace of work described as "shoot-the-chute," which more than doubled the bales stowed by hand. A spokesman in 1903 labelled shoot-the-chute a "menace to life and limb."

A screwmen's statement appealed for mutual respect of labor's and capital's "rights," invoking a "spirit of justice." But a 1903 *Picayune* editorial argued that soon "the screws themselves and the skill required for their operation will become worthless." Were screwmen to remain on the New Orleans levee, other ports would then beckon to merchants by offering faster, cheaper loading of ships. That must be prevented, the *Picayune* suggested in October 1903, "even if the screwmen must be eliminated as an obstruction to the progress of the port."[24]

A true difference in perception of "rights" emerged in the dispute. The steamship agents jointly wondered how workers could determine the method and pace of stowage aboard ships they did not own. Clearly, "the employee never can have the right to say what shall be the character of the work done."[25] Screwmen felt they should have a voice in these matters, which involved their jobs. How could they protect themselves? They accused employers of using the following tactic to impose a faster work pace and a greater work load in the 1890s and early 1900s:

> But note the manner in which this was done. At that time the screwmen worked in different parts of the ship, the whites in one section and colored in the other. The hirelings of the steamship agents would notify the white screwmen that the colored screwmen were working faster and doing a greater amount of work, and that unless they caught up with them that the agents would be compelled to discharge them. Immediately thereafter the colored screwmen

would be told that the white screwmen were doing a greater amount of work, and unless their results were the same, that their services would be dispensed with[26].

Black and white screwmen responded to the changes in the work pace and work load by formulating their half-and-half plan, a work-sharing agreement more far-reaching than other strategies fashioned by Black and white dockworkers in New Orleans. Their accord, in 1902, required the equal hiring (by union foremen) of Black and white, and their working abreast of each other in the same hatch. On the basis of the half-and-half agreement, the screwmen drastically cut back the pace of work.[27]

The new work agreement became the main source of levee controversy in the early 1900s. It initially shocked the steamship agents. The half-and-half agreement, an agent averred, "will prove the nigger in the woodpile. If that rule is to be enforced to the letter with all the hidden things it may conceal, then we may as well close up the port of New Orleans and get off the map."

Agents thought the agreement gave the screwmen too much power: it was "limitless in scope." Its possibilities, said one, "cannot be conceived by the human mind."[28]

The components of the labor force interacted. Traditional differences in skill and task perpetuated the division of dock trades. But certain skills, for example the use of the jackscrew, were apparently becoming unnecessary. And on-the-job interdependence bound all dockworkers together in the work process, skill notwithstanding. They carried their work-site cooperation into their organizations.

Organizations

New Orleans dock unions, essentially a product of post-Civil War times, came into their own at the turn of the century. Originating as benevolent societies, they became the vehicle through which laborers tried to shape their work and assert their interests in the city's most decisive business. Even though the various dock unions remained separate, most eventually affiliated with the ILA, and over time took steps toward mutual cooperation. Seasonality and unreliability of dock work also tended to induce cooperation. The organizations came to a general understanding among themselves and with others that their union cards would be mutually honored and that dock unionists might also use their cards to find work outside the levee in the off season.

Thus, a dockworker in good standing seeking a brewery job did not have to be initiated into the brewery union. Noting this procedure in New Orleans, labor editor Oscar Ameringer observed:

Such exchange of cards had been in vogue among the industrial unions of the Old World, almost from their inception. The Old-World unions were international: the union card of the Frenchman was good in Germany and Italy, as was the German card in England and Holland, and so on. Most American unions also call themselves international, but their internationalism is usually confined to members of the same craft and quite frequently does not extend as far as the next county.[29]

The separate dock unions formalized their cooperation in the interracial Dock and Cotton Council, founded in 1901. The council, which is fully discussed in a later chapter, was "not a general central union, but an *industrial union* of all workers on and about the docks," according to contemporary observer Covington Hall. The council united all workers engaged in handling cotton. It included the cotton teamsters (who were also members of a local Teamsters Council) but did not include the round freight teamsters who trucked sugar and rice. Sources suggest that the Black screwmen were the driving force in forming the Council. A white dockworker always served as president, a Black dockworker as vice president.[30]

The screwmen's locals were in fact the backbone of organized labor and workers' cooperation on the levee. As the oldest and strongest force, a labor paper commented, they frequently "entered the lists as sponsor for younger and weaker unions whenever championship and defense was necessary." The white Screwmen's Benevolent Association was formed in 1850. Aside from the screwmen, only one other union operated in New Orleans before the Civil War: the Typographical Union.

Following the Civil War, the white screwmen remained for a period the only organized body of dockworkers. The large-scale entry of Blacks into levee employment led to the formation of a Black longshoremen's union in 1872, the Longshoremen's Protective Union Benevolent Association. In the wake of the 1872 depression, with severe unemployment on the levee and fierce competition for jobs, the white screwmen's union helped found a parallel Black local: Screwmen's Benevolent Association No. 2. The Black local, formed in 1875, took shape after employers had used cheaper, unorganized Black labor to depress the wages of white screwmen; Black dockers were attacked by whites in race riots. Therefore, "in order to survive," observed a historian, the whites helped organize the Black screwmen and prevailed upon them to accept the following arrangement in 1875: "In return for equal wages, the colored agreed not to supply more than 100 men for work at any one time." This arrangement generally persisted through the remainder of the century, racial exclusion coupling with equal pay in the context of a rapid increase in the number of Black dockworkers and the development of larger ships, imperilling the special stowing skills of screwmen. Changing circumstances were later to contribute to labor's reconsideration of white-Black work arrangements.[31]

During the 1880s, aided at times by actual or threatened sympathetic actions by screwmen, other dock organizations emerged: the Cotton Yardmen (the white local in 1879, the Black local in 1880), Cotton Teamsters, Coal Wheelers, Round Freight Teamsters, Freight Handlers, and other unions. On several occasions, as in the July 1880 cotton yardmen's walkout, Black and white engaged in joint strikes. But Black longshoremen struck *alone* in March of that year.[32]

Relations Between Levee Unions

During the 1870s and 1880s, dock unions divided different stages of the work process. With some, the division of labor was clear, for example, between teamsters (who trucked frieght on wagons) and yardmen (who pressed cotton into bales) or screwmen (who stowed cotton in the ships). But what of the respective areas of responsibility of screwmen and longshoremen who both stowed cargo (although different types)? Even though linked at the same end of the work process, on the same ship, above and below the same hatch, these two unions clearly distinguished separate tasks during the 1870s and 1880s: screwmen stowed cotton and tobacco; longshoremen loaded sugar, rice, and other products.

Moreover, they agreed in 1889 that in the course of unloading ships the screwmen were to do no more than "break out" the cargo. Longshoremen were to do the actual unloading. Later, in July 1903, when screwmen insisted on doing *all* the unloading of the same type of freight they stowed (cotton and tobacco), longshoremen struck in protest. They stood by the 1889 agreement. Although the Black and white screwmen felt the 1889 division obsolete, they conceded the issue because as white president Robert Trainor declared, it would keep the "peace on the riverfront."[33]

A controversy emerged in September 1903 when employers, pressuring for simplification of the costly and complex division of work, actively implemented a contract clause that mandated longshoremen "to do such work as is required of them." They assigned longshoremen to stow cotton and tobacco, long the province of screwmen. The longshoremen refused and were locked out, inducing the screwmen, coal wheelers, cotton and round freight teamsters of both races to strike sympathetically. Eight thousand men stopped work. They succeeded in restoring the traditional division of labor, despite management's consequent lawsuit against the longshoremen's locals for breach of contract. Before dropping the case, stevedore John B. Honor collected $2,000 of a $12,000 award in the April 1904 suit, but longshoremen still refused to do screwmen's work. A prominent leader declared: "We can't think of it."

Screwmen and others also refused to work earlier in September 1903 while the longshoremen were engaged in an unsuccessful effort to expand work teams from four-to-a-hatch to eight to better cope with a faster work pace. Altogether, mutual cooperation on the levee held up two weeks of commerce in the heart of the busy season. Similarly, dock unions withdrew their men during freight handlers' (1902) and cotton teamsters' (1905) disputes. And although the various unions occasionally competed, cooperation generally prevailed, especially after the Dock and Cotton Council in 1901 was formed.[34] (See Chapter III.)

Screwmen's Organizations

Behind most efforts at cooperation stood the screwmen's organizations and especially the white screwmen's union. The Black screwmen, white and Black longshoremen, and other dockworkers, adopted many of the procedures of the white screwmen's organization.

The white union was open to new applicants older than age 21 but younger than 45 years old. (Until 1877, the maximum age for new members was 40.) Candidates submitted an application with a $10 fee and were required to have the commendation of three members in good standing. The application fee increased to $50 in 1887, which was a tremendous jump. By the late 1890's it was reduced to $25. For nearly 50 years, the by-laws listed no other requirements for applicants beyond the unwritten implication that they be white and the statutory requirement that they be decent and moral. In 1894, the union added that the applicant also be a United States citizen. An Investigation Committee discussed each applicant and reported to the membership for a final decision. If rejected, the applicant could reapply after six months.[35]

For the new member, obligations began with dues, which remained at 50¢ per month until 1877 when they rose to 75¢. By 1900, dues were no longer pegged at a specific figure, but constituted 5% of the wage, with deductions supervised by the foremen. By 1905, this generally amounted to $2.25 payable quarterly. Acknowledging the casuality of labor, the union, however, continued to assess members not working as screwmen (during the busy season) for the specific sum of 75¢ per month. Until 1887, when the union adopted the percentage system, unionists paid an additional assessment of 50¢ when a member died, 25¢ when a member's wife passed away. After 1887, only members doing nonscrewmen's work still paid this additional sum.[36]

Dues payments sustained the organization's benevolent work and paid the miscellaneous debts: bills for funerals, electricity (for the union hall: $2 monthly by 1900), garbage collection (from the hall: 75¢ per barrel in 1898), obituary notices in the *Picayune* ($1.50), postage, and telegrams. For decades, the white local sent handwritten reminders to members who fell behind in dues. In 1906, under the presidency of James Byrnes, the organization devised form letters and postcards to simplify the procedure. Suspension followed failure to pay quarterly dues; after two quarters in arrears, a member was dropped from the rolls.[37]

Benevolence constituted a major function of the white screwmen's local. Dues, application fees, extra assessments, and other funds supported aid to members and their families in cases of sickness and death. (The other dock unions operated along similar lines; the Black longshoremen for example, used funds "for all things necessary and legitimate to the carrying out of their humane and benevolent purposes": funerals, medical care, assistance to widows.) Throughout the local's history, including the first decade of the twentieth century, the dispensation of assistance "to such members as may be reported sick" lay in the hands of a Relief Committee.

And if "such members" were in good standing they received a certain amount of money every week. On a weekly basis, sick members received $6 between 1867 and 1877, $7 between 1877 and 1887, $4 between 1887 and 1894, $7 between 1894 and 1897, and $3.50 in 1897 and just after.[38]

Coverage at first extended for the duration of illness, but the union could not long sustain that practice. Therefore, in the 1870s, it began appointing two physicians, responsible respectively for uptown and downtown, to verify a member's condition; in 1894, the local imposed a 13-week limit for benefits. Uptown and downtown Relief Committees checked up and reported to the officers on the "Brothers Sick and Disabled." The union paid also for hospitalization, usually at the Catholic facility Hotel Dieu.[39]

Financial obligations constituted but one area of membership requirements. As the white screwmen's local gained strength and the labor movement evolved, the organization developed work rules that it required members to follow and sought to incorporate in contracts. Over time, the membership card became a "working card" entitling the bearer to privileges and holding him accountable to the rules. The earliest statutes said little about the work process itself. But the 1877 constitution mentioned for the first time that no member-foreman could hire nonmembers, and no member could work beside a nonmember. To guarantee compliance, the local established a Labor Committee with investigatory powers. In the 1880s, a set of rules appeared delineating the length of the work day (7:00 a.m. to 12:00 p.m., 1:00 p.m. to 5:00 p.m. or 1:30 p.m. to 5:30 p.m.), the scope of overtime, and the maximum number of bales each man could stow (75 per day, 38 per one-half day, and 19 per one-quarter day).

In the event of discharge for labor deemed unsatisfactory by management, the rules obligated a work gang to *remain* on the job until the local's Labor Committee, together with a member chosen by the employer, could investigate. The rules sought to protect members and to ensure that labor's voice would be heard in assessing the work quality.

Labor tried to incorporate rules of this type in contracts with management: otherwise they meant little. When Black and white unions began to collaborate more closely in the early 1890s and early 1900s, the rules were drawn up by a "Joint Conference" of each dock trade. The Conference worked out contracts with employers. The rules between 1900 and 1910 were quite specific, requiring a closed shop, disciplining of members who accepted *less* than their deserved pay, stipulating the size of gangs, and the length of the work day. The 1892 Black and white longshoremen's rules, for example, forbade members from taking on new work after 5:00 p.m., even though their day lasted until 6:00 p.m. These rules enjoined foremen to hire none but union members, as did the white-Black screwmen's rules in 1903, 1908, and 1909.

Contracts generally included the closed shop, at least on paper, and reflected compromise over the size of gangs, amount of work, number of hours, and rate of wages. Dock unions regularly insisted upon, and were conceded, contractual acknowledgement of their mutual interests. Rule 2 of the 1908 screwmen's contract, for instance, recognized their right to strike sympathetically with any "regularly organized and recognized Union connected with the shipping interest of the Port of New Orleans"; but, the same contract prohibited sympathetic actions with anyone else. The principle remained in the screwmen's contract as late as 1917.[40]

Style and Values

Solidarity followed from the fraternal and benevolent purposes of the Black and white organizations, and the developing need to act jointly in encounters with management. As late as 1907, union meetings were conducted along the lines of secret societies. In many cases unions met at the halls of such societies: Odd Fellows, Masons, and Pythians. They barred the press from most meetings; newspaper accounts relied upon observations, official statements, and the (often quite fertile) imaginations of journalists standing outside. Dock unions generally invoked the obligation adopted in the mid-nineteenth century by the white screwmen to keep union business strictly secret.

Thus, admitted the *Picayune* in 1903, actual dock union decisions were often difficult to report: "The difficulty . . . lies in the secrecy of the labor organizations, which are really secret societies, and which guard their business strictly." Reporters seeking entry to a Black-white cotton yardmen's strike meeting in 1905 were barred at the door by sentinels of both races. Seeking to argue their case in the 1903 dispute over the number of men constituting a longshoremen's gang, stevedores John B. Honor and William Kearney were barred from a meeting (to which key white longshoremen had been admitted) of the Black local. A Black member asked: "Did they really expect to get in? Are they members of the Longshoremen? Have they cards? We did not recognize the names, when sent in, as being on our membership list."

Oscar Ameringer spoke at dock union meetings in the 1907 strike, during which tremendous pressure was exerted to break the levee organizations. Of the Black locals, he remembered an intensification of security precautions:

> Coming to the door, behind which the union was in session, I would rap three times. A shutter would open. Through the round opening, two large white eyeballs and a husky voice would inquire who was the stranger knocking at the door, and what was his mission? . . .

> There followed some sharp knocks on an inner door. More mysterious whispering. By and by, someone gave a little marble-topped table a number of sharp knocks with a wooden gavel, and shortly thereafter, four guards armed with long spears appeared at the outer gate and escorted me into the inner sanctuary.

At critical meetings, consensus and unity inspired dramatic expressions, as in a gathering of the Black longshoremen's local in 1903:

> ...The closing act of the meeting was the singing of the old rally hymn of the organization, and every man in the hall joined in. The swell of voices could be heard for blocks away. It sounded like a revival meeting broken loose in the Longshoremen's Hall . . . [41]

Mutual concern began with benevolence, with sick benefits and visits, with funeral coverage. But the mutual benefits of workers meant more than this: It acquired a moral dimension.

The white screwmen called upon members to always treat each other with "due delicacy and respect," to avoid "all ungenerous remarks or sarcastic language," and to act in a spirit of "harmony, benevolence and union." in promoting "concord and good fellowship." The perpetuation of "the bonds of Unity and Brotherhood" was a "duty of every member of this Association," the union declared in 1877. Further, members ought "to aid each other" in and out of the union: any man "who shall inquire or attempt to injure a brother member shall be construed as violating the bonds of brotherhood."

Joint Black-white screwmen's rules in 1908 listed several violations of discipline: taking or receiving bribes, working while "in a state of intoxication," fighting and insulting other members, blackmail, coming drunk to meetings, and "using profane or indecent language." As far back as 1867, the screwmen's union had characterized drunkenness as a breach of discipline. In 1908, Black union leader Thomas R. Le Blanc denounced the frequenting of "dives" by many a Black docker, but noted ironically that such places were run by "white people who claim to be his superior." In dockworkers' organizations, trade unionism encouraged civil behavior, honesty, integrity and solidarity.[42]

Funerals

When a dock union subsidized a worker's funeral, it performed an inestimable service to his family. Funerals occupied a large share of union resources. Every dock union had a Burial Society or committee entrusted with filing an obituary, arranging for a ceremony, contracting with a band, and notifying the membership. The larger unions elected two burial societies, for the Upper and Lower Districts (uptown and downtown) respectively. White locals often used P. J. Donegan's funeral parlor, Black organizations made arrangements with the undertaker George Geddes (whose one-time clerk was longshoreman William Penn).

Funeral costs were too high for workers' families to afford. P. J. Donegan charged almost $4 for a carriage, $25 for a coffin, $20 for embalming, $5 for opening and closing a grave. A funeral might well tally $100 in expenses. The unions paid the bills, with the weaker organizations obviously less able to provide a fixed sum of money to the departed's family. Dock organizations commonly covered a portion of the funeral expenses for a member's wife.

Members of the white screwmen's local assembled an hour before a funeral and went together to the deceased's home carrying the union's banner — a silver star on a blue background — and wearing blue uniforms with silver stars over their chests. (The uniforms were also worn on Labor Day; such paraphenalia were well made and handcrafted, the banner and its accompanying black walnut poles themselves costing the union several hundred dollars.)

Funeral carriages were driven by members of the carriage drivers' union. When that union struck in 1905, Black and white dockworkers' organizations boycotted the use of nonunion drivers for funeral processions.[43]

Funerals of especially popular white dock leaders were also attended by Black workers (although evidence of the reverse could not be found). When white screwmen's president Robert Trainor died in 1904, Blacks came to the services. After white longshoremen's president Chris Scully died in 1910, Black and white longshoremen's locals stopped work at noon the day of the funeral; services drew members of the unions belonging to the interracial Dock and Cotton Council.

Like other Black working-class organizations, Black dock locals commonly hired a band to play at departed members' funerals. Funeral marches also gave opportunity to perform (and earn extra income) to Black dockworkers and other workers who moonlighted as musicians. The funerals of Black cotton yardmen, teamsters, and screwmen at the turn of the century brought exposure to musicians such as Buddy Bolden, whose style was based on the locally incubated blues-spiritual-march-derived idiom. If the departed had belonged to several unions or clubs — "Masons, Odd Fellows, Tulane or Zulu Club, the Vidalia, Veterans, Charity, and a few more" — each organization might supply a band for the funeral, and the streets would swell with music.

The funeral processions of Black dockworkers therefore demanded musicians of great stamina and strength. Musicians who performed levee or physical labor had the advantage. A contemporary construction worker-musician held that a true practicioner of the new music had "to be a workingclass man" out in the open all the time, healthy and strong." "Only a working man" had "the *power* to play hot": "You see, the average working man is very musical."[44]

Social Activities of Levee Unions

As union members, dockworkers participated in parades, sports, picnics, and social events, nearly all of which were segregated by 1900. Levee locals conducted festivals at the Fair Grounds. Unions regularly sponsored dances at Screwmen's Hall (owned by the white local), Odd Fellow's Hall (headquarters of several Black dock locals and of the CLU), and Longshoremen's Hall (where the Black longshoremen's local met). Unions of both races organized dance festivals and contests at these sites.

Performers like Buddy Bolden made their reputations at labor-hosted and union-sponsored social functions in halls "where for a dollar you could dance to music made by your neighbors." Although an occasional lawn party (in the Irish Channel, hosted by dock leader Joe Sullivan) was interracial, activities outside the workplace were generally segregated. White union members relaxed at Finnin's Cafe, Blacks at Tony's Bar. When, during a 1903 work stoppage, a white-only restaurant offered free soup and beer to both Black and white strikers, "they did not dine at the same table."[45]

By 1900, Labor Day parades and picnics, held on a massive scale, had also fallen victim to segregation. Joy L. Jackson points out that interracial parades of dock and other workers took place occasionally during the 1880s: "In 1881 two thousand white and Negro union members marched together in the funeral procession of Negro laborer killed during an outbreak of strike violence."

But Jim Crow prevailed by 1900, notwithstanding efforts by Black union leaders to revive joint white-Black parades and celebrations. Still, the Labor Day festivities of whites and Blacks marked an important public occasion for the union members and their families.

Unions commonly turned out en masse on Labor Day. Marching in contingents, workers wore blue or white uniforms and constructed floats representative of their trades.

A white screwmen's parade regalia included a blue merino scarf, gathered on the hip, with a small silver star on the front; trimmed in silver, the scarf matched a merino apron, which approximated in color the hefty gilded banner carried by white screwmen in parades since the 1870s. Black dockers also wore blue on Labor Day.

Brewery workers drove beer wagons, levee scalemen piled scales and sacks of coffee and rice onto floats, round freight teamsters did the same with hogsheads of sugar, and cotton teamsters did likewise with bales of cotton. Union officers rode carriages in the contingents.

The Labor Day parades of the affiliates of the Black CLU (whose leaders were levee unionists) found dock locals at the very front in 1904, 1906, and 1907: In 1904, dock locals constituted the Black parade's first six contingents. White dock locals comprised considerable sections of the Central Trades and Labor Council marches, but were not necessarily at the head of the parade. Longshoremen were second in line in 1903, but screwmen were seventh, and freight handlers nineteenth.[46]

Each contingent in the Black and white parades hired a band sanctioned by the musicians' union (although using nonunion bands was permitted when no union bands were available). Bands were essential to the participating organizations: the white longshoremen's and screwmen's locals declined to march on Labor Day in 1906 because they couldn't afford the rates charged by union bands.

Parading in the contingents of Black unions on Labor Day again afforded exposure for players of the new music: "In this important yearly parade each union had its own brass band. Nearly every musician in the city would have marched and some were probably imported from the country towns and plantations." (The last job — a breakdown and insanity soon followed — of the fabled Buddy Bolden, hero of the dances at Longshoremen's Hall, was, in fact, the 1906 Labor Day parade of the Black CLU). According to the *Picayune,* marchers in 1906 could be seen "prancing to the music with fancy steps." Here again, the musician were workers:

> . . . [T]here was something fine, something proud about watching those men, transformed from draymen and porters, barbers and stevedores, into bandsmen who could *play* that music, who wore uniforms that sported three rows of brass buttons.[47]

Labor Day picnics drew entire families to hear speeches, eat, dance, drink, and participate in various recreational activities. Each union sponsored events: sprints for men, women and children, rabbit catching, greased-pig chasing, baseball games, and baseball-throwing contests. Rufus Ruiz, popular white longshoremen, easily captured the Dock and Cotton Council's 100 yard dash in 1904; though aged 39, he "burned the wind." The Black freight handlers held a banquet, instead of a picnic, for members and their families in 1905.

Women attended Labor Day events as trade unionists, in the garment, shirtwaist, and domestic helpers (Black) unions; as members of auxiliaries, such as Ladies Longshoremen Benevolent Association and Cotton Yardmen's Aid (both Black) and others; and as community and family members. Social festivities helped inspire a family spirit of labor's togetherness. Later, in 1907 dockworkers' families would support the levee strike in ways demonstrative of a commitment that far exceeded participation in picnics.[48]

Fraternity

Dockworkers engaged in organized activities outside their unions as well. They belonged to clubs, societies, and churches in the early twentieth century. Evidence suggests that many, both white and Black, were active in fraternal organizations: the Odd Fellows, Druids, Knights of Pythias, Masons, Eagles, Moose, and Elks. (In 1894, the Catholic Church condemned three secret societies: The Odd Fellows, Sons of Temperance, and Knights of Pythias.) White longshoremen's president Chris Scully held membership in the Woodmen of the World, while former president Harry Keegan belonged to the Orders of Moose and Eagles. Prominent freight handlers' leader James Murphy was active in the Knights of Honor and the Ancient Order of Hiberians. Nor was he the only dockworker in an organization based on nationality: fraternal societies of Italians, Germans, and Portuguese also drew participation of levee laborers.

White dockworkers were members of a variety of other groups. Screwman Edward Paul was a Knight Templar, his coworker Emile Martin a member of the Orphans'Aid Association, and longshoreman Edward Ryan a participant in the Washington Avenue Swells Social Club. Longshoreman Oscar Patterson ran the Iona Social Club.[49]

Fostering economic and racial solidarity after the Civil War, Black fraternal societies also drew dockworkers at the turn of the century in New Orleans. August Meier submits: "Their activities probably reflect the thinking of the inarticulate majority better than any other organizations or the statements of editors and other publicists." W. E. B. Du Bois traced fraternal organizations among Blacks to the attempted suppression of the Afro-American church under slavery and the consequent rise of secret organizations for burying the dead.

From these organizations were derived other cooperative institutions — hospitals, cemetaries, and orphanages. And Black trade union locals carried over certain features of secret societies, consequent both to old traditions and contemporary antiunion activities of employers. By the middle of the first decade of the twentieth century, more than 4,000 Black Louisianians belonged to the Grand United Order of Odd Fellows. More than 6,000 were in the Knights of Pythias; membership reached 9,000 between 1908 and 1909.

Cotton yardman I. G. Wynn, a prominent trade unionist and public figure in the city, was a leading Odd Fellow for several decades. He represented his lodge at national gatherings of the Order. Screwmen's leader T. P. Woodland organized lodges in New Orleans and around the state, including and "Industrial Lodge" in Bossier City; in 1904, he was District Grand Master for Louisiana. Albert Workman, who became president of the Black longshoremen's local at the end of the decade, held a top post in the Order's "John and Jacob Lodge." Longshoremen's president William Penn, who died in 1902, held membership in a host of societies: Friendship Benevolent, Pure Friendship Association, Pilgrim Tabernacle, Young Men's Hope Benevolent, Young Men's Mutual Benevolent, United Order of Brothers and Sister of Love, and others.[50]

Church

Church-going dockworkers attended Catholic, Lutheran, Methodist, and Baptist houses of worship at the turn of the century. The majority of white levee workers were Catholic. Ethnic allegiances emerged in Catholic membership: Italians often attended St. Mary's; Irish joined St. Patrick's and St. Joseph's, Germans went to Holy Trinity. Dockworkers participated in Catholic organizations: Longshoremen's leader Harry Keegan was in the Knights of Columbus and the Holy Names and Ushers Society of Our Lady of Good Council Church. Thomas Brahney and Edward Powers, of the white cotton yardmen's local, and James Fitzgerald of the white screwmen, belonged to local societies of St. Vincent de Paul. Leading screwmen Thomas Harrison, one of the most important labor leaders in the city, and screwman-brewery worker Thomas Gannon held positions of honor in the mammoth golden anniversary celebration of St. Alphonsus Church in May 1908.

A number of German dockworkers belonged to Lutheran churches. Jacob Klundt, cotton yardmen's leader, attended the First English Lutheran Church, as did screwman Frederick Rubin, while yardman Henty Landwehr belonged to St. Paul's Evangelical, and screwman Charles Hartmann went to Congregational Lutheran.[51]

The New Orleans Catholic weekly, the *Morning Star,* expressed pro-labor sentiments at several points in the early 1900s. Although locating in contemporary levee disputes "an absence of the Christian spirit of charity on both sides," the paper supported labor's demands: All attempts at arbitration are futile until capital comes to a realization of the fact that the so-called dignity of labor is a farce and an insult unless it is based upon dollars and cents."

The paper urged employers to "fight Socialism" by being "just and Christian-like, to let the poor feel in a practical way that he is truly your brother; there is more wisdom and more soul in this method than in all arbitration laws and injunction planks." In July 1908, the paper printed without comment a speech contending labor unrest to be an expression of

> a working class struggle; it is sordid; it is material; it is really a struggle of the 'have-nots' against the 'haves'. Let it be so; so every struggle from the beginning has been. And howsoever we may disguise or try to disguise it, short of the possession of a certain modicum of material comfort, their is neither chance nor opportunity of spiritual and mental development. There must first be some *degree of material comfort.*

The "trouble about the rich," editorialized the Catholic weekly in February 1908, "is that basking in their seeming security they ignore the fact that wealth carries along with it an awful responsibility, a burden which must be discharged according to the law of Christ."

Violation of that responsibility — "corporate greed" and "business dishonesty" consequent to "departure from the principles of Christ" — led to the Panic of 1907.[52]

Such sentiments did not prevent the *Morning Star* from endorsing white supremacy, condemning miscegenation or "race suicide," and perpetuating "the memories" of the Confederacy's "great generals and heroes." Post-Civil War developments brought segregation into New Orleans Catholicism, with a resulting "decrease in the number of Negroes affiliated with the Catholic Church" (although the establishment of a Jim Crow Catholic Church for Blacks evoked strong protests from Afro-American organizations in 1895).

Sources indicate that Black dock locals had special relationships with Methodist churches in the city. Churches, assessed by W. E. B. Du Bois at the turn of the century at "the real units of race life," conducted annual salutes to each Black dockworkers' local. Huge crowds, including unionists and their families, filled Union Chapel, First Street Methodist, Wesleyan, Mt. Zion, and Leharpe Street churches to hear levee leaders report on the status of the unions. Highly respected longshoreman James E. Porter included an analysis of the Black local's financial health in his report at Union Chapel in 1899. "Great numbers" of longshoremen attended the program at Wesleyan Chapel in 1906. Such outstanding leaders as E. S. Swan (longshoreman), I. G. Wynn (cotton yardman), T. R. Le Blanc (freight handler), Joseph Coats (cotton teamster), and A. J. Ellis (screwman) addressed congregations in the early twentieth century. (The head of the small Black scalemen's union in the period was the Reverend Joseph Morehead.)

Refreshments followed the union reports, pertinent sermons, and formalities. First Street Church appointed "a little miss" to present the Black freight handlers' local with a banner and flag during the 1906 special services. Afterward, "the ladies of the First Church furnished lemonade and cake free to the great audience." The Mt. Zion choir greeted the cotton teamsters with a special performance in 1907, after which "the ladies" served "light refreshments" to the union members and their families.[53]

Although reporting favorably on trade union-church ties in the city, the local Black Methodist *Christian Advocate* did not always support the labor movement. Edited by the Reverend Robert E. Jones, a leader "of every big movement by the race in New Orleans for the past ten years" (according to the *Crisis* in 1916), the *Christian Advocate* was militantly antisegregation at the same time that it condemned the "agitation of labor unions" for the harm caused cotton commerce by the 1907 strike. It warned against strikes and boycotts. Such activities would turn the public against unions, eroding the sympathy won in the past: " . . . Then there will be a dark day for unionism." Ultimately, however, the main problems — "the Labor, the Negro and the Saloon questions" — were "embraced in the one question, namely the bringing of mankind to Jesus Christ, whom to know aright is life eternal."[54]

Summary

In New Orleans, all levee issues would converge in the productivity controversy. Dock labor was seasonal and uncertain, the shape-up hiring system competitive. Interaction among the workers nevertheless fostered mutual reliance, imbued with a fraternal morality of solidarity.

The work process originally united contiguous tasks and skills. Technology threatened to obliterate the most respected and valued of the crafts, cotton stowing. Trade union strength sustained that most crucial and apparently outdated category, the screwmen. Labor upheld traditional work divisions through the early twentieth century, despite steady pressure from management. Employers sought increasingly to do away with the best-organized, most-respected workers whose union had always backed the others. Elimination of the screwmen would make the organization — and control — of riverfront work easier and cheaper, depriving the unions of their traditional buttress.

Labor solidarity, of course, did not follow inevitably from the nature of the work or the pressures of the moment. It was hammered out through experience. Surely, the trades were interdependent. Cooperation between white and Black did not come easily, but it was achieved.

Chapter Three

Half-and-Half

. . . The whites had to amalgamate with the negroes or lose everything.

Thomas Harrison, white screwman, 1908

We were tired of being used as an instrument to starve our brother workmen, the white men.

Alonzo Ellis, Black screwman, 1903

The walking foreman shall hire half and half of the above-named Associations, shall distribute them equally in each hatch abreast of each other.

Rules of the Screwmen's Benevolent
Association and Screwmen's Benevolent
Association No. 1 (Colored), 1902[1]

During the early twentieth century, the half-and-half principle prevailed on the levee. Generally, it signified the equal sharing of work between white and Black locals in each trade. At the very least, it connoted interracial coopera-tion to some degree — even if not quite equal — to prevent employers from using the workers of one race to undermine the other's working conditions. Work-sharing arrangements in the early 1900s sought to ensure the simul-taneous employment of both Black and white men. The alternate hiring of Black and white workers in the mid-1890s had contributed to the 1894 levee race riots and the weakening of the unions.

But the half-and-half agreements went beyond the division of work: dur-ing the latter part of the nadir, white and Black dockworkers formed joint bodies, put forward joint demands, appointed joint negotiating teams, spoke in alternating sequence at meetings, constituted Black-white "juries" in intraunion judgements, and generally refused to take a single step on any issue without interracial agreement.

The issue of dockworkers' productivity and the city's competitiveness with other ports became paramount in the early twentieth century. City administrations, shipping corporations, railroad companies, newspaper publishers, and cotton merchants raised the alarm: the city would decline and all its citizens would suffer unless dockworkers labored harder and faster to send out more ships. Anything that was considered an obstruction to productivity — *especially the half-and-half agreements* — became increasingly controversial.

One scholar concludes that the 1894–1895 levee race riots, rooted in job competition after the 1893 financial collapse, marked the demise of local labor cooperation. The 1892 general strike, writes David Paul Bennetts, ended labor's "golden era in New Orleans." After the mid 1890s, Black dockworkers "drifted away from the unions," and came to an accommodation with employers. According to Bennetts, they followed "the direction of Booker T. Washington and his pro-employer, anti-union policies." Thus, Washington's 1899 visit to the city was, in fact, sponsored by the Black longshoremen. Where half-and-half arrangements thereafter occurred, Bennetts contended, whites often dominated and used them for their own purposes.

Indeed, in this regard, the white locals failed to agree that one-half of the *foremen* should be Black. (The subject will be discussed below.) Bennetts also observed that the "cotton yardmen's agreement provided that each two man team be composed of one Negro and one white worker. But if a third man were needed in the crew, the agreement stipulated that he always be white."

He further noted that in the early twentieth century, when Black workers became the majority of levee job seekers, half-and-half discriminated against them by continuing to provide one-half of the work to whites. Furthermore, Bennetts points out, joint meetings held under the half-and-half principles often found the delegates segregated in the hall. Blacks rarely became heads of joint committees.

Nevertheless, as a local Black unionist wrote W. E. B. Du Bois in 1902, the half-and-half approach in New Orleans promoted "unity of action among the longshoremen generally of that port." Half-and-half became a trade union instrument against wagecutting and strikebreaking. Although its application at times reflected white supremacy in the nadir, half-and-half arose to answer the racial splitting of white supremacist employers in ways the latter often found difficult to fathom. And even though its practice may not always have been truly equal, it diverged enough from what was expected to incur bitter hostility from those employers, the press, and local officials.[2]

Moreover, while Black dockworkers did not necessarily find or seek in half-and-half a road to equality, many had substantial experience in resisting certain broader incursions of segregation and had strong feelings on the matter.

Mutual white-Black competition, the ruinous experience of division, resistance to speed-up, and an on-going effort by local Blacks for livable conditions sustained cooperation. This chapter traces the unfolding of half-and-half in the years leading up to 1907 general strike.

Half-and-Half

Work-sharing arrangements between white and Black dockworkers dated back to the 1870s. The white screwmen helped establish a Black local in 1875 to prevent using Blacks as strikebreakers and to preserve their own monopoly on levee jobs. The work-sharing arrangement fashioned in 1875 limited the number of Black screwmen at work at any one time to 100. As Lester Rubin notes, the plan guaranteed whites the majority of jobs. Even though white and Black worked for equal wages, their employment opportunities were unequal.

Greater numbers of Black Orleanians sought levee work through the remainder of the nineteenth century. When employers in the mid-1890s depression began hiring Black screwmen in excess of the 100-man limit, whites struck in protest, attacking the Black longshoremen, and the militia was called in to restore order. Despite pledges to restore the white job monopoly, employers hired Blacks or whites whenever a dispute arose after that time.

Despite an overstatement of the number of deaths, Oscar Ameringer provided a useful description of the state of affairs in the mid-1890s:

> When the Negroes struck, the cry went up from the white man's sanctum, rostrum, and pulpit: 'White men, assert your supremacy, rescue your jobs from the niggers,' and white dock workers asserted their supremacy by scabbing and breaking the strike. This went on until both whites and blacks got down to sow-belly wages. In one of these last affairs, the white-supremacy strikers killed some ninety black strike breakers, where upon the white-supremacy Louisiana shot hell out of a similar number of white strikers.[3]

The experience led dock unions to consider how they might respond to management's policy. In the wake of the violent, divisive encounters of the mid-1890s, dockworkers evolved the half-and-half approach. The race riots of 1894–1895 became the point of reference for Black-white cooperation in the early twentieth century.

The early half-and-half experience can best be treated by examining white-Black cooperation in the levee disputes prior to the 1907 general longshore strike.

Half-and-Half among the Longshoremen

The longshoremen adopted the levee's *first* significant agreement dividing the work equally between Black and white in 1886. The two locals further agreed on a common contract and the same wage: 50¢ per hour. In 1892, under the leadership of James E. Porter and Rufus Ruiz, Black and white longshoremen reiterated the understanding. The phrasing of their half-and-half accord presaged that of all such levee compacts: "The stevedore or foreman shall hire half and half members of the above named Associations. The stevedore or foreman shall distribute them equally inside and outside, and on the deck."

The locals each chose 12 delegates to a joint committee of 24. They pledged in 1892 to furnish each other, as well as the other levee unions, with their respective membership lists four times each year.

But the 1894–1895 racial tensions on the levee disrupted the longshoremen's agreement. In the 1890s depression, Blacks found themselves excluded from an equal share of jobs. The heated competition for work produced the worst race riots on the docks in local history. Employers hired Black longshoremen at lower pay after the latter's appeal to the whites for equitable compliance with half-and-half went unheeded.[4]

And it was this, according to David Paul Bennetts, that led Black longshoremen to acquiesce in the cheap labor policies of employers, and to support the antiunion views of Booker T. Washington. Whites thereafter pictured Black coworkers as "employer-oriented," an image which Bennetts found "more accurate in New Orleans after 1894 than it had been in the 1880s."

But, in fact, Black longshoremen did not become antiunion nor did they "rely even more on the paternalism of the employer" as Bennetts suggests, but rather in the period 1901–1906 succeeded, with the whites, in adding new dimensions to cooperation.[5]

The 1901 Longshoremen's Strike

When the 250 "grain trimmers," members of the longshoremen's unions, demanded 50¢ per hour in the late summer of 1901, the Black and white locals resolved to strike any shipping line or stevedore failing to recognize union wages and conditions. On September 12 they struck, 2,000 strong: the Black and white screwmen at the same time pledged solidarity with the longshoremen (by refusing to accept cotton from strikebreakers). The Coal Wheelers, CLU, and the Central Trades and Labor Council declared support. The carpenters' union refused to work on the ships of the struck Harrison and Leyland Lines.

The longshoremen's Joint Conference Committee of 24 directed the strike from CLU headquarters. Black and white men staffed the office. Many Black and white strikebreakers quit work and joined the striking locals. Management failed to recruit Black roustabouts to replace strikers. The unorganized roustabouts, reported the *Picayune,* said "They are pledged to refuse to work on the ships, in the places of longshoremen, white and black."

So difficult was the recruitment of strikebreakers that the Leyland Line's M. J. Sanders put the following advertisement on the front page of the city dailies on September 20:

Wanted

250 Steady Laborers, White and Colored, for work on the Leyland-West India Streamers.

The Company *Guarantees* to pay to each Man at least *Fifty Dollars Per Month* and will contract for twelve months or longer. The rate of pay to be the same as the Cromwell Line, 30 cents an hour for a day work and 40 cents for overtime.

This means seventeen days work each month *guaranteed all year round,* and more time can be made if desired.

Apply and sign contract at the office of the Company, Room 5, Cotton Exchange Building.

The Sanders move elicited applications from many, but a number of new men came over to the strike: Sanders charged that they were intimidated.

Ultimately, the longshoremen won their ten-day strike. All firms signed contracts. The strike made a deep impression on shipping agents. One told the *Picayune* that he had rarely seen a walkout so carefully managed and planned. He "said that the men had everybody organized and he could get nobody to work."[6]

Emergence of the Dock and Cotton Council

Immediately after the successful, unified longshoremen's action came the birth of the most important half-and-half mechanism on the levee: the Dock and Cotton Council. The council united levee unions, particularly those involved in cotton handling, and drew delegates on a strict basis of half-white, half-Black. The 1901 longshoremen's walkout directly preceded its formation, but the council was not the product of a spontaneous brainstorm. Indeed, over a three-year period, the levee unions had taken tentative steps toward inter-racial collaboration to overcome, in the *Picayune's* words, "the unsatisfactory ending of the big strike of 1894."

Organized on October 4, 1901, the council was described at its inception as "a gigantic combination." The council respired on principles of solidarity, declaring its purpose "to protect all the labor on the pier front and in the cotton yards in case of any assault on any particular part of it."

Seventy-two delegates, 36 of each race, represented levee labor in the Dock and Cotton Council. Oscar Ameringer, who attended the council's sessions in 1907, recalled:

> And just as jobs on the docks had been divided fifty-fifty, between the races, so the offices of the Dock and Cotton Council were divided fifty-fifty. Delegates addressed each other as 'brother'. The division of officers was on the following order: President–white; Vice-President–black; Financial Secretary–white; Corresponding Secretary–black; and so on.

The council's first president was P. Murphy, a white screwman; James E. Porter served as secretary. Leaders in 1903 included president Harry Keegan (white longshoreman), vice president James Moore (Black screwman), recording secretary Porter, financial secretary Peter Clark (white cotton yardman), and treasurer John Reilly (white screwman). John Keith (white yardman), P. A. Graham (Black cotton teamster) and Edward Wiley (Black coal wheeler) constituted the Financial Committee. Equal Rights League member and screwman A. J. Ellis joined the Financial Committee in 1904; that year yardman and political activist Fred Grosz became Council president and Black teamster Joseph Coats, vice president. Generally, the foremost dock leaders were among the delegates to the council. In 1908, these included white unionists Rufus Ruiz, Chris Scully, and James Byrnes, and Black unionists I. G. Wynn, A. J. Ellis, E. S. Swan, and James E. Porter.

By 1903, the council embraced eight organizations with 10,000 members: the unions of white screwmen, longshoremen, and yardmen; the organizations of Black screwmen, longshoremen, and yardmen; and, the cotton teamsters and coal wheelers, whose members were Black.[7]

With the exception of the latter two, these unions conducted half-and-half arrangements of both work and organization. The Dock and Cotton Council oversaw the organizational, collaborative side of half-and-half. It helped ensure that unions abided by the agreements. Member unions informed the council of their relations with management. The council aided in negotiations and sanctioned appropriate measures of assistance. After 1901, levee labor therefore possessed a consultative, coordinating mechanism whose strength could be brought to bear in critical situations. The Dock and Cotton Council was the body with the power to call a general strike of the port.

The council's efforts at common action and cooperation extended beyond the city. In May 1903, it initiated a convention of Southern dockworkers in New

Orleans to establish common wage demands and end mutual "throat cutting." Delegates came from Galveston, Port Arthur, Mobile, Pensacola, and Vera Cruz, Mexico; Charleston, Norfolk, and Newport News unions cabled their support. Of interest was the *Picayune*'s observation that New Orleans levee men sometimes worked in major nearby ports when Crescent City trade slowed: "There are men who hold cards in both Galveston and New Orleans organizations."

The Dock and Cotton Council went all out for the convention. Member organizations delegated 50 representatives. Although the unification of Southern port workers promised, in the *Picayune*'s opinion, "to be one of the most significant moves in the labor world in recent times," it fell short. Other Southern unions were not as strong as their New Orleans counterparts. In 1907, the Dock and Cotton Council would renew its efforts.[8]

Further Experiences of Longshoremen's Cooperation

Cooperation among Black and white longshoremen, and between them and other levee workers, continued to develop in both organized and spontaneous forms. A wildcat walkout in sympathy with striking freight handlers in 1902 found white and Black longshoremen marching off the wharf together, "in a body."[9]

September 1903 brought a bitter dispute over the size of longshoremen's gangs. For years, gangs of four men had worked each side of a hatch. The unions' Joint Conference Committee in 1903 insisted on retaining the four-to-a-side (eight-to-a-hatch) work practice. But employers contended that one-half that number were sufficient, and proposed that the number of men be left open in the contract. On September 4, the shipping companies locked out the longshoremen.

The *Picayune* warned that if the unions' insistence on eight-to-a-hatch "without regard to the amount of room under the hatches, or to the character of the work" were conceded, shippers would have no choice but to do business elsewhere. During the controversy, shippers tried to establish a new levee union whose prospective members would perform all the tasks of screwmen, longshoremen, and freight handlers, thus rendering obsolete the unions of those trades. Agents emphasized that they wanted "an independent union of Levee workers" to "handle the port's shipping without recurring trouble."[10]

Great pressure was put on the longshoremen. On September 9, the United Fruit Company diverted 23 railroad cars of fruit to Mobile, for shipping to Bocas del Toro, Belize, and Port Limon. That night, Black and white longshoremen jammed every inch of space in the Black local's hall (with many unable to get in) and emphatically rejected the agents' proposal to reduce the size of work gangs.

Agents and stevedores threatened court action for losses resulting from the dispute and took steps to recruit replacements. But, Black longshoreman E. S. Swan explained, the men needed to have four-to-a-side, eight-in-a-hatch; their work was as hard as that in "a penitentiary": "We are not asking for more money but for more help."

The white and Black locals' joint statement of September 10 expressed concern for the health of the port, denying any intention to disrupt business: " . . . Upon the commerce of the port depends the living and sustenance of ourselves, our wives and our children." But longshoremen should not "be reduced to a condition a little less than slavery." If agents chose "to work a man to death," then perhaps "it would be better" than commerce "go elsewhere."[11]

The unions, however, did not get what they wanted. Legal threats and employer determination compelled them to concede. The new contract let the foreman decide the number of men in a hatch. Because the foremen were union members, labor scored a partial victory, but management made it quite clear that eight-in-a-hatch were generally "unnecessary" and would not be accepted. With the new agreement, employer threats of legal action for damages in the lockout were shelved.

The joint mass meeting called to vote on the concession was perhaps the largest dockworkers' meeting held up to that point in New Orleans. Chaired by Black local president John B. Williams, the meeting incorporated the 50–50 principle into the rules of order: "The whites and blacks took turn about in speaking and no advantage was shown either side."[12]

Several controversies put the longshoremen's half-and-half agreement to the test in 1904. In late 1903, stevedore John B. Honor filed suit against the two locals for their refusal to abide by the contract stipulation "to do such work as is required of them." Honor had asked them to do screwmen's work. In early 1904, a court awarded Honor $12,000 in damages from the financially weak white local. The local could either do screwmen's work or pay the award. Meanwhile, an award pended of $20,000 in damages from the Black local. The whites vowed to appeal their case. But they believed Honor would drain their treasury if he could. Some feared a deal between Honor and the Black workers, doubting that the latter would uphold half-and-half. One white unionist suspected Honor might contract solely "with the darkey" and shut out the whites "as it was done once before."

Honor probably considered lawsuits a useful instrument of pressure, for he initiated and called off many suits during 1900 and 1910. His frankly negative view of half-and-half emerged clearly during and after the 1907 general strike. In any case, Blacks in 1904 showed no disposition to betray half-and-half.[13]

Rather, they were inclined to enforce the principle across the board and this pointed to another potential conflict with their white partners in 1904. The *Picayune* reported on March 16 that the Black local had demanded that one-half of all foremen be Black. The paper predicted they would break off all agreements "unless the whites can assure . . . a more perfect working of the half-and-half system. The blacks think they are getting the small end of the deal."

To a number of white longshoremen and to the *Picayune*, the demand was unacceptable. Furthermore, the paper spoke of an "inherent" problem in the locals' Joint Conference Committee:

> A negro makes a charge against a white man and the white is tried before a jury composed of half blacks. The whites have come to resent this manner of trial and they are not satisfied to be sat in judgement over by the colored longshoremen. It is a piece of race friction that some think will not down and is inborn.

On March 31, however, the locals met jointly and reaffirmed the half-and-half jury system. Longshoremen's panel remained among the few juries still open to Blacks in New Orleans. The Black local at the same time chose not to pursue the foreman issue; actually, Blacks never achieved parity of foremen under the half-and-half principle.

But the locals emphatically repudiated rumors of imminent white-Black rupture at an April 5 meeting, which, in the *Picayune*'s words, "wound up in a love feast of resolutions and half-and-half enthusiasm." "Never more united than they are at present," the locals jointly affirmed their faith in "maintaining unionism," charging that levee "labor troubles" issued not from the unions but rather from "some other source."[14]

Reports of an impending Black-white longshoremen's split circulated in 1906. The contract approached expiration at the end of August and the Joint Conference Committee, cochaired by E. S. Swan and Chris Scully, called for restoration of the eight-in-a-hatch work gang system in the stowage of lumber and many other articles. They further asked for five hours' pay for men sent to work ships at Chalmette, Westwego, and Southport, whether they worked or not. Because the ships were often delayed, a trip to the downriver wharves might use a whole day, without possibilities of returning to the city in time to be hired for local work, but the men received pay only when they worked.

Blacks adopted a more conciliatory stance, according to the *Picayune*. As the agents rejected the new demands, warning that "the welfare of the entire community is at stake," Blacks opposed moves toward a strike. But a majority of whites also opposed a strike, making references to the uniquely "peaceful" wishes of Blacks unwarranted.

The locals reached a compromise with the agents: five hours pay for out-of-town trips (work or not), a Grievance Committee composed of four unionists (two whites, two Blacks), and three stevedores to determine if extra men were needed for gangs on particular ships.

While the unions reached agreement jointly, so too did rank-and-file workers jointly violate the new accord. Black and white longshoremen handling sugar sacks aboard the *Abyssinia* on September 10 defied the grievance procedure and stopped work to protest a work load they considered too heavy. They told employers, in effect, "to seek a climate where the thermometers are made without zero points." Similar incidents occured aboard the *Mexico* and the *Baroda*, and John B. Honor again threatened to file suit.

The local leaderships together appealed for compliance with the contract, for the situation threatened to become critical. Chris Scully, Harry Keegan, James E. Porter, and E. S. Swan met the agents on September 26 and agreed to take steps to ensure an end to the action. Two days late, the Joint Conference Committee unanimously upheld the contract and promised to consider any rank-and-file grievances, thereby effectively ending the contention.[15]

Freight Handlers and Teamsters: Black-white Cooperation

The all-Black cotton teamsters' local benefitted from the spirit of cooperation in the early 1900s. Local 254, led by Joseph Coats, had 400 members when it struck in early September 1905 for a consistent lunch hour from 12:00–1:00 p.m. and a starting time of 7:00 a.m. instead of 6:30 a.m. It was one of the smallest levee unions. The Dock and Cotton Council immediately declared support, but an apparent split developed within the council. The press reported that Black unions favored a general sympathetic action with the Black teamsters, while white locals were less eager. "Considerable race feeling" emerged: "racial prejudices" became "marked." The Black cotton yardmen's local in particular was "wild and rampant for a strike, wishing to support their black brethren." Yardmen pressed the bales that teamsters trucked to the docks, so their tasks and interests intersected, but white yardmen were reportedly slow to adopt supportive action.[16]

Nevertheless, on September 11, all Dock and Cotton Council member unions called a boycott of cotton transported by strikebreaking teamsters. Cotton unloaded at the dockside tracks by freight handlers and taken straight to the pier by longshoremen remained unaffected. The boycott, stated a prominent yardman, followed "the principles of unionism." At the wharves, Black and white yardmen, teamsters, screwmen, and longshoremen jeered nonunion drivers. A white strikebreaker was hit by a brick thrown by someone in the crowd.

The Dock and Cotton Council next interceded with the employers — the boss draymen — on the teamsters' behalf. It appointed a committee of five whites (including screwmen's president James Byrnes, longshoremen's president William Meehan, and cotton yardmen's president Jacob Klundt) and six Blacks (among them teamsters' president Joseph Coats, longshoremen's head E. S. Swan, screwmen's leader L. J. Obert, and freight handlers' president T. R. Le Blanc) to argue the teamsters' case before the draymen. The latter at first refused to see them; the council denounced this "discourtesy" and vowed support for the teamsters "to the very finish of the trouble . . . ."

Finally, the Cotton Exchange agreed to mediate between the Dock and Cotton Council and the draymen. The exchange proposed a 6:45 a.m. starting time and a straight 12:00–1:00 lunch hour, which the union found acceptable, but the employers (fearing it would interrupt work begun in the morning) did not. The council again upheld the union and, with the Cotton Exchange, implored Mayor Behrman to arbitrate. On September 21, the Cotton Exchange called upon the draymen to concede rather then "throw the whole cotton trade . . . into turmoil," which competitive ports would exploit.

Within a day, however, Behrman's chosen arbitrator settled the strike with the proposal that each teamster take a lunch hour sometime between 11:30 a.m. and 1:30 p.m. The Dock and Cotton Council's boycott ended.[17]

Three major freight handlers' disputes erupted between 1902 and 1906. Roughly equal numbers of Blacks and whites — several thousand in all — unloaded freight from the two major railroad firms owning docks in the city: the Illinois Central and Southern Pacific, both of the Harriman network. White workers at the Illinois Central's Stuyvesant docks belonged to Orleans Freight Handlers' Local 293, Blacks to Local 489. Southern Pacific freight handlers employed at the Morgan docks across the river in Algiers, however, belonged to the only integrated levee local in the city: Universal Freight Handlers' Local 402.

The Illinois Central freight handlers earned 16¢ per hour in 1902. When demands in November for 4¢ raise in pay went unheeded, the men struck with the endorsement of all the other dock unions. No sympathetic boycott materialized, however. Like the other dock unions, the freight handlers' locals had formed a joint white-Black committee. This panel conducted the strike.

The railroads were among the most capable and effectively run levee firms and utilized their own facilities to transport nonunion men to New Orleans during disputes. The Illinois Central sent more than 200 security policemen to protect 1,000 nonunion men, mostly Black, in mid-December 1902. The company brought them in very quickly and at great expense: the majority were very poor. Housed in segregated quarters on the Stuyvesant docks, they had for dinner on December 13:

500 long French bread loaves	100 gallons of milk
200 pounds of sausage	75 pounds of butter
300 pounds of port	half a barrel of sugar

5 barrels of potatoes	15 gallons of syrup
8 gallons of grits	100 bottles of ketchup
1 barrel of radishes	2 boxes of crackers
1 crate of celery	5 gallons of pickles
65 gallons of coffee	100 pounds of cheese
	half a side of beef

The *Picayune* termed this "a thing of wonder," and commented: "It is a saying about the place that everybody who goes to the dock gets a feed." Clearly, "they never had such good eating and as much fun as they are having there." Eight chefs, Blacks and whites working separately, prepared the meals.[18]

A number of strikebreakers quit work when they discovered a strike was in progress. But there appeared to be no end to the Illinois Central resources, and levee labor was reluctant to throw its weight into what appeared to be an uneven match. Longshoremen accompanied the freight handlers' joint committee to negotiations, and the CLU and Cotton Teamsters provided material support. But the striking locals could not hold out and conceded the strike on December 23, winning two smaller points: overtime pay on legal holidays and recognition of a grievance committee. The Illinois Center freight handlers also were able to have a half-and-half agreement put into the contract. It stated: "The work will be equally divided, as far as possible, between white and colored men." The railroad rehired all the strikers and sent home the strikebreakers.[19]

Nearly 1,000 Black and white freight handlers struck the Southern Pacific docks in Algiers in September 1903. Because they performed both longshoremen's and screwmen's work, they demanded wage parity with longshoremen through a 10¢ raise to 40¢ per hour. They called for union recognition and no antiunion recriminations, for a closed shop, and for eight-in-a-hatch, four men on a side. Limits on the number of cotton bales stowed daily did not enter into their demands, but they claimed to work harder and stow four times as many bales as the screwmen across the river in the city proper.

Algier's interracial Local 402 grew out of the amalgamation of the white Morgan docks' freight handlers and the Black Excelsior freight handlers in May 1903. Black freight handler Theodore Ternoir served as president, white freight handler William Trauth served as secretary. Union posts were equally divided and the strike committee in September operated on the same basis.

The Southern Pacific refused to negotiate with the local, hiring strikebreakers through the Thiel Agency in St. Louis. The railroad housed the men, most of whom were Black, on three company ships anchored in the river. One of these was the retired *Clinton*, with a long history of accidents.[20]

Announcing on September 2 that "we do not believe the dock workers are organized, in the first place," the railroad sought also to hire local roustabouts to replace strikers. But, as in the 1901 longshoremen's strike, roustabouts supported the white and Black strikers. One foreman indicated a strong aversion to subjecting himself to the likely "bodily harm" that would greet efforts at "drumming up laborers" from among the roustabouts.

Although the Southern Pacific evidently provided strikebreakers with ample food and tobacco, the strike committee charged that the nonunionists were held in "peonage" aboard veritable "floating arsenals" . . . "against their wishes." On September 5, the interracial committee demanded that the railroad send the strikebreakers home: they had been brought to the city "ignorant of a strike being on" and, besides which, constituted "an undesirable class of men." The union members, on the other hand, were "citizens and . . . tax payers here"; they deserved "consideration first." But the company withstood the strike and broke it. The members of Local 402 returned to work at the old rates. The Southern Pacific hired them back in groups of 250.[21]

As in the 1902 and 1903 strikes, Black and white freight handlers stood together when they struck the Illinois Central again in July 1906. This time they won a partial victory. Gains included a wage increase of 20¢ per day (up from $1.60 per day, but original demands had called for a 40¢ raise) and a raise in overtime pay. While feeling the issues might be settled without a walkout, the Dock and Cotton Council appointed James Byrnes, Chris Scully, Black cotton teamster Dave Norckham, and E. S. Swan to assist the strikers in negotiations. The council let the individual worker decide whether to touch goods handled by strikebreaking freight handlers.[22]

"Cooler heads" — Byrnes, Scully, Swan, and Ruiz — prevailed in the Dock and Cotton Council against "a general strike which would carry in its train all sorts of difficulties, complications and, perhaps, bloodshed, and the company, as well as organized labor, applauded their course."

The longshoremen *as a body*, however, began to implement the Dock and Cotton Council's "up to the individual" ruling by boycotting nonunion freight. And although not all business was affected, port commerce did suffer and freight accumulated.

A difference arose between Black and white strikers. The white freight handlers' local held out for the original demands. But on July 8, with partial victory apparently within reach, Black freight handlers voted to return to work. In this, they were supported by most levee unions. However, they did not return to work, but waited for further decisions by the whites. Meanwhile, no union member, of either race, broke the strike.

And, in fact, no member ever did, despite four days of reports that the Black-white split was irreparable. Ultimately, with the assistance of the longshoremen, the two freight handlers' locals and the railroad agreed on terms. The majority of the white workers supported the contract as the best possible.[23]

In general, the experiences of the early 1900s cast doubt on the notion that Blacks, due to the tensions with whites in the 1890s, were thereafter more likely to break ranks, or that the whites' distrust made joint action untenable. Setbacks as well as victories in pre-1907 disputes found cooperation intact, despite real or imagined problems between white and Black. Covered by common contracts, Black and white workers, in fact, labored under the same conditions and received equal wages. Thus, for example, Black and white cotton yardmen in 1903 both earned 7¢ for every bale weighed and sampled, and 2.5¢ for every bale reweighed; Black and white Southern Pacific freight handlers made 30¢ per hour in 1903 and 40¢ per hour for overtime and holidays; white and Black longshoremen received the same pay (40¢ per hour, and 60¢ for Sundays and holidays) in all contracts of that time: 1903, 1906, 1907.[24]

Yet on at least six occasions between 1903 and 1906, the press reported the termination of Black-white cooperation among (or in behalf of) the following: screwmen (Fall 1903 and Spring 1904), teamsters (Summer 1905, longshoremen (Spring 1904 and Summer 1906), and freight handlers (Summer 1906). The reports were untrue.

A New Twist: Half-and-Half among the Screwmen

The 1902 half-and-half agreement of the strongest organized levee force, the screwmen, produced a torrent of warnings of commercial chaos, abandonment, and the port's very collapse. In requiring that Black and white work *abreast* in the same hatch and in checking the acceleration of the work pace, it added new dimensions to the half-and-half concept. Tied inextricably to productivity, it bore crucially on decisive levee disputes, particularly on the 1907 general strike.

White and Black screwmen recovered slowly from the levee tensions of the 1890s. They began establishing joint contract demands and committees after the longshoremen had done so. No permanent working body or Joint Conference Committee appeared until 1902. No means existed to ensure support in labor disputes concerning one or the other local. The locals had separate contracts. The rule limiting Black screwmen to 100 at any one time remained in force after the mid-1890s, although by 1900 the two locals were roughly equal in size. While cooperation and half-and-half among the other levee workers undoubtedly influenced the screwmen, changes in the work process also pushed them to adopt a new arrangement.

But this, too, evolved slowly. When the two locals finally reached tacit agreement on equal division of work in April 1902, the Black organization signed a contract sanctioning the equal division that simultaneously forbade them to strike sympathetically or to strike for higher wages over a three-year period. Moreover, the contract placed no limit on the number of cotton bales to be stowed daily by work gangs.[25]

The ever-increasing capacity of steamships during the period made possible the stowage of more cotton. And, although they were still used, jackscrews declined in importance. Skilled hand stowing became the prevailing means of loading cotton. Gangs screwed 75 bales a day in the 1890s, but stowed much more by hand. By 1902, screwmen earned $5 per day, union foremen $6, regardless of how many bales were stowed.[26]

The labor-management debates and contract discussions of the early 1900s, therefore, focused on the number of hand-stowed bales. Employers pressed for slight increases in stowage by screw as well, but this issue stayed in the background. Management's introduction of a work pace increasing the number of hand-stowed bales fourfold brought matters to a head in the early twentieth century.

Workers named the new pace "shoot-the-chute." With several winches operating at once (and more quickly), more than 400 bales a day descended to the men in the holds. Men worried that shoot-the-chute "cut down the amount of work left to be done on other days" and left them idle. In 1903, the locals charged that employers sustained shoot-the-chute by playing off the Blacks and whites working in separate parts of the ship by threatening to replace one group with the other unless they worked faster.

Setting no limits on the number of bales stowed, the Black local's 1902 contract confirmed that the heavier work load actually affected both white and Black. The Black local's contract granted equal division of work at the same time that it extracted antilimit and antistrike pledges. But in actual practice, Black screwmen contended, shipping agents violated the equal-hiring clause of the contract.[27]

Assuming that a more effective half-and-half mechanism would prevent mutual undermining and help improve working conditions, Black and white locals met in October 1902. An increase in work-related accidents since the September 1 start of the cotton season and a work pace they felt incapable of surviving lent urgency to their meeting.

They decided to make their half-and-half agreement "complete and binding" by having whites and Blacks work in the same hold — abreast — instead of in separate holds as before. Even before the decision became public on November 1, news of what entailed began to trickle out: "If the man at a forward hatch is white, the one aft must be black. The division of the men working in a ship will be very strict." Half-and-half would now mean that "in a gang of four working in a hold two of them must be black."[28]

In this way, the workers said, "they can regulate the 'chutes', and . . . all will be serene on the levee again." Black and white screwmen announced that 100 to 120 bales per gang constituted a "good day's work." "When one was not afraid of the other 'doing' him," a certain measure of control might be exerted over the work pace. Screwmen reasoned, according to the October 30 *Picayune*, that they could make no viable demands "as long as the black was pitted against the white in the race for levee work . . . ."

Their joint meeting on October 21 lasted five hours and was filled with discussion. Several days later, the Black local met and unanimously endorsed the arrangement as the only way to end shoot-and-chute. On October 29, the two locals met again and elected a Joint Conference Committee. "The whites and the blacks are now amalgamated as they have never been before in this city," the *Picayune* indicated. Indeed, other levee workers who operated on the basis of interracial cooperation had "never entered it so thoroughly" as the screwmen.[29]

On November 1, the newly agreed-upon joint work rules were published for the first time:

> The walking foreman shall hire half and half gangs of the above-named Associations, shall distribute them equally in each hatch abreast of each other. The members of the above-named Associations shall not take orders from any one after going to work but the walking foreman.

These foremen were in all cases to be union members; they alone could order a gang to work. Under their supervision, half-and-half placed Blacks and whites in the same hatch, with whites "on the starboard side" of the hold and Blacks "on the larboard side."

The rules were termed "ironclad" and became effective on November 3. The steamship agents declared the new arrangement unacceptable. One agent urged the Black screwmen to violate the accord, but the local "would not consider the proposition of Mr. Graham and turned it down, sticking fast to the recent compact with the whites."

On November 3 and immediately after, Black and white screwmen struck all steamship lines which repudiated the new rules. Steamship agents insisted that the new larger ships made screwmen increasingly obsolete, that screwmen only fooled themselves if they thought they could control the work in a fast-changing industry that held no future for their skill.[30]

Employers condemned Black screwmen for breaking the antistrike, anti-sympathy, and by implication, antilimit clauses of their April contract. But the local felt the half-and-half pact to be "in strict accordance with the contract." For the agents had "repeatedly violated that part of the contract" giving them "one-half of all screwmen's work." Agents again charged Blacks with contract violation, but suspected the whites had goaded them: "The colored brother is the fellow who has sinned directly, but the white brother is the real instigator, and he was back of him in all the move."

When the charge surfaced again in the following spring, Black screwman and Dock and Cotton Council delegate A. J. Ellis responded bitterly:

We, the colored Screwmen, have not departed from any of our agreements except that we were tired of being used as an instrument to starve our brother workmen, the white men, and who have the same right to live that we have. We stood it for eight years; got nothing out of it but abuse, and depreciation of manhood. We did not go together to stop work and sit down in ships and draw money that was not earned. But we did go together to stop men from forcing us to starve other men and ourselves as well, and often to pay to our employers to occupy that position, which was an ugly one; which position we changed last Nov. 3.''[31]

The final six weeks of 1902 brought relative calm to the levee. Stevedores hired union foremen, the strike ended, and the half-and-half agreement went into effect without a contract. On Christmas Day, ship agents announced that screwmen's gangs were averaging 110 bales per day, down from the 400 to 500 daily before the half-and-half agreement. They threatened to change wage payment from the prevailing rate of $5 per day ($6 for foremen) to a *per-bale* amount but did not carry this out.[32]

The First Lockout

Two major screwmen's lockouts highlighted the emphatic renewal of the contention in 1903. Between April and October, screwmen and shipping companies battled over productivity, the latter seeking a return to pre-half-and-half stowage rates, the former insisting on their right and need to limit stowage.

On April 4, agents asked the screwmen to accept the following: no limits on the number of bales stowed daily; abolition of the half-and-half work gangs in the same hatch; restoration of the shoot-the-chute pace; and reempowerment of stevedores to give work assignments. Screwmen were given one day to agree, otherwise, a lockout would begin. The *Picayune* reminded readers of the dispute's recent twist:

The famous "half and half" agreement last fall, which caused so much talk, means that the whites and the blacks entered into a solemn compact that the work should be equally divided, and that the whites and blacks should work abreast of each other. Under the old regime the whites worked in one hold and the Blacks in another. They were naturally pitted against each other, and strove to outdo each other in a way. That was good for the man who was paying for the labor.

On April 5, the Screwmen's Executive Committee, including Thomas Harrison, Robert Trainor, and A. J. Ellis, unanimously rejected management's proposal. The two locals also met and seconded the decision. Arguing that the screwmen had no right to decide how stowage would occur on "ships which do not belong to them", and that "the employee never can have the right to say what shall be the character of the work done," shipping agents locked out the screwmen the following day.

Other workers responded. With Harry Keegan in the chair and James E. Porter as secretary, Black and white longshoremen declared their solidarity with the screwmen on April 8. The locals called their members out, bringing the total number of idled men to nearly 4,000. The Dock and Cotton Council, representing screwmen, longshoremen, coal wheelers, yardmen, teamsters, and others, promised moral and financial aid.[33]

The screwmen's locals soon issued a joint explanation of their stance. They accepted the employers' right to assign men to work, but asked that this be done with "reasonableness and fairness" through union foremen, without the "dictation and autocratic authority of the employer." They charged employers with trying in the past to reduce their status

> to that occupied by the pauperized labor or Europe. They sought to create trouble between the white and colored organizations, and finally succeeded in engendering a feeling of hatred towards each other, which culminated in the troubles of 1894. They succeeded at an enormous expense to both city and State, in obtaining the police and milita force to sustain them.

After 1894, the screwmen charged, agents who employed both Black and white workers strove consciously to divide them. White screwmen had been ordered to work faster or risk wholesale replacement by Black screwmen, while the latter had been told just the opposite. Adding that shoot-the-chute had reduced screwmen to "a wrecked condition," the locals asked employers to curb "the disturbing element" in their midst.[34]

Steamship agents answered that screwmen's gangs elsewhere stowed 100 to 125 bales by screw and 250 to 400 bales by hand "without any excessive strain on labor." New Orleans screwmen, on the other hand, averaged 85 by screw and 110 by hand, far below what they were capable of doing.

Agents supplied a detailed response to the unions' account of the events of the 1890s. A "period of peace" characterized the time between 1894 and 1902 on the levee. The 1894 strike opened up the job market to all comers. Unlimited cotton stowing obtained. Recognizing reality, agents agreed to divide work equally between white and Black in April 1902, only to find in November that labor intended to use half-and-half to impose limits on bale stowage. Now, local screwmen stowed far less than the more productive screwmen in other ports: Galveston averaged 80 to 90 bales per gang daily stowed by screw and 175 to 225 by hand; Mobile, 95 by screw, 200 to 225 by hand; Savannah, 80 to 100 by screw, 200 to 250 by hand; and Charleston, 82 by screw, and 250 to 300 by hand.

In mid-April, both sides called in the Cotton Exchange to mediate. Labor and management chose delegations to negotiate. The screwmen named five Blacks, including A. J. Ellis, and five whites, including Thomas Harrison. As tens of thousands of bales piled up on the levee the longshoremen remained out with the screwmen, the Cotton Exchange met with each side and then proposed a solution. It recommended that the screwmen increase stowage between 85 and 95 bales by screw and from 110 and 175 to 225 by hand, thereby resulting in approximate parity with Galveston. The half-and-half system of working abreast posed no problem, declared the Cotton Exchange, and could continue. But higher productivity was both necessary and possible.

Although falling short of their expectations, agents approved the proposal. Screwmen, however, rejected it out-of-hand, offering instead to stow 90 bales by screw, 150 by hand. The *Picayune* reminded the workers that larger ships and new cotton compresses made greater stowage possible and the screwmen's skill redundant: cotton screwing "will soon be one of the lost arts." If levee productivity remained low and wages high, the shipping lines would take their business elsewhere: Mobile, Galveston, Pensacola.[35]

The lockout lasted three weeks; the debate, seven months until resolution. By early May, workers were back on the job at the slower work pace effected by half-and-half. The Cotton Exchange's referral of the dispute to ILA head Daniel Keefe met with approval from labor and management alike, but the initiative never got off the ground. Keefe's choice of Black unionist James E. Porter to represent him in arbitration dismayed agents and Cotton Exchange officials who felt "that he could not serve as arbiter in matters where whites were concerned." The controversy's resolution was held over until the start of the busy season in September.

But in May, agents Alfred Le Blanc, Mathew Warriner, James Graham, and M. J. Sanders announced their readiness to divert ships to other ports unless September brought a settlement. New Orleans, said one, would soon be "absolutely barren of the big ships." The *Picayune* advised labor, "The old order of things is constantly changing, and men must accommodate themselves to the new conditions or step aside."

Labor's assessment became increasingly pointed. The agents were "unscrupulous and despotic tyrants who are watching for an opportunity to throttle organized labor," but would someday "rue their actions." In "absolute dishonesty," they had "deliberately, wilfully, and unnecessarily forced the issue . . . ." Reducing labor costs by using white against Black remained their objective: "The whites and Blacks both understood the tactics of the agents and united to defeat it."[36]

The summer witnessed a rush of predictions that half-and-half would not survive the approaching busy season. One paper hinted that white screwmen had reached an accommodation with the agents: " . . . The whites would get the bulk of the Levee business . . . ." The two locals jointly responded that "the affiliation between the two organizations is as fast as adamant and that nothing can sever it. They say the whites cannot do without the blacks and the blacks cannot do without the whites."

Employers and unions prepared for the upcoming negotiations throughout the summer, but a vast distance separated their positions. In mid-July, the screwmen's Tariff Committee of seven whites and seven Blacks began drawing up labor's proposal: although agents called for gangs to hand stow 175 to 225 bales daily, the Tariff Committee agreed to propose 150.

Reports of growing divergence between the stances of the locals circulated as September approached. These held that Blacks favored acceptance of a greater number of bales to be stowed, while whites stuck to the 150 figure. The truth here, admitted the *Picayune* was difficult to determine because the unions "are really secret societies . . . and guard their business strictly." Because agents promised a lockout without an agreement by September 1, the Black screwmen implied that differences with the whites had surfaced, but they had been resolved: "We all think alike now." Black president James Moore found the two locals "in perfect accord."[37]

The Second Lockout

The September 1 deadline passed without a settlement between labor and management. Union members worked at their chosen pace, Black and white abreast. Several shipping lines diverted ships to other ports or hired sailors to replace screwmen. Two firms rerouted railroad shipments of 12,000 cotton bales through Galveston, fearing "the most serious labor trouble in years" on the New Orleans levee. The *Picayune* asked the unions to adandon their "stubborn" and "inconceivable" position.

With the busy season well under way, differences between the white and Black locals apparently resurfaced. A Black screwman reported his local's readiness to stow 200 bales by hand. Let's "stop this monkeying," he insisted. Blacks wanted to work: "The opposition comes from the other side of the house." (Clearly, seating at the joint meetings was segregated.)

Nevertheless, the differences were apparently overcome. A joint mass meeting at the end of September reiterated the proposal for each gang to stow 150 bales by hand. The locals decidely reaffirmed their cooperation. "Good feeling," reported the *Picayune*, "ran like water in the open streets," and the races were "fully united" behind the proposal.

Nevertheless, the agents refused to consider the offer. They promised a lockout unless their terms were met by October 1.[38]

Thus, the second screwmen's lockout of 1903 opened on October 1. Agent Alfred Le Blanc was irate: "Owing to our troubles, Galveston is enjoying the heaviest tonnage in the history of that port." The Texas city's wharves hummed like "beehives." "Trade is slipping away from us," worried the *Picayune*: "The port of New Orleans must be placed in a position to compete on equal terms with Galveston, even if the Screwmen must be eliminated as an obstruction to the port."

The screwmen held fast. Despite behests to replace them, longshoremen supported the locked-out men. Cotton teamsters refused to truck cotton to the nonunion men hired to replace screwmen. One Black teamster, his locked-out friends standing with the whites and watching him, abandoned his cotton-laden float right at the levee: "There's too many of my friends standing over yonder for me to be monk'n around where a strike is going on, and I guess its high time for me to leave this yar float, cause it ain't mine anyway."

By the lockout's second week, several hundred replacements were stowing cotton. Several lines recorded up to 300 bales per gang stowed by nonunion men. The city provided ample police protection for the nonunionists, who (like the strikebreakers in the freight handlers' disputes) were housed on ships anchored some distance from the angry Black and white crowd on the wharf. The large-scale use of strikebreakers frightened several leading financial men, who implored the agents to stop. Cotton Exchange official Henry G. Hester begged Mayor Capdevielle to intervene, observing that "there is not a wheel turning on the river front" and expressing fears of commercial abandonment and "bread riots" unless the "present conditions" were relieved.

A number of strikebreakers quit when they learned of the lockout. Whites and Blacks jumped off the ships where they were quartered and swam off to join the cheering dockworkers on the levee. Strikebreaker Charles Goff of St. Louis described what happened when stevedore William Kearney escorted him and others (by tugboat) out to the "hotel" ship *Colonian*.

> We could see the big crowds over on the Levee, and we thought something was wrong. It did not look right. He [Kearney] said not be asking questions, and not to agitate the matter among ourselves, as all was right. But the crowd on the bank got bigger and bigger, and it looked like a strike. So the men plied him with questions, and he got more and more worried by us talking amongst ourselves. Finally, everybody was anxious.

> Then he was asked the question straight, if the men were not on a strike. He replied that they were only spectators. Others asked more questions, and Kearney, growing tried, fled to the upper deck. I followed him, and when out in the open I asked if it was not a strike, and told him I would positively

refuse to go to work. He told me that I must stay by the ship, and I could not leave it.[39]

The rapid deterioration of the levee situation prompted urgent pleas for conciliation. The Dock and Cotton Council turned down the screwmen's bid for a general dock strike and urged the men to accept a work load of 175 hand-stowed bales. When the screwmen dissented, a council committee of three Blacks and one white then met with the locals to find a compromise, while the city officials pressed shipping agents to be more flexible. Their efforts were successful. The nearly two-week lockout ended on October 11.

The screwmen and agents agreed on the following terms: 90 bales by screw, 160 by hand per gang, at $5 per man, during a nine-hour day. The smaller shipping lines prevailed upon the "Big Four" — Leyland, Harrison, Head, and Elder-Dempster — to accept the package, and the larger firms consented.

In crowded, stifling Screwmen's Hall, Black and white screwmen approved the contract after some debate. Thomas Harrison argued for 175 bales, others held out for 150, but the men ultimately compromised at 160 hand-stowed bales. The new accord was seen everywhere as a victory for labor.

The lockout cost the screwmen $50,000 in wages. While 10,000 bales had left New Orleans between October 1 and October 10, 1902, "not a single bale left the port" during the same interval in 1903. Shippers suffered more than $400,000 in losses.[40]

Cooperation Endures

Only a week after the settlement, news emerged of Black-white tensions in the screwmen's union. The problem was that debated by the longshoremen the following year: equal division of foremen. In the fall of 1903, a year after the birth of the screwmen's "half and half" accord, white foremen outnumbered Black foremen by 10 to 1, according to the Black local. But after opening the discussion the Blacks, fearful of upsetting cooperation with the whites, decided not to pursue the matter. Like the Black longshoremen, Black screwmen never achieved parity of foreman.

But for those who saw the doom of cooperation in every disagreement, one white screwmen had an answer. He found such men as the *Picayune*'s labor editor guilty of deliberately exaggerating the white-Black differences:

> How well he succeeded in helping the ship agents, the results have shown. Let him give up his fight. He ain't in it with both branches of the screwmen, for they are so closely welded together that it will require more energy and more ability in this line than appears to be the gift of this "noted" editor to separate them.[41]

In 1904, the locals attempted to impose further controls upon the work process. In mid-March they decided that any ship arriving after 2 p.m. would not be stowed until 5 p.m.: work would end at 6:45, with the total one and three-quarter hours constituting a half-day: at overtime wages. Previously, screwmen stowed such late arrivals from 3 p.m. to 5 p.m., with the two hours treated as a quarter-day. By changing the work rules, they hoped to compensate for prolonged idleness (without pay) during the day, due to the delayed arrivals of ships.

Agents reacted quickly, claiming that the present work rules already had them over a barrel: shippers had rerouted 300,000 bales of cotton through Galveston in 1904. Suspecting that the unions' proposal relied heavily on half-and-half muscle-flexing, they rejected the new rules outright. The unions realized they had gone too far and abrogated the rules, while reaffirming the half-and-half system of white and Black working abreast.

Tensions emerged during the slack spring and summer months of 1904, as jobs became hard to find. At a heated joint meeting in May, the two locals exchanged charges of violating half-and-half, but the issued petered out. In August, the press reported the locals at odds over the extension of the contract reached the previous October: the whites opposed extension, Blacks supported. Nonetheless, the locals agreed on a three-year extension and reiterated their cooperation. The contract would expire in September 1907, at which time all the festering wounds of the productivity struggle would open.[42]

Summary

In almost every instance, the locals jointly prosecuted disputes with management in the early twentieth century. Joint committees, tariff panels, delegations, and meetings prevailed among the screwmen. Five Blacks and five whites constituted the union jury

> whose duty shall be to try fairly and impartially members of either Association for any violation of the conference rules, and their combined decision in this respect shall be final, conclusive and binding on both organizations.

Meetings of the permanent Joint Conference Committee proceeded as follows: roll call, minutes of the last meeting, report of the Investigations Committee, initiation of new members, reports of officers and committees, motions, resolutions, and then the question, "Has any brother anything to offer for the benefit of this Committee" followed by adjournment.[43]

Dockworkers gained much experience in white-Black cooperation between 1901 and 1906. The thousands of Black and white workers who created and shared this experience were part of the nadir's real world of white supremacy, segregation, and anti-Jim Crow currents. Bitter past encounters with management and intensifying levee discord in the early 1900s led dockworkers to conclude that survival and improvement required joint action. By 1907, this conviction permeated the levee labor movement in New Orleans.

Chapter Four

Upheaval: 1907

The brewery troubles are likely to disrupt the entire labor movement of the city. . . .

New Orleans Daily Picayune, *June 5*

We have now come to the conclusion that a new central body is necessary, considering the treatment that the brewery workers and others have received from the Central Trades and Labor Council.

T. R. Le Blanc, *August 10, Black freight handler.*

An explosion rocked New Orleans on the eve of the expiration of the screwman's contract in September 1907. Amid mounting uncertainty over the forthcoming levee negotiations, a bitter craft versus industrial dispute erupted in the brewery industry. It profoundly shook organized labor, above all the dock unions. The brewery workers' resistance to the Central Trades and Labor Council's attempt (AFL-sanctioned) to reorganize them by craft evoked the strongest demonstration of labor cooperation since the 1892 strike.

Organized labor suffered a deep split in 1907. Repudiating national AFL policy, the dock locals led the majority of the city's unions into a new, interracial, industrial-unionist central labor council. Black-white solidarity on the docks grew in the process, at the point of renewal of levee controversy.

Organized Labor in 1907

Several strikes broke out before that of the brewery workers. Machinists struck for higher pay at 11 shops in April, with full Central Trades and Labor Council support. After four months, the nearly 200 strikers were still out.[2] Backed by the Building Trades Alliance, 100 sheet metalworkers struck in June for the closed chop, shutting down several major hotel and office-building

93

construction sites. Altercations between union and nonunion men occurred during both the machinists' and the metalworkers' disputes.[3]

Telegraphers walked out briefly in February for pay increases at the Postal Telegraph and Cable and Western Union companies. The local demands, which were partially conceded, echoed a national dispute which by June affected telegraphers in most major cities. In mid-August, New Orleans operators joined the national strike with grievances of their own: too-long hours, virtually no breaks, and no vacations. Local telegraphers' leader E. J. Ryan insisted: "Our life is one of uncertainty, we are away from our home and loved ones by day and by night."[4]

Swiftly replacing the strikers, Postal and Western Union companies suffered only a brief lull in activity. For a short time, the crucial Cotton Exchange quotations "were not sent out of this city to other markets." Although several unions, including the brewery workers, expressed support by boycotting the struck firms, the walkout of 200 collapsed in New Orleans after several weeks. Using nonunion workers, the Postal and Western Union companies substantially restored business by the end of August.

The strike involved men and women. Most remained out even when both local and national defeat loomed. From the start, the strike drew support from militant advocates of industrial unionism. Individual members of the IWW became something of a force in local labor in 1907. A large number of strikers joined the IWW, though the companies' policy of refusing reemployment to any striker in his or her home office made it difficult for local IWW members (Wobblies) to retain them.[5]

Despite early good relations with local radicals, the Central Trades and Labor Council wanted nothing to do with the IWW or industrial unionism. Leadership changes within the council, including the replacement of president Robert E. Lee by Boot and Shoe workers' leader Pat Welsh in 1906 and Lee's return in 1907, were not accompanied by policy changes.[6]

But dissension in organized labor became apparent in 1906 and 1907. On the initiative of well-known Wobbly Covington Hall, New Orleans unions formed a committee for the defense of miners' leaders Charles Moyer and Bill Haywood, then on trial for the murder of the former governor of Idaho.

Although Samuel Gompers condemned the trial, the AFL leadership abstained from the large-scale trade union campaign for their freedom that developed across the country. And when delegates from 31 local unions organized the Moyer-Haywood committee in March 1906, the Central Trades and Labor Council stood apart from, and even opposed, its activities. When the committee announced an outdoor mass meeting on the levee for April 14, the Council published a "Notice to the Public" declaring: " . . . The meeting called for tonight at Liberty Monument is not under the auspices of organized labor."

The "notice" infuriated many local unionists and served to swell that evening's riverfront crowd to 1,200. After several union leaders had spoken, Covington Hall rose to speak, to shouts of "Given them hell, Covington! Give them hell!" Hall, reported the *Picayune*, "set the crowd on fire with his speech." When he asked: "If Pat Welsh, President of the Council, and the other officers, were in the shadow of the gallows, condemned by a rotten power, would Moyer and Haywood refuse to help them?," the throng answered "No, no!" and hissed when he mentioned the Council. Then, led by a band, the crowd marched through the streets chanting "Moyer and Haywood shall not die!"

Amid reports of a move by the Carpenters and others to bolt the Central Trades and Labor Council, Covington Hall addressed an even livelier and larger meeting near the levee several nights later, at which Pat Welsh himself appeared. Welsh declared: "I will not stand for your attacks on the Council or myself." Hall answered that the Council was a public body and he had a right to criticize its acts "whenever I get good and ready." "If you do," Welsh retorted, "I will make it a personal matter with you." Hall countered: "Then you had better be quick. In the next five minutes I mean to rip into the Council for its action on the mass-meeting of the Conference." Later, Hall remembered:

> By this time the street was packed from wall to wall, and as far up as I could see. When I advised Welsh to be "quick" about it a tremendous roar of applause burst from the crowd. Knowing that the men were overwhelmingly members of the AF of L and Railroad Brotherhoods, I was as astonished as Welsh was. We stood there looking at each other in a dazed sort of way for a few moments; one of his companions caught him the arm, saying "Come on, Pat: there's some union men in this crowd anyhow!" They had to press through the packed crowd, and as far as I could hear they were cursed, "Yes, damn you, there's some union men in this crowd; and a damn sight better union men than you goddamn politicians ever were!" — and worse.[7]

Developments in 1907 were to show that the "bitter feeling of the rank and file, regardless of affiliation," was more than momentary.

Labor and Local Radicalism

Radicals had been a part of the local labor movement for some time and were well-respected by trade unionists. Eugene Debs spoke in the city in October 1903 under Central Trades and Labor Council auspices before an audience primarily of "workingmen." Council president Robert E. Lee escorted the speaker to the podium where Debs delivered "probably one of the strongest socialistic speeches ever delivered in the South, or ever heard in this city."

Newspaper accounts make Covington Hall's (1871-1951?) popularity at labor meetings quite clear. In 1903, Hall had written regularly for the council's *Union Advocate*. The paper gave free rein to his denunciation of the society where "little, helpless Christian children are fed to the dead fish of commerce."

Between "the people" and "the powers of vested wrong," Hall wrote in the *Union Advocate*, "there is no room for compromise" and "neither side can be conservative." The paper also published Hall's "Song of the Trust":

> I am the God-appointed — on my vested rights
>   I stand;
> By these rights I own the oceans and the wealth
>   of every land.
> Lo! all things are for and from me;
>   I've a right to all the earth,
> From this shining marble palace to the toiler's
>   humble hearth.
> To whom I will my bounty falleth; 'tis mine
>   to take or give;
> On my sufferance and charity the slaving millions
>   live.
> I am order, law and government, society and state;
>   I am master of my creator and
>   arbiter of fate![8]

The dynamic Covington Hall brought most unusual credentials to the New Orleans labor movement. An effective labor organizer, he was the son of a Presbyterian minister (a Confederate veteran) and a wealthy Southern woman from a distinguished family. Hall became Adjutant-General of the United Sons of Confederate Veterans of Louisiana in 1903. The *Picayune* felt he filled "all the necessary requirements" for the post: Hall's business experience (in the insurance field) would boost his effectiveness. The paper also noted his well-known views on "economic and social questions."

These were socialist views, increasingly prominent in his public statements. His ascent in the United Sons of Confederate Veterans paralleled the intensification of his early socialist activities. But his role in the United Sons was more than routine: Either alone or with other state leaders, Hall appealed for "the true facts concerning the Southern Confederacy and those who fought and died for her principles," attended state and regional Confederate reunions, memorialized the fallen, and pushed for a monument to Louisiana's soldiers. By 1905, Hall's term as Adjutant-General had ended, but he remained active through that year.[9]

Hall was the Socialist candidate for mayor in 1904 and Congress in 1906. Although he did poorly, he remained popular, newsworthy, and something of a social star. Oscar Ameringer described him as "the handsomest" and "best-dressed" young man in the city, the herald of new fashions.

The year 1905 marked the end of Hall's simultaneous identification with white supremacy and socialism (in February, he had favorably compared Russian revolutionaries with the Ku Klux Klan "that operated in the South during the reconstruction," wondering how the *Picayune* could praise the latter while condemning the former.)

After leaving the United Sons of Confederate Veterans, he devoted most of his time to labor organizing among Blacks and whites in New Orleans and later in the upland timber region of Louisiana. In particular, he established close friendships with dockworkers. Ameringer wrote: "To him, the perfect Southern gentlemen . . . belongs the credit for welding the black and white dock slaves of New Orleans into the solid body that raised them from the depths."[10]

Hall was an early leader of the Socialist party of Louisiana, founded in 1903. The party branch's advocacy of "the separation of the black and white races into separate communities, each race to have charge of its own affairs," delayed its charter from the national organization. Local organizer Peter Molyneaux argued that Socialist support of segregation was a matter of common sense in a state where white supremacy was law, practice, and custom. To do otherwise would ruin the party's chances of success, especially at the polls. Ultimately, the Louisiana branch dropped the "Negro clause" and obtained its charter from the Socialist party. Louisiana Socialists established segregated locals nonetheless, without further comment from the national officers.[11]

When the IWW emerged in 1905, local Socialists divided into "Red" (pro-) and "Yellow" (anti-) wings, with Covington Hall in the former. Hall moved into the IWW and helped launch a Wobbly local in June 1906. He helped build a local of perhaps 100 members by 1907. The local held regular meetings throughout the city, attracting the support of "a group of syndicalistic-minded Railway Shopmen, Screwmen and Longshoremen." Further, the local found sympathetic unionists in the Brewery Workers, the Dock and Cotton Council, and the Black CLU. "We were," said Hall, "a greater power and influence than our number indicated."[12]

The "group" of industrial unionists in labor's ranks in 1906 and 1907 included Black and white dockworkers. Hall showed a strong sympathy for inter-racial solidarity. Among the dockworkers closest to him and the Wobblies were the white screwmen's and brewery workers' leader Thomas Gannon and the Black cotton teamsters' president Joseph Coats.

As the brewery strike heated up in 1907, the Socialist editor Oscar Ameringer arrived in New Orleans from Columbus, Ohio, to cover and assist that strike. Ameringer's *Labor World*, transferred from Columbus to the Crescent City, promoted a frankly Socialist program and unequivocally advocated industrial unionism. It quickly became the forum for the local brewery strikers and later for the Dock and Cotton Council. Ameringer brought a snappy sense of irony to his work, filling his columns with pungent put-downs of employers and craft unionism. "In his prime," a coworker wrote, he "was a Debs kind of socialist, a fighter for the poor and oppressed," but with this difference: "Debs appealed to the heart; Oscar tapped the funny bone." After 1907, he became a labor organizer and editor in Oklahoma and still later edited the journal of the Illinois district of the United Mine Workers.

Ameringer became an integral member of the informal "group" of Hall, Coats, Gannon, and Brewery Workers' leaders who consulted frequently during the 1907 labor wars. An additional contributor to labor militancy was the local *Daily News*, published by local Democratic leader Robert Ewing. Ewing's labor editor, Peter Molyneaux (aged 24 in 1907) was a Wobbly who also wrote for the *Labor World*. Under the pressure of dock labor, the *Daily News's* daily "World of Labor" column increasingly reflected the dock unions' views in the city's internecine labor conflict: "World of Labor" endorsed the Brewery Workers, condemned the AFL and the Central Trades and Labor Council for trying to destroy the brewery union, and openly backed the trend for a new labor council. In July 1907, the *News* dropped the words "Official Journal of the Central Trades and Labor Council" from the masthead of the "World of Labor" column.

The Central Trades and Labor Council pressured Ewing to curtail Molyneaux's column in mid-1907, but a visit to the publisher by a dockworker's delegation prevented any change. Thomas Gannon recalled that Irish screwmen and longshoremen constituted Ewing's political base:

> Ewing knew this . . . So when a committee we had elected called on him to learn where he stood in the [brewery] strike, with us or the Central Council, he said: "I am not fighting you boys. What do you want?" The committee answered, "We do not expect to take over the *States* [Ewing's other paper], but we do expect fair reports in it. As for the *News*, we want Ameringer, Molyneaux and Hall to use it as they please, put anything in it they think best; if you don't agree to this, it will just be too bad for you in the next election."[13]

Socialists and militant industrial unionists became active figures in the 1907 New Orleans labor scene. Socialists and radicals were stronger in other parts of Louisiana (particularly the upland, piney-woods parishes of Winn and Grant, former populist strongholds), but for a time in New Orleans they also flexed a certain degree of muscle.[14] Levee workers and other trade unionists welcomed Hall, Ameringer, and Molyneaux to the labor movement: radicals were part of the movement. But it was the struggle of local labor's largest organized radical force — the brewery workers — that gave new influence and greater constituency to radicalism and industrial unionism in New Orleans in 1907.

Behind the Brewery Dispute

Adherence to industrial unionism made the International Union of United Brewery Workmen, in one scholar's estimation, something of a "forerunner" of the IWW.[15] Chartered by the AFL in 1887, the union affiliated with the Knights of Labor in 1893 and maintained dual affiliation until 1896. When the AFL threatened to revoke its charter, it broke with the Knights of Labor. Throughout the 1890s, the union worked to retain in membership the drivers, bottlers, engineers, firemen, and coopers employed by the breweries, against attempts by the unions of those trades to acquire jurisdiction over the separate crafts. The AFL convention in 1900 awarded jurisdiction to the brewery union over all workers in the breweries, except the coopers.[16]

As long as good relations prevailed between local radicals and the Central Trades and Labor Council, and as long as the AFL supported the union's industrial form, the predominantly German local Brewery Workers were accepted as part of the Central Trades and Labor Council. The union's assertive industrial approach notwithstanding, the council endorsed its contract demands in the early 1900s and helped bring into the world four locals: No. 161, Inside Workers; No. 215, Beer Drivers; No. 336, Box Repairmen; and No. 366, Beer Bottlers.

With 300 members by 1907, those locals comprised 10 divisions of brewery labor: malsters, brewers, engineers, firemen, steamfitters, electricians, bottlers, ice-handlers, oilers, and teamsters. Brewing, noted the *Picayune* in 1903, was booming in New Orleans. New methods of making and keeping ice encouraged production of the "practically nonintoxicating" drink, promising to make the local industry comparable to Milwaukee's. The Southern Brewers' Association met annually in New Orleans.[17]

Even before the AFL's 1900 jurisdictional award of most brewery trades to the Brewery Workers, the local labor council assisted the industrial union's organizing work. Prominent council leaders Robert E. Lee, Rufus Ruiz, and James Leonard served on a committee in 1900 to help "in harmonizing the Brewery Workers and perfecting their organizations." Local 161 entered the council in early 1901.

The council responded to the union's request in April 1901 to assist its "deliberations with the Brewery owners," establishing a committee (including Ruiz and Lee) for that purpose. The council backed the union's call for recognition and the closed shop.[18]

The council organized a boycott of nonunion breweries in 1901 and again in 1903. New Orleans, claimed Local 161 in August 1903, was "the only city of note in the United States where there are no strictly union breweries." The local expressed gratitude to dockworkers and unions for boycotting nonunion beer, singling out the Cotton Yardmen for special thanks. The Black CLU also supported the 1903 boycott.

As in 1901, the Central Trades and Labor Council in 1903 appointed longshoremen Rufus Ruiz and others to intercede with the brewing firms on the union's behalf. Lee and Ruiz urged unionists to adhere to the boycott: reports in the fall of 1903 indicated that screwmen were patronizing nonunion beer, despite their union's support of the boycott. The Central Trades and Labor Council encouraged compliance with the boycott, even as the local Brewery Workers expressed views at variance with those of council leaders, as in their definition of Labor Day:

> It means that the day of the arrogant employer is fast coming to an end; it means that they that earn their bread by the sweat of their brow shall have a right to say under what terms they shall earn their bread; it means the passing of the employer who has nothing to arbitrate; it means one goal nearer the emancipation of the toilers from wage slavery.[19]

In mid-1904, the eight New Orleans breweries recognized the union and granted a wage increase. Throughout the four-year fight for union recognition, the Central Trades and Labor Council sustained the union's industrial character. The 1904 victory, however, marked the passing of good relations between the council and the union.

Indeed, under pressure from the Stationary Firemen and the Stationary Engineers, the 1903 AFL convention had ordered the Brewery Workers to relinquish the right to organize engineers and firemen in the breweries. The Central Trades and Labor Council supported the AFL's renewed craft approach to the brewery union, but the local union retained its industrial outlook, endorsed the IWW's work, and continued to proposed societal change. The left-led union's national identification with organized socialism was public. Across the masthead of the *Brauer-Zeitung* appeared the words "Workingmen of all Countries UNITE!"; and the "SP Items" column offered weekly news of Socialist activity.[20]

In accordance with AFL policy, the local labor council in 1905 ordered the organization in the breweries of Stationary Firemen's and Teamsters' locals. The council encouraged firemen and beer drivers to leave the brewery union and join the new craft locals. Thus began the local jurisdictional dispute.[21] In 1906, the AFL warned the national brewery union that failure to allow brewery employees to be divided organizationally by craft would result in the union's exclusion from the AFL. Controversies arose in important centers of the industry: St. Louis; Milwaukee; Columbus; Belleville, Illinois; and New Orleans. (More than 400 jurisdictional disputes occurred in the industry between 1890 and 1924, according to historian Philip Taft.)[22]

Emphatic assertion of the craft union approach distinguished the AFL's position in the matter. Although the brewery union could report tremendous growth (and in fact, according to historian Hermann Schluter, better conditions than rival craft unions), President Gompers told the 1906 convention that "efforts to prematurely bring workmen of kindred trades into cooperation or amalgamation have aroused greater hositility and resentment and driven them farther apart." When that convention's demand that craft divisions be conceded went unheeded, calls for charter annulment followed. C. L. Stamp, leader of the Stationary Firemen, wrote AFL secretary Frank Morrison: "We insist upon revocation of the International Brewery Workers Charter for failing to comply with the [1906] St. Paul decision." Miners' head John Mitchell cabled the AFL: "The decision of the [1906] Minneapolis convention should be enforced at all costs."[23]

The Dispute in 1907

Now the struggle developed in earnest. In 1907, the Central Trades and Labor Council threw its weight squarely behind the craft unions, particularly Teamsters' Local No. 701, which challenged the Brewery Workers Union Local No. 215 for the right to represent beer drivers. The Teamsters' local underbid the Brewery Workers' local in negotiations with employers: drivers in the teamsters earned $50 to $60 monthly; in the Brewery Workers, $80 monthly.

Finding the Teamsters' contract terms attractive, employers encouraged, and in some cases told, beer drivers to join Local 701. Although complicity with employers was at first denied by Teamster organizer Pat McGill, others later admitted that "the bosses had put up a dollar apiece for men to join the new union in order to get protection from the outlawed Brewery Workers' Union."[24]

Early in 1907, the AFL revoked the charter of the Columbus, Ohio, Trades and Labor Assembly for supporting the local brewery men against Teamsters', Firemen's, and Engineers' jurisdictional claims. AFL Executive Council members were informed in early January of the Trades and Labor Assembly's stance; a poll of the members indicated broad support for revocation. The expelled central's newspaper, Oscar Ameringer's *Labor World* (Ameringer left Columbus for New Orleans in July) denounced the "cowardly and knavish" American "Separation of Labor," labelling the AFL's supporters in Columbus "an unhappy combination of dirty scabs, drunken Gomperites and a job lot of local imbeciles whose heads serve only as a knot to keep their backbonds from unraveling."[25]

The crisis in New Orleans developed apace. While Gompers warned national brewery union leader Louis Kemper that charter revocation loomed, national recording secretary Joseph Proebstle journeyed to the Crescent City to encourage the beer drivers to resist Teamster encroachments. A socialist (like Louis Kemper), Proebstle found the great majority of drivers committed to Brewery Workers' Local No. 215, rather than Teamster's Local No. 701.[26]

The AFL gave the brewery workers' union until June 1 to release drivers, firemen, and engineers from its locals around the country. The situation deteriorated rapidly through the spring. The union's very survival was at stake, cried the *Labor World*. All brewery tasks were linked in the labor process: "To divide an industry like that in crafts is the highest kind of stupidity." The *Labor World's* portrayal in May conveyed the anger of industrial unionists:

> It is proposed to dissect the Brewery Workers' organism. The boiler or stomach is to be handed over to the Stationary Engineers; the feeding organs, teeth, tongue and saliva are to be presented to the Brotherhood of Firemen; the legs, Beerdrivers, will be generously assimilated by the Teamsters; the balance of the body may remain in possession of the Brewery Workers, provided they behave themselves.

The brewery workers' union polled members across the country on compliance with the AFL's mandate; the vote was 34,707 against and 367 for. New Orleans members stood with the national majority, convincingly, 267 to 0. But the AFL and Gompers remained firm, the latter asking union leader Louis Kemper one final time "whether the decision of the Minneapolis Convention will be complied with by your organization."[27]

The last week of May witnessed the descent toward the brewery strike in New Orleans. Brewery Workers' Local No. 215, beer drivers, headed by Edward Aime and the militant screwman Thomas Gannon, voted unanimously to remain in the brewery union. It vowed to oppose any Teamster attempt to organize beer drivers. On May 24, the Columbia Brewery locked out Local No. 215. Teamsters' Local No. 701 called upon the breweries to dismiss drivers belonging to the brewery union. The Central Trades and Labor Council's top leaders endorsed the Teamsters and notified the public that Teamster-delivered beer was the only union beer in town.

The discontent evident to Covington Hall and Pat Welsh in 1906 now broke the surface of the New Orleans labor movement. Immediately, the white screwman's and longshoremen's locals condemned the Central Trades and Labor Council's move as "premature, arbitrary and unjust," and announced: "We are compelled to give our unqualified endorsement to Local 215 in their struggle for better conditions."

Central Trades and Labor Council president Robert E. Lee minced no words in his reply, assuring the brewery union of a fight to the finish to determine "whether the American Federation or the Industrial Workers [of the World] are the strongest in this section of the country."

Both the Black and white levee unions in the Dock and Cotton Council voted to back Brewery Workers' Local No. 215. The Dock Council statement was equally clear:

> The Industrial Workers of the World having been brought into the controversy between the Brewery Workers and the so-called American Federation of Labor by President Robert E. Lee of the Central Trades and Labor Council . . . and other strikebreakers and union disrupters, we deem it our duty to state to you (the public) our position, which is as follows:
>
> > The IWW is in no way affiliated with the Brewery Workers, nor they with us, but whensoever we see a labor organization striving to perfect its power, to unify the workers, all our sympathy is with it, and we pledge ourselves to aid the Brewery Workers by every means in our power. Our voice, our pen and our last cent is theirs if they wish it. We are both against Gomperism and for Unionism.[28]

The Brewery Strike

On June 1, the New Orleans brewery strike opened (concurrent with the AFL's revocation of the national union's charter), affecting all local breweries but one. A strike committee headed by Thomas Gannon began working to ensure unity and to seek assistance. At several breweries, employers replaced strikers with nonunion men. The union charged the Central Trades and Labor Council and Local No. 701 with recruiting these men, an accusation denied by Robert E. Lee. The Brewery Workers, declared national secretary Joseph Proebstle in New Orleans, would stay out as long as necessary: "until doomsday."

The Brewery Workers' appeal for help evoked an immediate response, particularly from levee men. The joint white-Black committee of the Illinois Central freight handlers gave "unqualified indorsement" [sic] to Local No. 215 of the brewery union in its "struggle for better wages and conditions." The white screwmen hosted the brewery workers' strike meeting on June 3. The Tailors, Retail Clerks, Bricklayers, and Elevator Constructors backed the Brewery Workers; the Electrical Workers declared the Central Trades and Labor Council's and AFL's actions "an injustice to organized labor."

When Robert E. Lee demanded apologies from defiant Council affiliates, the dispute took a new turn. Six days into the strike, the white screwmen's and longshoremen's unions let it be known "that the feeling among the members of these powerful organizations was so strong against the Council" that they would quit the Council before apologizing.[29]

The outcry puzzled regional AFL organizer James Leonard. Particularly dismayed by the statements of levee unions, he wrote AFL headquarters that IWW influence seemed greater in New Orleans than previously suspected. The Wobblies' effort "to create dissension in the ranks of labor in this city . . . will prove a dismal failure as far as this town is concerned," Leonard predicted. Writing to Samuel Gompers on June 9, Leonard suggested a strong AFL letter to the dissenting unions "for a great many of them do not understand the principals involved" and were under the brewery workers' sway. The leader of the "opposition" in the Council, Leonard informed Gompers, was "Thomas Harrison, a member of the Screwmen's organization, affiliated with the International Longshore, Marine and Transport Workers' also a delegate to the AF of L convention from that organization."

Although the IWW local in the Crescent City endorsed the Brewery Workers early in their strike, powerful unions and labor leaders unrelated to the Wobblies (including movers and shakers like Thomas Harrison and Rufus Ruiz) were nevertheless opposed in their own right to the Central Trades and Labors Council's antibrewery union actions. The Brewery Workers were *right*, the council and AFL *wrong*, Harrison told a stormy council session (chaired by Robert E. Lee) on June 7. Interestingly, the IWW local urged brewery men to *accept* exclusion from the AFL: the Federation was "organized defeat." But levee and brewery leaders demanded reversal of the AFL/Central Trades and Labor Council position and reinstatement of the Brewery Workers in the AFL.[30]

Samuel Gompers assumed that the anti-council trend in New Orleans labor would soon dissipate. As late as June 12, with levee and other unions on record in fierce opposition, Gompers directed organizer James Leonard (then on a working visit to Birmingham) to "turn the New Orleans matter over to some one in that city in whose discretion and ability you have full confidence"; or, to "wait a little later when you may be better able to return to New Orleans for a day or two to make an investigation and report."

A week later, Gompers cabled Leonard to return to New Orleans to "take up matter referred to you in previous letter."

The situation was worse than expected. Leonard arrived to find a beer boycott supported by the city's labor majority and anti-council sentiment at a new height. He contacted Gompers for advice: Might an accomodation be considered? Gompers's cable, slow in coming, offered no possibility of compromise: "When question remains unanswered, don't you think there's a reason?"[31]

On June 25, Leonard put a full page advertisement in the city's major dailies, informing the public that the boycotted breweries were not "unfair" to organized labor. The following day, waning negotiations broke off between employers and labor. Several days later, a mass rally took place at the head of Canal Street, behind the levee. Speakers included members of the Brewery Workers, Screwmen, and Electrical Workers, as well as Covington Hall of the IWW. Denunications of the Central Trades and Labor Council came fast and thick; a parade followed. On July 1, the white screwmen quit the Central Trades and Labor Council: The resolution passed "with a whoop."[32]

Solidarity

Until this point, only the Illinois Central freight handlers, among the levee unions, had issued a joint Black-white statement of solidarity with the strikers. All levee unions had expressed support, and dockworkers of both races respected the beer boycott. But in early July, the Central Trades and Labor Council and James Leonard inadvertantly triggered the organized extension of interracial levee cooperation to the field of solidarity with the brewery workers.

Stung by charges that he was recruiting strikebreakers for the breweries, Leonard organized 100 nonunion men into a "Federal Union" at a meeting in Typographical Hall. Hundreds of strikers and dockworkers protested outside. The new union signed a four-year contract with employers.

Leonard's action precipitated the strike's first interracial solidarity meeting, chaired by Thomas Gannon, on July 3. Five speakers took the floor, four of whom were dockworkers: Black leaders E. S. Swan and I. G. Wynn, and white leaders James Byrnes and Rufus Ruiz. From a Screwmen's Hall rally the next day (Independence Day), Ruiz, Wynn, Swan, Byrnes, Louis Kemper, Thomas Gannon, longshoreman Chris Scully, and several others cabled Samuel Gompers:

> Dear Sir and Brother:
> Owing to the present controversy of brewery workers and teamsters in our city we feel it our duty as representatives of the various organizations, who are part and parcel of the American Federation of Labor, to petition you to instruct Brother James Leonard, or others, to hold matters in abeyance in reference to organizing any brewery workers. We feel that if such is done it will be done to the interest of all concerned. Please wire instructions if this meets with your approval.

Gompers cabled disapproval:

> Not being on the ground am not able to form correct judgment of local situation. However every true unionist should help faithfully carry out decision Minneapolis Convention of the American Federation of Labor, the highest court in American labor movement.[33]

Opposition intensified. Leonard's memos to the AFL no longer attributed the dissension to the IWW alone, or in the main. The "colored organizations . . . don't understand the situation," he complained; but at the same time he located a likely source for dockworkers' identification with the brewery workers' union: " . . . The reason is their busy time is during the winter. In the summer they go into the breweries and work during their dull season." The teamsters' jurisdictional challenge to the brewery workers had caused these dockworkers — who belonged to the brewery workers' union — to lose their summer jobs.

During the first week of July, the presidents of the white and Black levee union locals, along with several other labor leaders, issued a call to a convention to discuss the crisis. Held on July 10 and 11 at Screwman's Hall, the convention was open to all organized labor representatives. Sixty unions sent delegates. When Robert E. Lee agreed to participate only if Covington Hall and Peter Moyneaux were excluded, the two Wobblies offered to withdraw. But the assembled delegates demurred, shouting: "If they [Lee and his associates] are too good to associate with good union men, let them stay outside!"

Brewery workers' union leader Louis Kemper addressed the convention, proposing a compromise: The union would concede its drivers to the teamsters if employers pledged to rehire all strikers. The debate went on for two days until delegates reached consensus in favor of Kemper's proposal. The convention sent a delegation of three whites — Louis Kemper, James Hughes, and Rufus Ruiz — and two Blacks — James E. Porter and Thomas Le Blanc (president of the CLU) — to the white Central Trades and Labor Council to explain the proposal and obtain its support. All but Kemper were leaders of dock unions.

Because Porter had other commitments, the other four constituted the peace mission to the Central Trades and Labor Council on July 12. Ruiz (regular council delegate for the Longshoremen) got into the session without a problem, but Hughes and Le Blanc waited three hours before being invited inside. When told that Kemper (as leader of a union no longer in the AFL) was unwelcome, Hughes and Le Blanc refused to participate. Kemper commented: "I, a man who always stood for Union labor, was kept out, but Mr. Leonard, who organized 'scabs', was admitted. That's a nice proposition, isn't it."

The council voted down the labor convention's compromise proposal and endorsed James Leonard's "Federal Union." President Robert E. Lee warned Rufus Ruiz for the last time that the longshoremen would be expelled from the council if their support for the brewery workers' union persisted. Expulsion did come, in August.[34]

By mid-July, most unions stood behind the Brewery Workers, concentrating their fire on Leonard's Federal Union. The Black CLU, including nine levee locals, declared full support for the brewery men. "The colored delegates," observed the *Picayune*, "have stood up to a man for the striking brewery workers"; Black unions fined members violating the beer boycott. The cotton teamsters' union, all-Black and the largest Teamster affiliate in the city, also denounced Leonard.

From the left-wing labor press of other cities came sharp criticism of Leonard. Oscar Ameringer's *Labor World,* soon to be published in New Orleans, called the Central Trades and Labor Council and Leonard "a scabby bunch." The *Dallas Laborer* opined: "Unfair, unjust, uncalled for — what word is strong enough to describe this action on Mr. Leonard's part?" *Appeal to Reason* declared Leonard's unionization of strikebreakers "one of the most infamous assaults ever upon organized labor in this country." From another Mississippi River port, the socialist-oriented *St. Louis Labor* exclaimed that "ruin and disaster in the American trade union movement" would result if the AFL "sanctioned or tolerated" the strikebreakers' "union" in New Orleans.

Toward the end of July, the CLU took the unprecedented step of inviting the Central Trades and Labor Council to a formal meeting to work out a common position on the brewery dispute. Even though the two centrals stood at opposite poles (the CLU, noted the pro-labor *Daily News,* had "done all that it could to bring about a settlement, while the Central Trades and Labor Council had continually poured oil on the fire"), strike supporters of both races yet hoped that high-level talks might prove useful.[35]

The Central Trades and Labor Council balked at first, then, "after a stormy meeting," accepted the invitation. For the first time, the two councils agreed to meet officially. Hitherto, explained the *Picayune*, the white council "drew the color line," precluding such a get-together. Now, "the bars were lowered," but "only in the interest of peace."

The councils set the session for July 29 and prepared their delegations. The white central chose Pat Welsh (Boot and Shoe), John Stadler (Railway Carmen), W. H. Sims (Carpenters), R. James (Machinists; Robert E. Lee's union), and Philip Hoffman (Barbers). The CLU sent James E. Porter (Longshoremen), E. S. Swan (Longshoremen), Thomas Le Blanc (Freight Handlers), Dave Norckham (Cotton Teamsters), and Joseph Morehead (Scalemen).

The historic meeting failed. With Robert E. Lee and James Leonard sitting in, the white council reiterated the AFL position on the brewery workers and defended the new Federal Union. The conference broke off abruptly. The Black and white centrals were officially at loggerheads.[36]

In August, the Central Trades and Labor Council asked the AFL to revoke the charter of the CLU and to rescind Rufus Ruiz's organizer's commission. It also requested the chartering of the new Federal Union in the breweries. Gompers referred the CLU case to the AFL Executive Council and deferred decision on the Federal Union matter, but took action against longshoreman Ruiz.

Informing Robert E. Lee on August 17 that he was unable to personally investigate the strike, "which you say is fast assuming serious proportions and may result in serious losses to the trade union movement," Gompers then wrote to Ruiz directly. Pointing out that a volunteer organizer's commission required the approval of one's own central labor council, Gompers said he had no choice but to revoke the commission. Ruiz, he added, had "lost his usefulness" as an organizer.

When Ruiz, a founder of and longtime delegate to the Central Trades and Labor Council, refused to return his commission and asked Gompers for the specific charges against him, the AFL president quoted Robert E. Lee's complaint of his "persistent activity against this Council." Further, continued Gompers, the AFL Executive Council respected the Central Trades and Labor Council's opinion. He found Ruiz's defiance of AFL policy "inconceivable," due not "to a wrongful influence of the heart," but rather to a failing in "your otherwise good judgment."[37]

Ruiz was finished as AFL organizer, but neither he nor the other dockworkers stopped supporting the brewery workers' strike that continued in the meanwhile. Due to the beer boycott led by dock labor, reported the *Brauer—Zeitung* in early August, many saloons no longer sold nonunion beer. According to James Leonard, brewery owners told the Central Trades and Labor Council in September that the boycott "has done some damage to their business." More unions, including the Stereotypers and the Blacksmiths, endorsed the brewery workers' union. The Railway carmen, Electrical Workers, and the Cotton Teamsters (led by David Norckham and Joseph Coats) joined the list of organizations fining members for violating the boycott. The *Brauer-Zeitung* saluted the Cotton Teamsters:

> That the teamsters' and loaders' local union is taking such a decided stand in our favor is very significant. This union is the strongest local affiliated with the International Brotherhood of Teamsters in the city of New Orleans, its members are colored people. It is a well-known fact, particularly in the South the colored people are considered far below the standard of the white working-men, but in this case those colored members of [the] teamsters' and loaders' union showed a remarkably sound conception of right and justice which is certainly to their credit; the action of these colored men ought to put the white leaders of our enemies to shame . . . . By this action the colored men show their conviction of their being of equal standing with the white men as human beings, and show their determination to fight for the recognition of their equal standing.[38]

The newly arrived Oscar Ameringer wasted no time entering into the dispute. So bitter were his denunciations (in the *Daily News, Labor World,* and *Brauer-Zeitung*) of the Central Trades and Labor Council ("hell bound to separate labor on the color line"), that Robert E. Lee accosted him on the street. Surrounded by their respective friends, the two came to blows; Lee's nose was bloodied. No charges were pressed. Teamsters' organizer Pat McGill, however, took Ameringer to court for libel. The case opened in September and culminated in Ameringer's conviction the following February.[39]

The situation spun out of control. During Robert E. Lee's visit to Washington at the end of August, Gompers promised more support but deferred action on chartering Leonard's Federal Union, to Lee's disappointment. The revocation of the Black CLU's charter was likewise put on the back burner. Lee's own international president, James O'Connell of the Machinists, "bawled him out" for the state of affairs in New Orleans. In the Crescent City, James Leonard realized that AFL enthusiasm for the Central Trades and Labor Council was waning. Signals from the AFL were having "a demoralizing effect": the "outlook is gloomy and looks very much like the IWW and Brewery Workers are getting the best of it." Were we wrong?, Leonard asked the AFL.[40]

Resolution

Under fire from many quarters, the AFL indeed changed its position on the Brewery Workers. As strikes and lockouts of brewery men festered in Columbus, Peoria, Belleville, St. Louis, and New Orleans (where dockworkers and brewery strikers attacked strikebreakers in September), AFL leaders reconsidered their stance. Thus, the AFL convention in November voted to restore the Brewery Workers' charter and to recognize the union's industrywide jurisdiction. In the convention's Adjustment Committee, James Leonard admitted that local beer drivers had been organized in the brewery workers long before the birth of teamsters' Local No. 701. Further, President Gompers denied that he had ever encouraged the organization of strikebreakers in New Orleans breweries into a Federal Union.

A host of city centrals and unions had opposed charter revocation. So great had been the outcry that Gompers, while reiterating craft union principles and resisting "premature" amalgamation, suggested solving jurisdiction disputes "in that broad spirit that shall *tend toward the cooperation or federation* of the organizations in interest in the hope that wherever possible they may eventually amalgamate, thereby working for the individual and common good of all."

While the convention set the tone for resolution in New Orleans, settlement did not immediately follow. Gompers cabled national brewery union leaders and told James Leonard in December: "You are expected to cooperate in bringing solution of local situation." But *Brauer-Zeitung* appeals such as "Money is needed to carry on war. Assist your brothers in Peoria and New

Orleans, La.," persisted through March 1908. By cable, Gompers helped get the brewery owners, Central Trades and Labor Council and brewery union together in the spring. Agreement came in June 1908: Beer Drivers' Local No. 215 again became the sole union in the field, Teamsters' Local No. 701 disbanded, and the Brewery Workers rejoined the Central Trades and Labor Council.[41]

Soon after its start, however, the intense local brewery conflict had begun a relative decline in the public eye before a wave of more profound labor developments. In August 1907, a new central labor council rose on the crest of the brewery contention. Just ahead lay the critical screwmen's negotiations and, with their collapse, the general levee strike.

The United Labor Council

In 1907, the emotions ignited by the brewery controversy catalyzed a movement, sparked by the local brewery union, the dock locals, and the CLU, for a new central body. When plans for a convention on August 15 became known, the pro-labor *Daily News* attributed decisive impetus to the Black CLU: "It was of some of the members of the Central Labor Union that the move originated and they have been working tirelessly ever since." CLU president Thomas Le Blanc assessed the course:

> Yes we have been working head and shoulders with the brewery workers since the beginning of the fight, and we have now come to the conclusion that a new central body is necessary, considering the treatment that the brewery workers and others have received from the Central Trades and Labor Council. The levee unions will heartily support this new move and many others, and it will aid in getting the majority of the labor movement closer together, so that strikes might be won in the future.[42]

Freight handler Le Blanc, screwman Thomas Harrison, and longshoreman Rufus Ruiz helped map out the convention. On convention day, the *Daily News* predicted that 20 unions, "very evenly divided between white and colored organizations" and including all dockworkers' union, would attend.

The convention bore out the prediction. A total of 80 men from 20 organizations attended. Dockworkers comprised one-half of the delegates. Every dock local in the city, with the exception of the white Cotton Yardmen, took part of promised support. Others present included the Brewery Workers (all four locals), Clothing Clerks, Blacksmiths, Plasterers, Tailors, Elevator Constructors, and Electrical Workers.

A "Who's Who" of levee leadership attended: white screwmen Harrison, James Byrnes, and Thomas Gannon (secretary of the Beer Drivers); white longshoremen Ruiz, Chris Scully, and John Reilley; Black teamsters Dave Norckham and Joseph Coats; white freight handler Ethan Duffy; and Black cotton yardman I. G. Wynn.

The assembly elected freight handler F. J. Francis chairman and Rufus Ruiz (well on the way to losing his AFL organizer's commission) recording secretary. Francis opened with an appeal for a central body without "foreign" allegiances, enabling loyal workers to "better their own condition." He asked Thomas Harrison to take the floor.

Evoking cheers in the packed Screwmen's Hall, the longtime levee figure, political influential, and Central Trades and Labor Council mainstay called for a new council, for labor unity against the AFL's "unjust rulings" and "encroachments." Rufus Ruiz followed Harrison to the podium, adding his endorsement to the proposal. James Byrnes, Chris Scully, I. G. Wynn, Joseph Coats, John Reilley, and the Blacksmiths' George Spence all took the floor and spoke in favor of a new council.

The motion to establish a "United Labor Council" was put to the house and unanimously approved, with much enthusiasm: "Three cheers and a tiger were given that might have been heard a square away." The assembly established an Organization Committee and a Constitution / By-Laws Committee. Coats, Harrison, and Ruiz, among others, were elected to the former; Byrnes and Wynn participated in the latter.[43]

The next day Robert E. Lee called upon the AFL to revoke the charters of all its affiliates in the new United Labor Council. Rufus Ruiz denied the new body's opposition to the AFL as such, insisting that the United Labor Council stood for labor cooperation; addressing a brewery workers' rally, Oscar Ameringer "kept the crowd in good humor" while asserting that only *international* unions, such as the ILA, could revoke a *local's* charter. But the white Cotton Yardmen attacked the new council, refusing to "be a party to secession."

The United Labor Council's committees soon met to discuss leadership and statutes. A huge session on August 23, with the Black Longshoremen (represented by E. S. Swan), Universal Freight Handlers (of the Southern Pacific), and the Scalemen among the new member unions, heard the report of the Constitution / By-Laws Committee. Delegates adopted a constitution markedly different from any document ever issued by local labor. Article 5 enjoined member unions from signing any contract that forbade a sympathetic strike. Article 6 empowered the United Labor Council to call a sympathetic or a general strike.

The Constitution / By-Laws Committee also introduced a preamble, probably drafted by Oscar Ameringer. Adopted by delegates along with the Articles, its tone was fiery:

. . . We declare:

First, that in order to emancipate themselves from the influence of the class that is hostilely [sic] arrayed against them, the Working Class must organize and oppose the power of capital with the power of organized labor . . . .

Second, The United Labor Council is in a position to exercise a great influence on production, on wages, on the hours of labor, and to uphold its members in various emergencies.

Third, the struggle which we naturally have to wage with the organized power of capital brings us to the recognition of the fact that individual unions must unite in one large league, which shall proclaim the unity of the interests of all and give mutual support. Soon thereafter will come the recognition of the fact that our whole system of production rests exclusively upon the shoulders of the Working Class, and that this latter can, by simply choosing to do so, introduce another and more just system.

The class-conscious power of capital, with all its camp followers, is confronted with the class-conscious power of labor.

Fourth, there is no power on earth strong enough to thwart the will of such a majority conscious of itself. It will irresistibly tend toward its goal. It has natural right upon its side. The earth and its wealth belong to all. All the conquests of civilization are on an edifice the rearing of which all nations for thousands of years have contributed their labor. The results belong to the community at large. It is organized labor that will finally succeed in putting these principles into actual practice, and introducing a condition of things in which each shall enjoy the full product of his toil.[44]

No evidence is found showing who in the new council (aside from the Brewery Workers and levee men Joseph Coats and Thomas Gannon, who were close to Oscar Ameringer and Covington Hall) shared the ultimate aims suggested in the preamble. But to the extent that it expressed the principles of solidarity and industrial unionism, it reflected the overall mood of the upheaval.

Since it had the support of the CLU and the powerful Dock and Cotton Council, the new central, Covington Hall noted, "rapidly became the center of working-class power in New Orleans, and was so recognized (by all except the heads of the AF of L Central Council) to the ending of the rebellion." James Leonard wrote Samuel Gompers that the United Labor Council was organized by Rufus Ruiz, Thomas Harrison, "and a few dissatisfied members of the Retail Clerks and Brewery Workers." "Comment," replied Gompers, "is unnecessary." But Leonard later noted that dock unions, not leaders alone, supported the United Labor Council.

On August 30, with a membership now of 30 unions, the new central chose its leaders. Delegates elected an executive committee of ten, of whom four were Black and seven were dockworkers. The new council, the *Brauer-Zeitung* asserted, proved that "in the city race prejudice is waning." The United Labor Council was, in membership and leadership, the first interracial central body in the city since the 1892 general strike. In a structure akin to the Dock and Cotton Council's white-Black division of posts, Thomas Harrison became president; I. G. Wynn, vice president; Thomas Gannon, recording secretary; Black freight handler Henry Baptiste, financial secretary; and James Byrnes, treasurer. Rufus Ruiz and representatives of the retail clerks, brewery workers, and Black cotton yardmen completed the executive.[45]

Labor Day 1907, witnessed the smallest-ever Central Trades and Labor Council celebration, a picnic without a march, that drew 3,500 people. Many United Labor Council supporters participated in the brewery workers' picnic, swelling it to about the same size. But the Central Labor Union marched, 8,000 Black unionists in blue uniforms passing by the reviewing stand.

In his Labor Day address, Robert E. Lee expressed his bitterness. The United Labor Council was "a 'tower of Babel and a confusion of tongues'." Moreover, "the lack of intelligence amongst the white men shows when they appeal to the colored brother to guide and direct them."

Several weeks later, the Central Trades and Labor Council issued a statement on the local dispute and the nature of the United Labor Council. The brewery union had colluded with "Industrial (Wonder) Workers of the World" to "stir up strife against the AFL." Their efforts had produced the new council, "composed of the Brewery Workers' Union and a few disgruntled malcontents."

The new council represented substantially more than that. By September, it included the dock unions (except the white Cotton Yardmen) and the Bakers and Confectioners, Tailors, Carriage and Wagon Workers, Clothing Clerks, Retail Clerks, Electrical Workers, and Plasterers and several other construction unions.[46]

The United Labor Council lasted about one year. In 1908, longshoreman Rufus Ruiz replaced Thomas Harrison as president, but that year's resolution of the brewery contention greatly reduced the new central's influence. Significantly, when the Central Trades and Labor Council finally conceded the Brewery Workers' industry-wide jurisdiction in June, it made withdrawal from the United Labor Council a precondition for readmission. The Brewery Workers consulted the United Labor Council, however, before reentering the Central Trades and Labor Council.[47]

Nevertheless, in the summer and fall of 1907, the United Labor Council was the vigorous expression of an upheaval of thousands of workers concerned with labor's strength, health, and organization. The city's intrinsic labor force, the levee men, brought their experiences in solidarity, especially Black-white cooperation, to the upsurge: They opposed AFL craft policy, boycotted beer, demonstrated support for brewery strikers, and fought for a new interracial labor council.

Talented speakers and organizers, Socialists and Wobblies (several of whom were workers) helped strengthen collaboration among the growing ranks of labor's dissenters during 1907. The labor movement in New Orleans possessed its own tradition of cooperation, particularly on the levee, a tradition to which radicals uniquely contributed. But principles, not "troublemakers," motivated the 1907 developments.

Occuring along the fault line of solidarity, the 1907 upheaval put levee controversy into new perspective. On the eve of the general strike, the spirit of militant solidarity of the levee was at its highest.

Chapter Five

The General Levee Strike

The white men and colored men are standing together as solid as the rock of Gibraltar and there is no chance of a break in the ranks.

E. S. Swan, Black Longshoremen, October 8, 1907

To the black laborers and their steadfast support of the white labor leaders is due the victory of the carpetbag principle.

Times-Democrat, *November 1, 1907*[1]

The decade afforded no greater test of the "carpetbag principle" on the levee — Black-white cooperation — than the 1907 general levee strike. Described as "the most massive of the period," "one of the most stirring manifestations of labor solidarity in American history," and "the greatest ever won in the South," the strike occurred during the torrid labor upheaval and paralyzed New Orleans. "Nothing," remembered Covington Hall, "could affect the public more than a general strike on the levee, unless it might be a street car operators' walk-out."[2]

The screwmen's contracts ran out in late summer. The contracts of other key dock unions — Teamsters, Longshoremen, Cotton Yardmen, and Southern Pacific Freight Handlers — expired at approximately the same time: summer and fall. In the center of this unprecedented concurrent expiration stood the issue of screwmen's productivity, more bitterly and decisively contested than ever before, but with an added feature: employers now strove purposefully to eliminate first the Screwmen, then the other dock unions. A lock-out of the Screwmen precipitated a general sympathetic strike on the waterfront on October 4. In the eyes of both labor (which reaffirmed it) and management (which sought openly to disrupt it), only interracial solidarity stood between the survival and the destruction of levee unionism.

115

Preliminaries

Supremacy over the Galveston port resurfaced as a concern of employers as the September busy season approached. Not only did the Texas port's cheaper labor costs threaten New Orlean's commercial health, commercial interests charged, but further, Louisiana's more stringent laws subjected an exorbitant number of cotton bales to condemnation: "The same cotton which is threatened by rejection by the ship here goes without challenge via other routes and through other places," leading to "the upbuilding of Port Arthur, Pensacola, Brunswick, Texas City, and the increase of other ports . . . at the expense of this city." Although "inspection is a necessity," declared the Cotton Exchange after the 1907 levee strike, it was also "a hardship . . . and if continued in the same manner will only add to the present discord."[3]

Amid fears of commercial desertion, several levee unions presented demands. The Cotton Teamsters insisted on renewing their contract (due to expire on August 31), opposing the boss draymen's call for cutting lunchtime in half. The Black and white Cotton Yardmen jointly demanded a wage of 10¢ for each compressed bale, a 1¢ increase. The *Picayune* found the outlook for levee peace "very uncertain" in mid-August and "gloomy" at month's end.

The Teamsters' and Yardmens' demands were overshadowed by a Longshoremen's contract war and the hovering Screwmen's negotiations. In August, steamship agents and stevedores proposed to elminate from the Longshoremen's contract the guarantee (won in 1906) of one-half day's wages for men sent to ships downriver at Chalmette and Westwego, regardless of whether they worked. At the same time, agents and stevedores forwarded a proposition to the Black and white screwmen's locals that entailed a 40-bale increase in daily work, from 160 to 200 bales per gang. "If they only desired to," claimed management, screwmen could easily stow 200 to 225 bales per gang daily.[4] On the night of August 26, ten days after the birth of the United Labor Council, the Longshoremen's and Screwmen's unions met on different floors of Screwmen's Hall and delivered simultaneous rejections. With no settlement between either the Cotton Yardmen and the press owners or the Cotton Teamsters and the boss draymen, the port was headed for crisis.

Temporary abatement came when the Black longshoremen again appealed for a half-and-half division of foremen. The ensuing controversy delayed the joint Black-white repudiation of management's contract offer. A. J. Ellis, former screwman and now a leading longshoreman, elucidated the Black local's position: the 50-50 division of foremen would enhance labor's strength. Longshoremen "could not effect the ends they seek without power over themselves." Equal empowerment of the Black local would augment the joint strength of the two organizations.

Both the white local and the employers opposed the demand, the latter declaring that white men resented having "a negro boss over them." An emotional meeting of the two locals, chaired by Chris Scully and E. S. Swan, witnessed sharp white resistance to equalization of foremen: "We'll have no niggers bossing us as foremen!," and "I'll drive a dirt cart before a nigger'll boss me," pledged white screwmen.

Expecting "cooler heads" to prevail within the Black local, the *Picayune* blamed the trouble on "a few belligerent Ethiopians who believe in the theory that Ham's descendants are as good as the white man in every respect." Anti-Black statements were challenged during the joint meeting by a Black longshoremen who, according to the *Picayune*, gave "a general arraignment of the white race." He protested the "screening [of] the colored brother off to himself in the street cars," charged that whites "generally denied him his rights," and promised that the Black worker would achieve equality "on the levee if he can have it no place else." A white worker answered: "You black _____ , you'll never get it!"

That the *Picayune's* reporter was, by union statute, not in the hall and that the paper had in the past forecast splits that never materialized, did not, however, rule out actual white resistance to the proposal. Once again, the Black local dropped its demand for equalization of foremen. This pleased the editor of the *Picayune*: "It is well to remember that this is a white man's country."[5]

The longshoremen's organizations now jointly rebuffed management's contract offer and readied for a strike. The Black and white screwmen's locals had, in the meanwhile, pledged to continue stowing 160 bales per gang rather than the 200 bales asked by management. Even though the Cotton Yardmen and their employers had reached an agreement on the aforementioned 1¢ raise, the Longshoremen's contract controversy combined with the Cotton Teamsters' lunch-hour dispute to introduce the first stage of port paralysis in early September. The teamsters walked out on September 3, immediately affecting the yardmen (from whom they received baled cotton) and the longshoremen (to whom they delivered the bales), but the situation worsened on September 5 when the longshoremen's locals struck together. One-half day's pay, work or no, for assignments to nearby Chalmette and Westwego and the right of longshoremen (rather than lower-paid members of a projected "sack sewers" union) to repair damaged cargo constituted the points of contention.

Now the screwmen (their own issues far from settled), in solidarity with the longshore locals, refused to stow cotton handled by nonunion longshoremen. Although the United Fruit Company and Puerto Rico ship lines and stevedore John B. Honor reached accord with the longshoremen, allowing some work to continue, most lines did not settle. The bulk of levee commerce ground to a halt. Sympathetic action with the longshoremen threatened to become a general strike. Mayor Behrman called longshoremen's officials to his office the evening of September 5. The mayor asked those present (among them

Chris Scully, Harry Keegan, E. S. Swan, and James E. Porter) to concede a five-day grace period in which longshoremen would work and negotiations proceed.

E. S. Swan was amenable to the mayor's proposal, but the others were not. The mayor got to the crux of the matter: "It's the advertising this city of ours is going to get that will hurt us. It will be carried all over the country on the telegraph wires that the port of New Orleans is tied up, and trade will be diverted from us."[6]

The following day (September 6), the minimal levee labor continuing, longshoremen's leaders and employers met at Mayor Behrman's office. Along with the joint white-Black union committee came Thomas Harrison, president of the United Labor Council and secretary of the white Screwmen. Steamship agent William P. Ross warned that local trade "will certainly be deviated elsewhere," and stevedore William J. Kearney complained that workers were undisciplined, ready to stop work at the smallest trifle. Kearney suggested that to further undermine the foreman's role the whites had refused extension of half-and-half to Black foremen.

Perhaps Kearney had intended to provoke dissension between white and Black unionists, then and there, by raising the recent dispute; in any case, white longshoreman Harry Keegan thought so. His blunt response implied that press reports distorted matters: "I'm sorry to see Mr. Kearney take up that question. I want to say to Your Honor [Behrman] that whoever told Mr. Kearney that the white men of the Levee refused to work under negro foremen is the damnest liar the Lord ever put on earth!" Behrman interrupted, "Hold, Mr. Keegan; you must not use such language." Keegan went on:

> Excuse me, Your Honor, but when a man stoops so low as to misinterpret facts it demands strong talk. If Mr. Kearney thinks he can come here and make trouble between these two unions, he is mistaken. They are standing together for mutual protection, and are going to see that they get justice.[7]

The longshoremen stayed out for a week. The locals jointly reaffirmed their demand for renewal of the old contract. On September 10, Illinois Central freight handlers refused to unload pig iron destined for stowing by non-union longshoremen; the all-Black Coal Wheelers began a boycott of the affected steamship lines.

In mid-September, employers conceded the sack-sewing and downriver labor issues and agreed essentially to renew the old contract. The locals accepted and the strike ended. Because the Cotton Teamsters' lunch-hour dispute had been resolved in the meantime, levee labor was almost back to normal by the third week of September.[8]

Galveston

Their significance and impact notwithstanding, the foregoing disputes preceded the developing screwmen's storm as preliminaries to a heavyweight title fight. Even as the longshoremen's strike ended, the massive Leyland Line hired sailors to stow cotton and tobacco in its ships, triggering a boycott of the line by levee unions. The screwmen's negotiations had deteriorated through September. On the steamship lines not struck by the longshoremen, screwmen's gangs had continued to stow 160 bales, far below employer demands. Screwmen's leaders rejected invitations to several meetings called by the Cotton, Sugar, Stock, and other Exchanges — the Joint Conference of Exchanges — to discuss an increased work load.[9]

The impasse featured a revival of claims that screwmen of other ports were more productive. Agents particularly mentioned that Galveston workers stowed 300 bales per gang daily, nearly double the work load of local screwmen. "Why not look into this?" asked the *Picayune*.

The question seemed reasonable to local screwmen. They dispatched James Byrnes and Thomas Harrison of the white union and T. P. Woodland and Nelson Shepard of the Black local to Galveston in late September, after the longshoremen's walkout. While awaiting their return, dockworkers maintained the boycott of the Leyland Line, but even the work at unaffected ship lines remained at low ebb because the busy season had started slowly and late.

"Galveston," Covington Hall reminisced, "was pictured as a port where everybody, including workers, was happy, satisfied, and working together solely for the public good." But when the screwmen's leaders returned, they had a different story to tell. Harrison and Byrnes reported that Galveston screwmen rarely stowed 300 bales per gang. Gangs in the Texas port handled as few as 150 and as many as 270 bales.

T. P. Woodland's version complemented this account. After observing and talking with Galveston screwmen, he was more than ever convinced that a five-man gang could not stow 300 bales in a day without dropping from exhaustion. He himself had once helped stow 200 bales: at quitting time he was "half dead." If Galveston men stowed 200 or more a day, there was a reason, Woodland ventured: "In Galveston . . . the white and colored screwmen are fighting each other, and to that circumstance is largely [due] the conditions that prevail there."[10]

Galveston dock organizations had not scored gains in developing cooperation like those registered by their Crescent City counterparts. Black longshoremen had received some white support during an 1898 strike, but employers had not ruled out the exclusive hiring of whites, suggesting then that "the days of the negro on the wharf will be a thing of the past." A 1903 dock strike for recognition of a Grain Handlers union failed when the Screwmen and Freight Handlers remained at work.

Three thousand workers, including 1,000 Black men, comprised the Galveston levee force, but joint white-Black bodies do not seem to have developed in the early twentieth century. Amid recordbreaking cotton, corn, and wheat shipments, white and Black dockers were segregated on the job. (Like New Orleans, Galveston in 1907 was generally segregated and its Black population disfranchised: 500 of 10,000 Blacks voted in the city in 1906.)

Black screwmen, reported a Leyland Line representative, also did longshoremen's work in Galveston: by 1908, the Longshoremen's union no longer existed. The Leyland stevedore hired only Black screwmen; whites, he felt, were lazy and inclined to drink. Freight handlers, on the other hand, were all-white. The *Picayune* reported that the "entire work" at the Texas port's "Southern Pacific wharves is done without even a Senegambian in evidence."

Though estimates of average stowage in 1908 ranged from 200 to 275 bales, Black screwmen in January 1908 set a "world's record" by averaging 338 bales stowed per gang in one day. Twenty-seven gangs loaded 9,146 bales on January 1.[11]

New Orleans levee employers had good reason to insist on "parity with Galveston" in working conditions and cotton stowage. Fears of diverted trade were real and were invoked to reduce union strength in the Crescent City. Covington Hall observed that in their "war on workers," New Orleans steamship agents pointed to Galveston as example and rival, for the Texas port enjoyed cheap labor and better machinery, newer wharves, more conveniences. This, commented Hall, "was used by the agents" in New Orleans "as an excuse for imposing lower wages."[12]

Dead-End

Steamship agents ignored the reports of overworked, divided Galveston levee men presented by screwmen Byrnes, Harrison, Shepard, and Woodland upon their return to the city. Agents threatened a lockout in all shipping lines unless screwmen agreed to stow 200 bales per gang. Acting on the agents' behalf, the Joint Conference of Exchanges put the 200-bale demand to the screwmen's locals at a meeting on September 26. Labor men present included Byrnes, Harrison, Shepard, Woodland, and longshoreman James E. Porter.

The Black and white locals deemed management's position intolerable. The cost of living had risen 35% in five years, contended Harrison, and wages had not kept pace. Shipping lines had meanwhile recorded great profits: "If any shaving is to be done, should it not be from their end?" Harrison spoke heatedly:

> Is it not singularly strange, that when it comes to reducing the cost of anything, in this instance we will say, the cost of loading a ship, the laboring man must bear the brunt of that reduction, the cut must be made in his wages? I contend that the laboring man has stood for as much reduction and squeezing as he can. I have not seen the agents show in the papers what they make. Examine the assessment rolls for yourselves: you will find that they have grown rich out of what the laborer has made for them.

In a joint session on September 27, the white and Black screwmen's locals rejected the 200-bale demand and threatened to stow fewer than the 160 bales stipulated in the last contract. In turn, the exchanges announced that 200 bales was the *minimum* and that stowage of 230 to 240 per gang was soon to come. The *Picayune* admonished the screwmen not to be stubborn on September 30.[13]

With the agents now sworn to achieve parity with Galveston, and levee labor sustained and inspired by the experience of recent and continuing upheaval, the crisis developed precipitously. On October 1, another steamship line, the Austro-American, joined Leyland in hiring sailors to stow cotton, locking out union screwmen. The solidarity spirit and mechanism, fortified in preceding weeks, now went into motion. Illinois Central freight handlers, Black and white, refused to "unload any cars having freight aboard" for the two lines. Black longshoremen's president E. S. Swan warned: "If the Screwmen were by themselves maybe they [employers] would beat them, but the minute strikebreakers are put to work everybody on the levee quits!"

When, in an unrelated controversy, the Southern Pacific freight handlers struck on October 1 for a wage increase, the port faced the closing of both banks of the levee: Algiers and cityside. Mayor Behrman called in the screwmen and the agents one last time on October 3, as levee unions blacklisted the Leyland and Austro-American Lines. William P. Ross, chairman of the Joint Conference of Steamship Agents and Stevedores, told the mayor and the union leaders that a 240-bale work load was the only acceptable solution, the only guarantee of parity with Galveston. The following day, all steamship lines locked out the screwmen, driving the levee unions to the ultimate response.[14]

The Strike Begins

Responding to the appeals of the Dock and Cotton Council, 9,000 dockworkers struck the port on October 4 at 6:00 p.m. Two thousand stave classers, pilers, and drivers walked out a day later. The initial breakdown of participating unions read as follows:[15]

White Screwmen	800 men
Black Screwmen	1,000
White Longshoremen	1,400
Black Longshoremen	2,100
White Cotton Yardmen	523
Black Cotton Yardmen	700
Coal Wheelers (Black)	310
Cotton Teamsters (Black)	200
Freight Handlers (mixed)	1,100
Cotton Markers and Inspectors (white)	110
Stave Classers	300
Stave Cart Drivers	75
Round Freight Teamsters	200

The 1907 general levee strike was a sympathetic industrywide action of solidarity with the screwmen. Joining their own wage demands to the screwmen's cause, Southern Pacific freight handlers made the cessation of levee life complete on both banks of the port. The strike affected every steamship line and both dock-owning railroads, the Illinois Central and the Southern Pacific. The action became more extensive and absolute than any work stoppage in the decade. It challenged in the same breath several of the world's largest shipping concerns (particularly Leyland and Harrison, both British-owned) and railroad companies.

"The first purpose of the steamship companies and railroads," wrote Covington Hall, "was to destroy the Screwmen's Association." The aim came into clear focus in the *Picayune* and the *Times-Democrat,* which were the city's most influential papers. (The venerable *Picayune,* dating from 1837, consistently reflected extreme white supremacist views, while taking somewhat less hostile positions against the levee unions. The equally racist *Times-Democrat* — an 1881 fusion of the formerly Republican *Times* and the anti-Reconstruction *Democrat* — claimed in 1907, "A larger Circulation Than Any Other Newspaper South of the Potomac and Ohio Rivers": It was strongly antiunion.) The *Picayune* reported on October 5: "The employers again stated as individuals yesterday that the Screwmen would probably be done away with entirely in the fight and things would be reconstructed on a basis that would do away with the different classes of labor."

The *Times-Democrat* related, "Around the Cotton Exchange the sentiment was unanimous that the fight should be made for the extinction of the screwmen's organizations," and editorialized on October 8: "The present fight is to do away with the screwmen, to abolish an extinct, useless, expensive and dangerous organization . . . ." The idling of 10,000 men, roaming the streets with energy to burn, was proof positive of the "menace to the peace of the city" posed by "irresponsible unions," the *Times-Democrat* maintained. (In a similar vein, the *New Orleans Item* advised strikers: "Above all, don't drink.")

"Suppressing" the screwmen, stated the *Times-Democrat*, would equalize wages and conditions between Galveston and New Orleans. Southern Pacific agent E. E. Lamberton told the press that the Freight Handlers would also be wiped off the map: "We have never recognized any union in these sheds and we don't intend to now." The *Picayune* elaborated, explaining that if management triumphed, "there will not only be no more screwmen's unions, but the longshoremen's unions, the freight handlers' union and the coal wheelers' unions will not be recognized as separate or individual organizations, any body of workmen being employed to do any character of work." Under such an arrangement, employers would feel "safer."[16]

The unions in the Dock and Cotton Council issued their own endorsements and instructions to members. The screwmen, acknowledged a dock leader, would be crushed if they were alone: "strikes are won by unity" and "lost by lack of proper mutuality." The Black longshoremen unanimously voted to support the strike. E. S. Swan reported: "The white men and the colored men are standing together as solid as the rock of Gilbraltar and there is no chance of a break in the ranks." The Black and white yardmen's locals and the Cotton Teamsters jointly asked their men "to remain away from their former place of business." After the joint yardmen's endorsement, Black local president I. G. Wynn announced they would "stand by the strike to the last."

The Dock and Cotton Council acquired two strike organs at the very outset: The *Daily News* and Oscar Ameringer's *Labor World*, distributed free to strikers. The United Labor Council supported the strike from the beginning, prompting rumors of a citywide general strike. That action failed to materialize, but the Central Trades and Labor Council, even though bitterly estranged from dock labor, declared support. The October 6 *Times-Democrat* carried a remarkable statement by Central Trades and Labor Council president Robert E. Lee:

> We are bound to recognize the negro as an economic factor in the labor situation here, and that is the difference between the situation here and in Galveston. In Galveston, the negro and white longshoremen are competing with each other, and the condition of that port practically amounts to slavery.

New Orleans, moreover, was larger and its cost of living higher, "to a point where the laboring man can scarcely support himself and his family on what he earns. If competition were to prevail between the negro and the white laborers, starvation wages would be the rule."[17]

Dockworkers reported to their union offices for strike benefits soon after the walkout began. Economic burdens remained substantial, however; employers expressed confidence that hardship would pressure entire families and bring strikers to their senses. A stevedore predicted: "Their wives will win the strike for us, for I have been told that they do not sympathize with the idea of stopping work when the season is just commencing."[18]

Later events would belie his forecast, for woman and children not only supported the strike but also participated in key confrontations.

Strikebreakers

Employers, however, did not rely on an increase in hunger to bring the strike to an end. They introduced thousands of strikebreakers. Although Governor Newton Blanchard at first vowed to send in the militia to ensure continuing commerce, he did not follow through (and was, in fact, discouraged by Mayor Behrman); therefore, the shipping companies and railroads provided their own security.

During the first week, replacements unloaded freight trains and stowed cotton. Ship crews initially performed the latter task, but the Thiel and Pinkerton agencies soon provided nonunion men (from points north) in abundance. The Illinois Central, itself a beneficiary, subsidized the transportation. News of the food provided the obviously desperately hungry men appeared in the *Picayune's* human interest story, "Hungry Strike Breakers Hold the Sandwich Record.":

> Dining car officials of the Illinois Central Railroad said yesterday that they had seen droves of cattle eating up prairies of grass and had heard of boa constrictors and other wild animals satisfying their hunger with enormous quantities of food, but that the sights they had witnessed within the past few days had surpassed not only the records of their observations, but the strangest stretches of their imagination.

The strikebreakers were Black and white. The whites, noted the sharp-eyed *Picayune*, comprised — "by appearance" — Irish, Germans, Austrians, Scandanavians, and Italians; the October 10 *Times-Democrat* reported the arrival of "Yiddish and Greeks" from St. Louis and Chicago. Strikebreakers of both races were poor, labeled "dirty" by the press. Most were "unfortunate men to whom most any job anywhere held out the promise of three meals per," according to Oscar Ameringer.[19]

Housed on ships and in freight sheds watched over by well-armed guards particularly at the Illinois Central docks, where 200 company police carried rifles and hickory sticks, and at the Southern Pacific wharves, where 50 rounds of ammunition were available to Winchester-toting detectives), many initially stowed several ships at a rapid clip, some gangs averaging 200 bales in the strike's first days. But predictions that they could stow 300 to 400 bales per gang were not borne out, nor did the men prove able to work consistently. The *Picayune* noted on October 9 that they were "not as handy as they might be." Most had not labored at all in recent months. "By their general attitude," said the *Picayune*, many showed "that they were hardly on speaking terms with any kind of work."[20]

Inexperience in dock labor and congested living quarters produced accidents and illness. A nonunion longshoreman was knocked into the river by a cotton-laden float. He drowned: "The body has not yet been recovered." Aboard the hotel ships *Magdalene* and *Endeavor*, men suffered from food poisoning and exhaustion.[21]

Perhaps persuaded by the booing and jeering interracial crowds of dockworkers on the wharves or by the several physical confrontations with Black and white strikers, many strikebreakers quit work. Furthermore, many had not known a strike was in progress and stopped working when they discovered that fact. To strike participant Covington Hall, the "rebellions" of scores of non-union men against the shipping and railroad firms constituted "one of the most unusual mixups." During the strike, Oscar Ameringer met a Chicago socialist who claimed to have been taken from a jail cell (to which he had been consigned for drunkenness), "pushed and jostled" along with cellmates "into a waiting train," and sent to New Orleans as a strikebreaker.

Groups of sailors, members of European, particularly British, seamen's unions, refused to load and unload cargo. Over drinks in a riverfront bar, Irish and Swedish seamen told dock leader Rufus Ruiz that they had been forced to do dock labor at the risks of their paychecks, a charge denied by steamship agents. Aboard the United Fruit Company's *Anselm*, reported the *Picayune*, "the sailors . . . refused to load cargo yesterday, declaring themselves in sympathy with the striking dock workers." For a day, stevedores themselves performed the work. They then hired replacements, seven of whom quit almost immediately, while others remained. Those remaining on the Anselm, the *Times-Democrat* stated, "were Russian Jews mainly, while the quitters were Americans."

Several days after the walkout opened, 65 strikebreaking freight handlers quit the Illinois Central docks and sent a delegation of 30 to see the Mayor Behrman. They had come to New Orleans unaware of a strike, informed by the railroad that freight handlers were needed and jobs abundant. Several such repentants obtained passage home via boxcar and caboose, courtesy of railroad unionists who supplied passes reading,

This is to certify that the bearer of this card was brought to New Orleans on the promise of a legitimate job. Discovering on his arrival that he was to act as strikebreaker, he refused. We kindly ask all good union brothers to assist him in returning to his home in_____.

Within a short time the mayor's office was besieged by other strikebreakers. Replacements doing screwmen's and longshoremen's work claimed that they had been brought there on false pretenses. They were neither receiving the agreed-upon wages nor "doing the kind of work they had contracted to do."[22]

Now indeed, a growing pool of idle and angry ex-strikebreakers walked the streets. Amid reports of stealing (clothing) from storage sheds, editorials protested the importation of "the roughest, toughest and dirtiest bums that the country affords." A cry went up to send them home at railroad expense. At this early point in the strike, Mayor Behrman entered the fray forcefully and in a somewhat antimanagement frame of mind. He feared that the use and misuse of nonunion men endangered the security of the city.

Behrman contacted the Illinois Central, relating his talk with strikebreaking freight handlers and their charge of company distortion of the actual situation on the New Orleans levee. Please arrange for their return, the mayor asked:

. . . The city must not be made to suffer further by dumping in our midst a lot of tramps and hoboes who claim to be brought here under misrepresentation and left to prey upon the community, because of their unwillingness to work and inability to return to the points whence they were brought here.

The railroad's reply, to the effect that nothing obligated it to pay the fares of "indigent persons," prompted Behrman to cable the Interstate Commerce Commission (ICC) for a ruling. He explained: "The men brought here by the Illinois Central Railroad are now a public charge and danger . . . . The railroad cannot be the judge of the law. I ask your construction."

A visit by Oscar Ameringer and four refugees from the hotel ship *Magdalene* did nothing to relieve Behrman's consternation. The former strikebreakers said they had not been permitted to take their clothes with them when they left the ship. Behrman notified Police Inspector E. S. Whitaker bluntly, "You will please to detail a man to accompany Mr. Ameringer to get these men's clothes."[23]

Awaiting the ICC's ruling during that first week, Behrman became increasingly concerned about the strike. Notwithstanding management's claim that strikebreakers were doing fine, freight piled up on the levee. No dock unionist had returned to work: the Dock and Cotton Council was in firm control and, as far as the mayor could see, was conducting a generally peaceful action. But what of the harm caused by the prolongation of the city's agony?

"Undesirables" were "dangerous as long as they infest our city"; but worse, "the commerce of the port is being made to suffer and is threatened with absolute ruin." "There is serious danger," wrote the mayor to the Joint Conference of Exchanges, of trade "never being recovered if we do not take immediate steps to remedy all abuses once and forever." Noting that labor had kept things peaceful, Behrman suspected "that those who have been clamoring loudest for the prevention of acts of violence are really those who are more than anxious to have them occur."

Backed by the Dock and Cotton Council, the screwmen meanwhile declared parity with Galveston out of the question. If anything, they preferred the *upgrading* of Galveston's working conditions to achieve *parity with New Orleans*, at a higher standard. As employers yet envisioned parity of a lower sort, the impasse thus deepened. On October 11, Mayor Behrman declared: "We are face to face with a condition which will not admit of extenuation of any kind."[24]

The Second Week

The next week found the strike solid, its effects wider. The port, Oscar Ameringer wrote, "was completely tied up":

> Fruit steamers from the tropics could neither coal, nor discharge their cargoes. Thousands of tons of bananas and citrus fruit were dumped in the river. Thousands of workers not connected with the strikes were thrown out of work. Business of all kinds suffered tremendously.

"Not a bale of cotton was sold at the Cotton Exchange" on October 15, the *Picayune* reported: "This is certainly not a pleasant fact to contemplate."[25]

The strike's second week witnessed attempts to split the strikers, accompanied by reports of infighting and division among them. To prominent cotton merchant J. G. Duncan, the other dockworkers' solidarity with the screwmen was incomprehensible. How, he asked, could longshoremen, teamsters, and others join a strike which did not concern them? Since the other levee men had "no grievance against their employers," it was "folly" for them to risk "loss of wages" and "present and eventual suffering" simply for the principle of solidarity.

To weaken the strike, steamship agents called for the revival of the White League, spearhead of the famous 1874 coup attempt against the Reconstruction government (heralding the demise of Republican rule three years later). Designed to intimidate Black strikers and to stoke the apparently cooling furnace of "white solidarity" among white unionists, the appeal received an immediate rebuff from the strike's unofficial voice, the *Daily News:*

'What's sauce for the goose is sauce for the gander' and if, as they declare, they are going to organize a new White League to break up the so-called 'conspiracy' against the port by the Screwmen, let them get after all such conspiracies and break them up.[26]

But the strikers remained united as the walkout entered a new phase with an exchange of peace proposals. Backed by the Dock and Cotton Council, on October 11 the white and Black screwmen offered to return to work at the 160-bale rate, pending a settlement on the basis of a port investigation. Mayor Behrman urged the Joint Conference of Exchanges to endorse the proposition and to launch a "full and complete investigation of all port charges, right now and at once." The *Daily States* editorialized, "Nothing can be fairer than this," appealing to the steamship agents to now "do their share towards relieving the general burden," while the *Picayune* added its endorsement. But management found labor's "flexibility" rigid and unacceptable. Indeed, the Exchanges agreed to investigate only if the screwmen returned to work at the 200-bales per gang rate — the demand that had precipitated the strike in the first place.

Stories of vacillation among the levee unions now surfaced, key leaders apparently considering the screwmen too unyielding. "Persistent rumors," several of which "came from the steamship agents," spoke of the Dock and Cotton Council's impending desertion of the screwmen's cause. One leader told the *Times-Democrat* on October 13:

> We are tired of this thing. Our treasuries are depleted by a strike which does not concern us and can do us no good . . . . The other labor leaders are getting tired of pulling the chestnuts out of the fire for them [the screwmen]. They are the aristocrats of the levee and they have never done anything but harm. We all want to go back to work. Our wives and families are starving because we have no food to give them and we can't get any until we go back to work.

The papers reported that contention arose during the Dock and Cotton Council's discussion of the exchanges' counteroffer, as "the peace-lovers in the body" shouted down the motion for rejection put forth by "a mulatto" of "insolent temperament," whose "reputation as an agitator is well-established." Overall, however, according to the *Picayune*, Black unionists were "most clamorous" for an end to the screwmen's unrelenting stance.[27]

Nevertheless, the Black and white screwmen (spurred by "the whip of discipline," the *Times-Democrat* stated) unanimously repudiated the exchanges' proposal at an October 14 joint meeting; the Dock and Cotton Council, equally accordant (its "conservative opposition was stifled," the *Times-Democrat* charged), upheld them. The exchanges, declared a screwman, "must think we are a lot of kids to swallow any such proposition as that made in their reply to the Mayor's letter." The screwmen's joint session greeted the reading of the 200-bale proposal with derision: "Turn it down!" "Throw it in the waste basket!" "We stand for 160 bales."

In a letter to the mayor, approved by the meeting and signed by presidents James Byrnes and T. P. Woodland, the screwmen found the latest proposal lacking in "fairness, equality or justice." Upon adjournment, the men retired to the alley alongside Screwmen's Hall and continued to assail management, one screwman observing that the exchanges' offer "had no parallel in labor history." Another curbstone debator asserted:

> Were we to go to work . . . it would practically amount to accepting conditions that were one of the issues to be arbitrated. We will go to work stowing 160 bales as of yore while they investigate and arbitrate, but no 200 bales for us.

The fidelity of dock labor's most oppressed component, the Black workers, made a particularly vivid impression on Oscar Ameringer: "As strikers, there could be no better. I saw some of the boys lose the shines of their skins, grow thinner as the weeks went on, but they stuck." Whenever he addressed Black dockworkers' meetings, Ameringer encountered emphatic commitment:

> As the audience warmed up, there came responses such as 'Now he's talking, now he's talking. Tell 'em. Tell 'em.' Their responses were harmonized somewhat in the manner of Negro spirituals. An eerie picture, these chanting black men, their white eyeballs shining under flickering gas jets. But once I heard them chanting, I knew they would stick for another week. Their unionism was far more than a matter of hours and wages.[28]

Events during that second week indicated, however, that dock labor was not impervious to compromise. On October 17, Mayor Behrman appeared before a joint white-Black screwmen's session and practically begged the locals to accept a 180-bale work load, pending arbitration. Denying that the unions disrespected law and commerce, the mayor termed antiunion attacks by press and management "slanderous and unfounded." He labelled their proponents "insidious" and "obstinate" for refusing "to remove the barriers in their insistence for 200 bales before even taking up the open investigation of port charges."

The screwmen acceded to the 180-bales figure, but to Behrman's dismay, as a *final* settlement, *pending nothing*. They thereby evoked new indignation among employers and prompted new rumors of opposition to their "inflexible" decision within the Dock and Cotton Council. Reports notwithstanding, Black and white dock locals endorsed the screwmen's vote. Nothing could divide the strikers, asserted Black longshoremen's president E. S. Swan:

I wish to deny that there is any danger of the Longshoremen breaking away from the Screwmen and going back to work. The whites and negroes were never before so strongly cemented in a common bond and in my thirty-nine years on the Levee, I never saw such solidarity. In all the previous strikes, the negro was used against the white man, but that condition is now past, and both races are standing together for their common interests. New Orleans cannot be compared to Galveston, as in Galveston a condition of slavery exists because the races are at variance. If the two would combine there as they have combined here, they would get better conditions.

But when the Dock and Cotton Council (noting that 160 bales was preferable and that the screwmen had conceded much) unanimously endorsed the screwmen, the pro-employer *Times-Democrat* opened fire as never before: "This is a battle decisive in its way as Waterloo was. Surrender to the handful of men who use a mass of negroes to block the progress of the city should be put out of the question forever."[29]

Confrontation

Important developments in using strikebreakers occured in a span of several days. The Southern Pacific, whose union freight handlers had combined the sympathetic strike with their own wage demands, announced victory on October 15. Reports suggested strikers would return but without union recognition. The Illinois Central, too, declared victory over its sympathetically striking freight handlers, after strikebreakers unloaded a record 110 railroad cars on Sunday, October 13, and a more incredible 134 cars on October 14. The nonunionists, stated the railroad, had won permanent jobs; but, for their comfort and protection, the Illinois Central provided "copious supplies of water and soap," round-the-clock Thiel Agency guards, and an emergency lighting system in the event of a citywide general strike.[30]

Despite the railroads' announcements and a concurrent steamship agents' report that strikebreakers had learned to stow cotton "in a remarkably quick time, . . . with almost as much precision as . . . the screwmen" (and several gangs averaged 260 bales per day), port commerce was crippled by the general character of the walkout. Dock labor embodied a process, each of its adjoining components dependent upon coordination and cooperation with the others. The massive cargoes unloaded by strikebreaking freight handlers did not necessarily find immediate transfer into ships as in the usual freight handlers-longshoremen's-screwmen's chain of tasks. On the contrary, freight accumulated on the levee. Black roustabouts refused a whopping 50¢ per bale to assist in cotton stowage. The *Times-Democrat* quoted one: "We wouldn't tech a bale of that cotton, 'cus we promised our 'sistance and wouldn't hurt the screwmen's cause. No boss, not f'r a dolla bale."

Spreading illness and fatigue among the strikebreakers on the hotel ships undermined hopes to conduct business as usual. And even as Mayor Behrman learned from the ICC that the Illinois Central was *not* obliged to pay strikebreakers' return fares, refugee nonunionists continued to ask his assistance in returning home.[31]

In the meantime, a crucial leg of the work process had not operated at all: unremedied by nonunion labor, the compressing and transporting of cotton bales to the docks had broken down completely during the first week of the strike. Special problems attended the use of strikebreakers for this work, normally the labor of cotton yardmen and cotton teamsters. The cotton presses were near the levee, in residential communities: union teamsters customarily conveyed the pressed bales to the docks through city streets. They passed houses and shops on the way. Among those residing along the routes were dockworkers and their families.

Using strikebreakers in this realm of the labor process was a risky proposition. But ten days after the strike began, the cotton factors and boss draymen attempted to get things moving again. To cut down expenses and labor, they announced that a certain amount of the *unbaled* cotton (unloaded from trains at the Illinois Central tracks) would be brought directly to the ships and stowed "flat." Significantly, this avoided using yardmen and teamsters altogether.

But, because greater profits accrued to the tight, full stowage of ships that only cotton pressing made possible, strikebreakers for both the presses and the conveyances, or floats, had to be found to handle the balance of the cotton.

To do yardmen's work, men were brought in (by arrangement with the Illinois Central) from rural Louisiana. Most were Black. Housing facilities included camps in the cotton yards and an old building two blocks from the river. Cotton factors added to Mayor Behrman's anxieties by asking police protection for the arriving nonunionists at the railroad depot and at the sites of accomodation. (Interestingly, the shipping and railroad companies preferred to hire security men rather than use the police to guard the wharves and hotel ships. Covington Hall suggested that in fact city police could not be trusted to protect strikebreakers: many policemen also worked as longshoremen and screwmen and were members of levee unions.)[32]

The boss draymen hired as teamsters local men who knew the routes from the presses to the docks. All were Black. All were in their teens. Their first day of work was October 14; their last day, October 15. Their experiences en route to the levee forced the abrupt cancellation of an entire field of levee commerce for the duration of the strike.

The press reported five attacks on the young strikebreakers, all by Blacks; women participated in four of the incidents, youth in one. The wives and mothers of Black dock unionists, Oscar Ameringer reminisced, played an important role in the strike: "Many of them worked in white men's kitchens, and supplies they carried home at night under their aprons contributed greatly toward holding out."[33]

All the family, social, church, recreational, and fraternal dimensions of levee unionism that gave it community worth and made it moral, crystallized in the events of October 14 and 15.

The mother of one strikebreaker gave him a public beating, despite the "protestations" of a policeman "who did not understand the situation." She pointed out that her son was not yet 16 years old, that "she had a right to do whatever she pleased with him." Not far from the stables where the nonunion men picked up the mule teams, one father caught up with his son, "called him off the float and ordered him to go home."

The press supplied droll, abusive descriptions of a confrontation in the Irish Channel community. "An old negro mammy," "of the Amazon type, big and burly," approached her son "who was driving one of the drays." She cried out, "Listen ter yoah mah!" According to the *Picayune* the ensuing scene unfolded:

> 'A son ob mine take de place ob a union man!' Smash and the exclamation was punctuated by a sock on the nose — 'mah own flesh an' blud drag mah grah hairs down ter disgrace.' bing! another on the breadbasket. 'Why you trashy nigger, run yer life!' and to make peremptory the last injunction, the huge wench raised her No. 10 foot, connected with her son and heir's anatomy and lifting him clear off the float, sent him 'ker-plash' into a slimy puddle that claimed the center of the roadway.

Farther uptown, a nonunion teamster driving through "the poorer quarter" came upon a crowd of women. When they rushed toward him, he jumped off the float and ran. The "infuriated mob bedraggled, evil-smelling negresses" was led by "an ebony-hued Antiope." Because the object of their anger had fled, the women proceeded to destroy the vehicle. With knives, they cut the traces of the harness (allowing the mules to escape), "and then by sheer strength lifted the float from the muddy street and held it suspended, while others of the band, skillfully using wrenches, removed the wheels. The float was left a wreck in the middle of the street . . . ."

Fearing hysteria, Mayor Behrman accused the press of exaggerating the incident and produced a message from a cotton merchant to clarify events. But Charles W. Shepard's brief, less evocative, statement suggested that this incident had occured as reported, and that more than one vehicle had been ruined:

> We have endeavored since Saturday to move some of our cotton . . . to the Creole Line at Eighth street. We were able to secure the labor and the floats.

We moved to Seventh and Annunciation streets, where they were set upon by a mob, wheels removed from the drays and the harness literally cut in pieces.

Like the latter experience, the next took place uptown, near the levee, in an integrated community. A group of "women, girls and boys" stopped a passing nonunion teamster and drove him from the float. They "unhitched the mules and drove them up to the street. They then took the wheels off the wagon bed and left it in the street." Police inspector E. S. Whitaker's official report confirmed the newspaper stories: "When a crowd of boys and women crowded around the negro, hissing him, he got frightened and ran away. Some of the boys drove the flat into the gutter, against an electric light post and took one of the clinchpins out of the wheel."

Therefore, the boss draymen abandoned hauling cotton from the presses to the levee. Merchants confessed inability "to comply with our contracts." The cotton factors diverted new consignments of flat cotton to cotton press establishments in Natchez, Vicksburg, and Mobile.[34]

Towards a Settlement

Although the strike's third week found "the city in the midst of an unusual period of depression" and "financial New Orleans suffering badly with the blues," new moves buoyed hopes for settlement. On the day they accepted Mayor Behrman's 180-bale proposal, minus the arbitration clause, the screwmen amended their decision.

A Dock and Cotton Council delegation met with Behrman to announce the screwmen's readiness to stow 180 bales pending the investigation initially suggested by the mayor: the unions opposed arbitraton. They insisted, moreover, that the investigation analyze all port conditions, not only wages and work load. Behrman favored the move. The *Picayune* as well call for the agents to concede a point or two, but the *Times-Democrat* considered the mayor "misled"; the paper preferred arbitration.[35]

The arbitration versus investigation controversy lasted several days. Stories circulated that other levee unions supported arbitration and found the screwmen too uncompromising. But again, the other unions, most notably the longshoremen's and yardmen's locals, upheld the screwmen. A Dock and Cotton Council leader reiterated: " . . . we are all standing together, and if we are defeated, we'll go down together."

But commercial loss continued, despite reports that strikebreakers had made "progress." The Harrison Line wharves swelled with un-shipped molasses, lathes, and lumber. The United Fruit Company docks stood barren, most of its ships having been diverted to Mobile. Thousands of unpressed cotton bales piled up at the head of Canal Street by the river. Bales likewise backed up at the wharves of the Southern Pacific, which had claimed victory over union freight handlers. On October 20, 65 "unkempt, unwashed" men who "didn't like hard work" quit the hotel barge *Magdalene*.[36]

Commercial stagnation lent urgency to Mayor Behrman's appeals to management. On October 21, he sent a concrete port investigation plan, based on labor's overture, to the agents. Chaired by an impartial umpire, a committed of eight would conduct the inquiry: two agents, two stevedores, two white screwmen, and two Black screwmen. This latter conformed to the half-and-half principle. The committee would investigate shipping costs and rates, railroad charges, stevedores' rates, screwmen's work and wages, pilot fees, and wharfage charges, among other items, and would make a comparison with other ports.

Steamship agents still favored arbitration and opposed the plan, especially resisting any role for labor in resolving fundamental problems of commerce. One agent could "not see how any body of laborers could think themselves capable of selecting four of their members as judges of so intricate and difficult a task as they had announced a willingness to undertake."

Agents failed at first to consider as well that part of Behrman's plan involving Black screwmen in the investigation, but the *Times-Democrat* recognized it immediately and set the tone for management's subsequent behavior on this score: "The suggestion that ignorant negro laborers be permitted to sit in judgement on the commerce of New Orleans, is little short of blasphemy."[37]

But when prominent stevedores broke with the agents and endorsed Behrman's recommendation, great pressure was brought to bear on the steamship companies. Observing that unions and stevedores had shown flexibility, the *Daily States* expressed a growing sentiment: "The real obstacle to a settlement of the troubles on the river front is the steamship agents."

Behrman's condemnation of the *Times-Democrat's* "war-to-the-knife" effort at "the undoing of the screwmen" further isolated the agents. On October 22, the steamship agents decided to drop the arbitration demand and endorsed an investigation. Accord now seemed possible. Only the *Times-Democrat*, angered at the proposed inquiry's "black and tan feature," regretted the agents' acquiescence. The agents' refusal to endorse investigation of *all* port conditions, as labor and the mayor preferred, delayed settlement for a day; but on October 23, the steamship firms acceded to the mayor's plan *in toto*.

Meeting jointly, Black and white screwmen voted to go back to work. The Dock and Cotton Council called off the general strike. The hundreds of Black and white dockworkers outside Screwmen's Hall greeted the announcement with cheers.[38]

Assessments

The general levee strike ended on October 24, after 20 days. (The freight handlers' strike for higher pay at the Southern Pacific endured until November 5: The men retained union recognition but lost the strike. Contrary to company reports that they would not be taken back, the Illinois Central freight handlers returned on October 26). Assessments of the walkout appeared immediately. All sides thanked Mayor Behrman for his concern and hard work.

William P. Ross, chairman of the Joint Conference of Steamship and Agents Stevedores, termed the strike's generally peaceful conduct "most unusual," "remarkable." Leyland Line agent M. J. Sanders agreed and felt the unionists should be "congratulated upon their attitude throughout the trouble." Illinois Central superintendent O. M. Dunn hailed the "gentlemanly" spirit of the struggle, which agent W. H. Hendren found "unique in the history of strikes." Both sides, stated stevedore William Kearney, "showed the proper spirit in reaching a basis of settlement." The Joint Conference of Exchanges' chairmen E. F. Kohnke believed that "general good will result."

Pointing to the hunger and want resulting from the walkout, the *New Orleans Item* found frugality to be the chief "lesson of the strike." Had workers economized beforehand, they would not have suffered: "The first thing that should be done when the rent man and the grocery man are paid is to begin to save."

The *Daily States*, on the other hand, eschewed the ridiculous. Having initially adopted a neutral position, it had become thoroughly antiagent by the end. The strike revealed a "deep-seated disease" in the port and heightened suspicions of commercial interests: "the whole system is poisoned." Over time, "a change . . . had taken place in the popular sentiment here." The comprehension of their consequent isolation had brought the shipping companies to the negotiating table.

Labor drew conclusions. The Dock and Cotton Council's quasiorgan, the *Daily News*, editorialized:

> It was a struggle without its equal in the whole of the annals of organized labor in this city.
>
> It is probably unique in the history of organized labor in this country.
>
> Ten thousand men on strike for three weeks and not in this country.
>
> Ten thousand men on strike for three weeks and not even a fist fight.
>
> Its chief lesson is the value of solidarity.

White longshoremen Rufus Ruiz agreed: "Together they accomplish much; singly their power is seldom felt." Colleague Chris Scully declared: "This strike presents features that make it extraordinary. Nearly three weeks of it, with never a break in the ranks, and not a single act of lawlessness or violence."

"All the men stood together," stated Black longshoremen E. S. Swan: "The screwmen showed the proper spirit all through this controversy, and diplomacy, and not brute force, was used to settle things, which condition should always obtain in a civilized country."

Oscar Ameringer gave his assessment: "This fight shows what is to be accomplished by the industrial form of unionism." From Cincinnati, the national Brewery Workers enthused: "This is the strike of the future." The socialist-leaning *Cleveland Citizen* editorialized: "The victory was probably the greatest ever won in the South and the principle of industrialism is spreading among the rank-and-file." The conservative *Mobile Register* was impressed: "The strike was remarkable for the length of time it lasted without a single act of violence having been recorded."

Back in the Crescent City, Dock and Cotton Council president James Byrnes was both proud and critical:

> I am glad the strike is over. It has been a tremendous strain on everybody directly concerned in it, especially the labor leaders, who had pledged their word to the Mayor that there would be no violence. We have kept our word, but great praise must be given to our men, who have shown fine self-control in the face of great provocation at times . . . .
>
> As the president of the Screwmen's Benevolent Association, I must say that the screwmen showed a conciliatory spirit all along, and had the steamship agents shown the same spirit, the strike might have been settled a week ago.[39]

The dockworkers defeated the antiunion effort so cogently expressed by parity with Galveston, which connoted intensive speed-up and expansion of workload, on the scale of the pre-half-and-half days of shoot-the-chute. Parity meant antiunionism, nonunionism, and the open shop. It signified the segregation of white and Black on the job and in the unions.

That the successful resistance to parity with Galveston owed its strength to an interracial cooperation that defied rumor, threat, slander, and strikebreaking did not escape the attention of steamship agents. As long as Black and white were confident that neither would break ranks, dockworkers could presume to bring the size and scope of the workload under their jurisdiction, assuring that its augmentation would proceed at a snail's pace, if at all. These "limitations," wrote a prominent agent, prevented the shipowner "from deciding what class of work he desires to be done in his steamers."

To make matters more difficult for the companies, the levee unions soon offered to help the white and Black dockworkers in Galveston establish a Dock and Cotton Council. Similarly, they agreed to help those in Savannah, Mobile, and other ports. One white unionist's explanation could not have failed to further upset the steamship agents:

It is a matter of self-protection with us, and it is absolutely necessary that we get all of the dockworkers of all the Gulf ports together. We have got to do this or be forced down to their level in wages and conditions. In the white supremacy strike some years ago, we learned the lesson that the white and negro workers had to get together, and in subsequent little squabbles we were taught the necessity of uniformity of action on the part of all the unions connected with the levee through the Dock and Cotton Council.[40]

Against this concept and practice, employers took aim in the immediate poststrike period.

Unity Assaulted

Mayor Behrman's investigation scheme foundered and died on the "race question." Before labor and management chose their delegates — two agents, two stevedores, two Black screwmen, and two white screwmen — business representatives declared they would never meet with Blacks. Perhaps they had not take seriously that point in Behrman's plan. Yet it was derived from the levee's half-and-half norms and had initially appeared natural to nearly all but the wary *Times-Democrat*.

But the strike had been over only four days when the "business and commercial circles" preparing for the inquiry denounced "such a move as placing negroes on the committee" as "not only impolitic, but almost out of the question." One agent averred that "if negroes were appointed there would be no investigation at all and . . . the committee would fail in its mission entirely."

As the Black and white screwmen deliberated separately to nominate committee men — later to be jointly ratified — rumors circulated of an impending split in labor's ranks: key white unionists "discouraged the idea of having negroes on the board in such an important matter." Agents were sure of Black-white rupture: they attributed the pressure for Black representation to a certain "class of negroes" in the unions which strove single-mindedly toward that end.

But white longshoremen's president Chris Scully reported otherwise: "We are satisfied to leave everything in the hands of the screwmen. It's their business and they alone have the right to form the investigation from their ranks." Black screwmen, moreover, found the possibility of their exclusion incredible. One insisted: "We have just as much right as our white members, and I think those Carondelet Street agents have a gall to cry out that they do not want any 'niggers' on that committee."

The likelihood of white-Black labor representation grew, as it appeared to enjoy dock union consensus. The meetings to designate the four screwmen proceeded, while management issued stronger warnings and direct appeals to white supremacy. An employer declared:

> It is unwise, very unwise of the unions considering a negro in this matter. This Committee may accomplish many things if it is properly appointed, but if the unions force the matter to obliterate the color line, well I know some men likely to be approached who will decline to serve as agents' representatives.
>
> The Committee will have many important things to look into, and I, for one, can't see how a negro belongs on it.[41]

Mayor Behrman, too, came to oppose his own proposal for the inclusion of Black workers. On the eve of the screwmen's decision, he launched an "earnest appeal to the organizations" not to choose "colored men." Nevertheless, after separate consultations, the Black and white screwmen's locals on October 31 ratified the nominations of Black representatives John Granderson (a future leader) and Edward Gray, and whites James Jemison and Edward Nestor (former head of his local).

Terming the move "a most unwise one" (amid the *Picayune*'s cry, "Levee Peace is Again Threatened"), the mayor upbraided the screwmen. "This won't do, Shepard," he told the Black screwman who brought him the news: "Take these demands back to your Association and let the members know that interests demand that there shall be no colored men on the Committee." But in keeping with the mandate of those the *Picayune* called his "Senegambian brothers," Shepard insisted (according to that newspaper), "They wants representation, Mr. Mayor."[42]

The *Times-Democrat* exploded. The "carpetbag system of government for the levees" was responsible for the impasse. In their past surrender to the "black and tan coalition," steamship agents had blown "the opportunity to draw the color line in this levee controversy." The paper conjured up memories of Reconstruction:

> To the black laborers and their steadfast support of the white labor leaders is due the victory of the carpetbag principle. It would be ingratitude of the rankest sort, if the white screwmen refused recognition of their puissant allies. More than that: such refusal is beyond their power, for, having recognized the equality of the blacks in the unions, the latter can avail themselves of an overwhelming majority to carry the point. The carpetbag theory works out in commerce as in politics. During carpetbag days, Louisiana had a black executive and the negroes swarmed in official places, not necessarily because the white carpetbaggers would have it so, but because the system left no alternative . . . .
>
> The whites who accepted the carpetbag yoke on the levee and in the strike must eat of the fruits of surrender, however indigestible they may be. The

protest against the seating of black committeemen is based neither upon law nor upon equality. Carpetbaggery was nominated in the bond and the bond must be kept.

Management's proposed delegates — E. T. George, Mathew Warriner, W. H. Hendren, and J. C. Febiger — immediately announced they would not negotiate with Blacks. "With all the instincts and traditions of the true Southern gentleman," George resigned his nomination. Febiger stated, "I would not like to serve on a committee with negroes. There were plenty of good white men that might have been chosen for such a duty," while Hendren ("son of a major in the Confederate Army") invoked his genes, citing his Virginian heritage as reason enough "to withdraw from the committee if the negroes are successful in their efforts to form a part of it."

Oscar Ameringer suspected that the "real purpose" of management's opposition was "to destroy the solidarity of the two races." After all, employers had dealt exclusively with one or the other race in pre-half-and-half days:

> What could be easier for the emissaries of the employers than to spread the idea among the blacks on the outside that they were being sold out by the conspiracy of white men behind closed doors? Isn't the Negro always sold out when white men put their heads together? Don't be fools, black men. Get your jobs back before those white men behind closed doors take yours. And hurry — hurry.[43]

In any case, Mayor Behrman rushed to address an emergency session of the Dock and Cotton Council. Speaking at great length, he implored the Black screwmen to withdraw for the sake of the port, but he directed his remarks to both white and Black. He had the comfort of knowing he was perceived as a friend of labor. Applause greeted his plea and Behrman hoped for the best as he "repaired downstairs to await the action that would be taken upon his suggestion."

He waited a long time in the lobby of Screwmen's Hall. Finally, a white longshoremen and "a mulatto" — the latter reputed to be an "agitator" — came down to tell Behrman "that his mission had borne no fruit."

The Dock and Cotton Council had voted unanimously to endorse white-Black representation in the investigation committee. Oscar Ameringer, who witnessed the Council debate following Behrman's appeal, remembered that "every white speaker declared himself opposed to the withdrawal" of the Black designees: "There was no need for a roll call."

Behrman could not believe the news. Didn't the labor leaders know the score?

I tried to make these people understand that they would display bad judgement should they insist on colored men being on the committee. As a matter of fact, there are many other interests to be investigated than the wages and amount of work to be done by screwmen. I told them very plainly what the sentiment of the community is as to having colored men figure so prominently in public matters.

I suggested that surely there must be some white men in whose hands they might entrust their case . . . . Despite all that I said to them, they have persisted in being represented by men of their own race. Of course, under the terms of the agreement . . . , they can not be denied this representation. My sole purpose was to try to have them appreciate the sentiment of the community on a question of this kind.[44]

The *Picayune* outlined the stakes involved, accusing the "sons of Ham" of "simply trying to pull down the barriers which bar them from equity in all things with the superior race." In fact, "the darkey in Committee thinks he sees a step in gaining his ambition of equal rights." The Black workers' desire "to mingle with the whites" had put "a kink into things, as tight as some of their scalplocks."

But Blacks had been in labor delegations before. Why, asked Black unionist E. S. Swan, was there a problem now?

I do not see why the four men have now refused to sit with the two colored representatives on the committee. It is necessary to have colored representatives on the committee. The white screwmen want the colored members represented and the colored screwmen mean to fight for representation on the committee.

Black freight handler and CLU head Thomas Le Blanc took the argument further:

There being a controversy relative to the acceptance of negro representatives . . . , and as such a step will not only be an injustice to the thousands of negroes who constitute a majority of the laboring organizations of New Orleans, but will tend to make a settlement of the present trouble more difficult, it is to be hoped that the objections . . . will be abandoned.

Since the beginning of the labor unions, the negro always and at all times arrayed himself against any cause which would injure or be a detriment to the commercial interests of this city. It is he who forms the greater number of laborers and any act which will debar him from a voice as to the welfare of his organization is both untimely and unjustifiable.

Let those who decline to sit with negroes be assured that while the negro does not in a measure demand to be a part of the committee, they at least expect it as a right.[45]

Behrman's investigation plan collapsed. The new antagonisms forced the annulment of the mechanism agreed in strike negotiations: thus, fully a week after the strike, no instrument functioned to settle fundamental problems.

On November 4, the mayor suggested, however, that the state legislature conduct the investigation. He forwarded the proposal to Baton Rouge in a Memorial to the General Assembly. In mid-November, both houses approved the measure; the legislature elected a joint House-Senate committee to investigate the port. The Port Investigation Commission would visit other ports too, interview representatives of management and labor, and seek to resolve conclusively the outstanding issues of the general levee strike.[46]

The signal theme of the 1907 general strike was solidarity. Steeped in a tradition of half-and-half that transcended the perfunctory and the token, New Orleans levee cooperation withstood great pressures and retained its power and organization. White supremacist fulminations in the press, invocations of "Black Republicanism," steps toward a new White League, lurid descriptions of assault on nonunionists, threats of commercial diversion and loss of jobs, and importation of strikebreakers in untold numbers failed to break white-Black cooperation.

Concerted efforts at intimidation and division, for all intents and purposes, fell on deaf ears in Jim Crow New Orleans in the heat of the general strike. In the ensuing poststrike controversy, new attempts to split the races were unsuccessful. The editorials and influential avowals constituted a veritable primer in white supremacy, administering a refresher course in the elementary logic and natural law of segregation. But the races met and acted jointly, whites defended Black participation in leadership and investigation. Black dockworkers declared: We are an integral component of the labor force — we should not and cannot be excluded from matters pertaining to the port.

White unionists agreed. The 1907 general levee strike and the investigation dispute convinced employers more emphatically than ever that Black-white cooperation interfered with commercial ascension.

Chapter Six

Investigation and Aftermath

*One of the greatest drawbacks to New Orleans is the working of
the white and negro races on terms of equality.*

Report of the Port Investigation Commission to the Louisiana
General Assembly, May 28, 1908[1]

The 1907 general levee strike marked the high point of dockworkers'
strength and cooperation in the early twentieth century. Union influence,
powered by half-and-half, operated after the strike, but suffered gradual erosion
under the insistent pressures of Jim Crow and antilabor efforts by employers.

But ten years after the strike, the screwmen were still stowing cotton at
a rate far below the employers' 1907 demands. Having ofttimes cited the current
and growing redundancy of screwmen's work, management imposed heavier
work loads in the late 1910s and early 1920s. In protest, massive levee strikes
broke out in 1921 and 1923, but employers crushed these efforts and built the
open shop on the ruins of dock unions.

Clearly, however, dock unions strength did not decline precipitously after
the 1907 strike. And this was despite a ferocious white supremacist attack by
the Port Investigation Commission in 1908. With commission members and
levee employers cheek-to-cheek, the investigation put white-Black levee cooperation on trial. The investigation constituted a five-month assault upon, and a
concentrated appeal to whites against, the half-and-half practice.

The Commission

Charged with probing the commercial and labor conditions of New Orleans
in comparison with other Southern ports, the Port Investigation Commission
comprised six members of the state's General Assembly: State Senators C. C.

Cordill (Tensas Parish) and T. C. Barret (Caddo), and Representatives Swords Lee (Grant), John Oge (St. Landry), Fritz Salmen (St. Tammany), and George Terriberry (Orleans). Along with commission attorneys W. S. Parkerson and Samuel Gilmore, they met in December 1907 and approved visits of inquiry to Galveston, Savannah, Jacksonville, Pensacola, and Mobile, as well as sessions in New Orleans. Before adjourning until the January convocation in Galveston, the Commission elected C. C. Cordill chairman.[2]

An examination of several commission members suggests the orientation of the investigation. C. C. Cordill set the tone. To the Commission's interrogation of levee unionists, he brought impeccable credentials of white supremacy. A leading Tensas Parish Republican during the Reconstruction Era, he later rejoined the Democrats and headed the local party organization. In 1878, he organized the violent suppression of an interracial poor farmers' party — the Country People's Ticket — in his home parish.

During the investigation, Cordill repeatedly expressed the antilabor, antiBlack views that had become the determining sign in his astrology over a lifetime of distrust of the lower classes. Cordill and his sister owned several of Louisiana's largest sugar and cotton plantations in the predominantly Black Tensas Parish. Of his sister's heavy losses during the 1907 dock strike, he did not hesitate to hold forth. The wealthy Senator considered labor organization anathema and interracial cooperation insidious.

In the early twentieth century, Cordill also became a Crescent City presence, investing heavily in choice local real estate on Canal Street, and his holdings included a major department store and a 13-story office building. Although familiar to some, he cut a figure during the investigation that few Orleanians had seen in person:

> Senator Cordill was the composite portrait of the Kentucky colonel seen in whiskey advertisements. He was topped by a shock of beautiful white hair. He sported a silvery mustache and goatee. He had a florid complexion, suffered from high blood pressure and fell frequently into the role of Shakespearian hero, such as Mark Antony declaiming over the body of Casesar . . . .[3]

Commission members Swords Lee and Fritz Salmen were lumber operators. Lee came from the piney woods region, the center of the state's lumber and timber industries. The Mississippi-born Lee represented Grant Parish, a former Populist stronghold. Aided by disfranchisement — the parish was 30% Black — Lee won election in 1902. His outlook in 1908, however, appeared dim. Socialist and radical sympathizers in Grant remained strong and Eugene Debs would capture 30% of the parish's 1912 presidential vote. Timber workers of both races would soon join forces in an IWW-backed "Brotherhood," confronting Lee and other lumber operators.[4]

Galveston and Savannah

The Commission began working in the dead of the 1907 – 1908 winter, with New Orleans still reeling from the levee strike. Jobless men from other cities, seeking work in the wake of the 1907 financial panic, found nothing in the Crescent City, despite rumors to the contrary. Mayor Behrman asked the mayors of St. Louis and New York to discourage their unemployed from coming to New Orleans: "It would be unjust and cruel to send men here in the false hope of securing work. The local demand for labor is far from sufficient for our home supply."[5]

With C. C. Cordill chairing, the Port Investigation Commission opened in Galveston on January 9, 1908. Steamship agents took the commissioners on a tour of the port and informed them of recordsetting cotton, wheat, and corn commerce in recent months. Commissioners noted that Galveston's harbor was shallower, giving New Orleans a distinct advantage in accommodating larger ships. Galveston's storage facilities moreover, appeared less durable than, and inferior to, those of the Crescent City. Commissioners observed that the New Orleans port enjoyed superiority as a railroad terminus.

Nevertheless, the bulk of exportable crops produced in Arkansas, Indian Territory, Oklahoma, western Louisiana, Texas passed through Galveston. It was revealed that fewer cotton bales were condemned in Galveston than in New Orleans. Bale size and density in the Texas port were more consistent, and pilot charges were cheaper.

The commission began probing the conditions of labor and unionism in the city. The testimony of steamship agents established that Galveston was "less labor union ridden"than New Orleans. Three screwmen's unions operated, two Black and one white. The white union stowed ships bound for other United States ports, the Black organizations stowed craft headed abroad. Only the screwmen of the Southern Pacific enjoyed a closed shop. Many nonunionists labored on the levee and for far less pay than union members. At the same time, segregation prevailed on the Southern Pacific wharves: whites unloaded cotton from trains at the dockside tracks; Blacks stowed the bales aboard ship.

Several employers testified that they preferred Black dockworkers to white, considering the former more disciplined and less inclined to drink. Generally, however, workers were loyal and unlikely to break contracts. Where both whites and Blacks stowed cotton, they worked on separate ships or in different hatches.

A Leyland Line representative reported that the Black men in his employ averaged 275 hand-stowed bales per gang. A Southern Pacific stevedore claimed his screwmen averaged 200 bale-stowed bales per day. Screwmen also performed longshoremen's work, stowing timber, oil, and sugar in addition to cotton. Employers informed the commission that the longshoremen's union no longer existed in Galveston and that management's efforts to consolidate the various dock unions into one, "such as the steamship agents and stevedores of New Orleans hoped to see born during the general Levee strike of September and October," had been largely successful.

Sifting through the data and testimony collected in several days of hearings, the Port Investigation Commission left Galveston with mixed impressions: Dockworkers there were more productive and better disciplined, but substandard storage, poor railroad access, and a shallow harbor inspired doubts about the long-feared supremacy of Galveston. Now uncertain of the "threat" posed by the Texas port, the commissioners predicted that in Savannah would be found conditions seriously rivalling the New Orleans port.[6]

Nevertheless, when the Commission convened in Savannah in early February, it found conditions inferior to those in Galveston and New Orleans. The harbor was too shallow, the channel to the Atlantic Ocean "long, narrow and tortuous." Savannah (where, despite protests, segregation had become entrenched in stores, schools, bars, streetcars, and theaters), the commission learned, had no labor problems: there had been no dock unions for 15 years, since the last strike had been defeated. The strikers then had been all white, earning 30¢ per hour; their permanent replacements now earned 15¢: all were Black. No whites worked on the levee. (The same situation existed in Brunswick, Georgia's other major port.)

Notwithstanding the amount of work possible under these conditions, the commission gave low marks to the quality of labor: "The labor is underpaid and not of the class found in New Orleans or among the white men of Galveston."[7]

Jacksonville, Pensacola, and Mobile

Between February 6 and 8, the commission visited three key ports, the final stops before opening the New Orleans phase of the investigation. In Jacksonville, Florida, some 26 miles from the Atlantic Coast (on the St. John's River), investigators found a rapidly developing cotton trade. Blacks and whites performed dock labor: There were no unions.

At Pensacola, on the Gulf Coast, a thriving commerce in lumber made a strong impression on commission members. The city had been free of levee disputes for years: work teams were segregated, but the port was a closed shop. The union responsible for lumber stowage handled 350 40-foot logs daily per gang of 17. Gangs of six or eight (New Orleans gangs used five) cotton screwmen stowed 240 bales daily. At $4 per day, they earned $1 dollar less than their Crescent City counterparts.

Although the harbor was very shallow at some points and advantageously deeper at others, the commissioners agreed that Pensacola had great potential. New Orleans lumber commerce, handicapped by inadequate storage facilities, could benefit from a careful study of the Florida port.

Nearing the end of its out-of-town itinerary, the Port Investigation Commission paused in Mobile. The commission found a port dependent on timber and lumber trade. Dockworkers belonged to segregated ILA locals. Blacks only handled lumber, earning $2.50 to $4 daily. Whites stowed cotton and timber exclusively. The all-white gangs of cotton screwmen, earning $5 per man per day, stowed bales by screw alone, not by hand. Hence, the investigation recorded a 90 to 100 bale stowing rate per gang, far below the work load elsewhere.

The lumber and timber trade, however, was paramount in Mobile. Employers, noting a recent strike of Black timber handlers which resulted in a shorter working day, told the commission that the port otherwise encountered few labor disputes. White dock unions belonged to a Workingmen's Cotton and Timber Association, which excluded Black levee organizations. When Blacks struck in 1903 for higher pay, the association issued an endorsement, promised a sympathetic boycott, and offered $500 in material support: but the boycott fell through, the money was never delivered, and the strike collapsed.

Here, too, felt the investigators, a close examination of Mobile's port operations would benefit New Orleans. Mobile indeed had great possibilities.[8]

Indictment of the Dock and Cotton Council

Meanwhile, New Orleans screwmen continued to work at the agreed-upon pace at the end of the 1907 strike, pending the investigation's conclusion, which was 180 hand-stowed bales per gang. Levee disputes broke out here and there, but few endured more than a day or two. Late in November 1907, Chris Scully protested the payment of longshoremen's wages in scrip by steamship lines yet to recover from the strike. And, although the *Picayune* feared that the white longshoremen might "trot back to the Othello class again," the controversy was resolved.[9]

A more critical dispute in February had a bearing on the forthcoming New Orleans hearings of the Port Investigation Commission. When the locally based Central American Line hired nonunion men to load the *Habil* on February 10, the Dock and Cotton Council directed the coal wheelers' union not to supply the fuel necessary for the ship's departure. Although the ship later sailed, the steamship line's director appealed to the federal grand jury for redress.

The grand jury responded on February 14 with the biggest federal indictment in the city's history. It charged the 36 Black and 36 white Dock and Cotton Council delegates by name with together violating the Sherman Anti-Trust Act of 1890. In keeping with similar antilabor measures, the indictment accused James Byrnes, Chris Scully, E. S. Swan, I. G. Wynn, A. J. Ellis, and the others of forming a "combination" in restraint of trade. In response, the council defended its custom of solidarity with aggrieved member unions and denied interfering with nonunion men fueling or loading the *Habil*.

The indictment threatened to disrupt the Port Investigation Commission, for the upcoming witnesses included union leaders. Even the *Picayune* declared the indictment unfair and groundless, too sweeping an invocation of the Sherman Act.

Subsequently abrogated, the indictment provoked indignation in labor's ranks. The Central Trades and Labor Council appealed to the United States Congress to reverse antilabor legislation. Most importantly, the indictment created a furor that left the tempo and direction of the port investigation in doubt. Only one month later, when it became clear that the Dock and Cotton Council would not be tried, could the commission open the most significant phase of its investigation.[10]

Labor Testifies

James Byrnes, president of the white screwmen's union and of the Dock and Cotton Council, took the stand on March 10. A 20-year veteran of the docks, the 39-year-old Byrnes fielded questions for two hours. He sketched the mechanics of screwmen's work, asserting that insecurity of employment remained a constant preoccupation: "The screwmen in the dull season when there is no cotton to load get work wherever they can." The current 180-bale work load was difficult for five-man gangs to handle. That Galveston's screwmen stowed more could be attributed to larger (seven-man) gangs and overwork.

The commission now turned to racial matters, querying Byrnes on the sources of half-and-half among the screwmen. He described how the Harrison and Leyland Lines had formerly hired either whites or Blacks, precipitating the 1894–1895 levee race riots. Afterward, employers had hired Blacks and whites, but disproportionately; furthermore, gangs were segregated. Moreover, whites had earned $5 daily; Blacks, $1.50.

In response, the white and Black screwmen had forged a half-and-half agreement in work and organization. Byrnes estimated that there were now twice as many Black screwmen as white. His own local comprised 600 members.

Byrnes' testimony irked the eloquent planter, commission chairman C. C. Cordill. Why, he asked Byrnes, did the screwmen strike last year? Byrnes answered, "We had no strike, Senator. We were locked out!" Coming swiftly to the point, Senator Cordill broke in:

> Do you think it is fair for 600 men to enter into an alliance with a band of negroes to bring about a disastrous strike, and cause the men who grow

cotton to lose $15 on each bale? Suppose the growers would organize, and say we will ship any cotton as we please? It would be an unequal contest, and you wouldn't have a chance to win, and I tell you that's what we are going to do.

Byrnes replied that the men in good conscience could not have accepted a hazardous and unmanageable work load. Cordill reiterated: "No 600 men can in justice amalgamate with negroes and tie up this port." Cordill scorched the levee unions generally: " . . . You run things to suit yourself. You are the czar . . . We work in the country producing cotton and we can't get it off the wharf without your permission." There were no more questions.[11]

The next day, dock leader A. J. Ellis, "as black as any of his race ever comes, even from the heart of the Congo," testified.[12] Aged 58, Ellis belonged to both the longshoremen's and the screwmen's unions — whose local Black memberships he gave as 1,300 and 900 respectively — and was a fixture in the Dock and Cotton Council. Replying to questions, Ellis traced white-Black cooperation to the 1894–1895 levee race riots. He charged the Harrison and Leyland Lines with fostering racial enmity to destroy levee unionism. Black screwmen had taken the initiative in proposing a half-and-half accord to their white counterparts. When the whites had agreed, Ellis recalled, Leyland agent M. J. Sanders had "told him personally that if the whites and blacks amalgamated . . . he would discharge both as he was not going to stand for friendly relations between the races."

Black dockworkers, Ellis maintained, sought protection, not "social equality," in half-and-half. Mutual resentment of the employers' practice of requiring workers of both races to borrow money from them at "usurious" rates of repayment lent further impetus to cooperation; through joint agreements, unions sought to check the arbitrary powers of management. For his contribution to solidarity on the levee, concluded Ellis, he had lost his position as foreman for the Leyland Line.[13]

The "usury" charge was not new on the docks: As far back as 1903, the Cotton Exchange had proposed the discharge of any stevedore who loaned "money to the men at interest," bribing workers in exchange for job guarantees. But Ellis's public denunciation in the austere halls of the Port Investigation Commission created a stir.[14]

Ellis had just finished testifying when Senator Cordill threw out a possible solution to recurring dock labor disputes: *Let the contracts expire in the dull season instead of in the busy season.* If contract talks collapsed in May rather than September, then consequent labor actions would not seriously damage the port. In all likelihood, disputes that arose in May would be solved by September, and the cotton traffic — the *alpha* and *omega* of the busy season — would proceed unimpaired,

But from the back of the hall came a cry of protest from union leader

Thomas Harrison. Cordill called him to the stand. Harrison charged that holding contract talks in the dull season would rob unions of effective recourse in defense of the needs of dockworkers. Levee work was hard, Harrison insisted, the living conditions of those who performed it already difficult: "Longshoremen eat turkey in the fall and winter, his bones in the spring and the feathers in the summer!" (Harrison would later testify formally.)

Unconvinced, Cordill turned to A. J. Ellis and surprised the hall with another rationale for signing contracts in May. Did not the busy season, with labor disputes threatening commercial disruption, customarily also witness racial tensions on the levee? Would not the Blacks therefore benefit from signing contracts in the spring? Addressing Ellis, he observed that spring contracts would "take out all the sting; you know when you people have a controversy with the whites, you generally get the short end of the poker."[15]

The commission interrogated the prominent longshoremen Chris Scully and E. S. Swan on March 13. Swan spoke first. His testimony shocked commission members. He had to be reminded "that he was only a negro and that he should not overlook the fact." The commission, however, obtained Swan's support for renewal of contracts in May.

The commission probed the phenomenon of solidarity. Swan confirmed that work rules required that members boycott ships loaded or unloaded by nonunion labor. Did he realize how seriously that practice impaired commerce? He knew indeed that much freight had been diverted to Galveston, Mobile, Savannah, and elsewhere, that the New Orleans levee "looked like a cyclone had struck it." Swan submitted this own theory about the greater "productivity" in other ports: laborers there "were little better than slaves, because the white men and the blacks are fighting each other, and each strives to load more than the other."

Commission attorney W. S. Parkerson conducted the questioning. The "slave labor" charge aside, would Swan admit that dockworkers elsewhere stowed more cotton? Perhaps, Swan answered, but "not like it should be stowed. They might throw it in promiscuously." Wherever white and Black remained divided, he went on, labor was overworked. Swan knew the time when "the whites wouldn't work with the negroes" and workers were segregated. Employers would tell the whites, then the Blacks, that the other race was working faster: " . . . They kept war to the knife, and knife to hilt, between the two races . . . ."

In those days, Swan remembered, gangs stowed 200 bales and more: "It was a case of slavery, the agents wanted to break up the unions, and the agents and stevedores were getting all the money." In response to these conditions, Blacks and whites "amalgamated."

But, attorney Parkerson warned Swan, the unions had obstructed Crescent City commerce for the last time: Orleanians would not tolerate white-

Black labor cooperation to the detriment of business. Swan, however, gave no ground. He insisted that blacks had "to stay with the white men," even if and when the latter were hostile. Otherwise, Swan asked, "what are us niggers going to do?"

To the attentive Senator Cordill from Tensas Parish, Swan's logic was bizarre and difficult to follow, so when he now interjected he asked about something said five minutes before:

> Do we understand you to say that in Galveston and other places where the whites and negroes work separately, a condition of slavery exists? Can you give us an instance in history where the Anglo-Saxon allowed himself in subjection?

"No sir, I can't do it," answered Swan, and Cordill continued: "Yet you can say that an Anglo-Saxon must lower himself to the grade of a negro to be free?"

Swan said nothing, but Cordill moved on to something else that had bothered him: Hadn't Swan claimed during last year's strike that Black dockers would control the port and put "the white men up against the Blue Ridge Mountains?" Not quite, Swan responded: He had in fact suggested that the "steamship agents and stevedores were up against the Blue Ridge Mountains with 10,000 [Black and white] laborers against them."

On that note, Swan's testimony concluded.[16]

White longshoremen's president Chris Scully, a 14-year levee veteran, spoke in the afternoon session on March 13. The commission again focused on the why's and wherefore's of solidarity. Attorney Parkerson asked about the longshoremen's refusal to do screwmen's work. Scully described the traditional division of labor: screwmen loaded cotton and tobacco, longshoremen handled grain, sugar, and timber. By offering the former's work to the latter, steamship agents endeavored to break the powerful screwmen's unions. Longshoremen had even refused, Scully confirmed, to do screwmen's work on the very eve of the 1907 general strike, in the full knowledge that the port faced disaster.

Scully appeared wary, clearly uncomfortable. "Don't answer me reluctantly," Parkerson admonished: "Your attitude is hostile to me but I don't want to hurt you."

Questioning now turned to labor cooperation. Within the past few months, the agent for the Mobile and Gulf Line had approached Scully to ask if the union would interfere with nonunion men unloading cotton from Mobile and Gulf Line ships. Why, Parkerson inquired, had Scully brought E. S. Swan to the meeting when the agent had not requested Swan's presence? Scully explained that Swan belonged in discussions concerning levee labor.

Scully and Swan had promised noninterference, but they gave no guarantee that the contiguous union dockworkers — longshoremen, teamsters, and yardmen — would touch the cotton. Consequently, observed Parkerson, the Mobile and Gulf Line had abandoned the port altogether; thereafter, it would send ships to Pensacola and Mobile.

The commission dismissed Scully and resummoned E. S. Swan to the stand for a special statement. Clarifying his earlier suggestion — so irksome to Senator Cordill — that whites had to unite with Blacks to achieve better conditions, Swan denied casting aspersion on white superiority. Blacks cooperated with whites for mutual protection "against the bosses," with no ulterior motive: " . . . There is no question of equality here. Is that satisfactory, Mr. Parkerson?"

But Senator Cordill's dissatisfaction persisted. Affirmation of white superiority, even Swan's concluding "I believe in the white man," still left interracial labor cooperation standing, though swaying. Cordill wanted it down for the count. He reminded Swan: " . . . You know that whenever your people have a controversy with the whites they come out at the short end of the horn."

The day's final witness, white screwman James Daugherty, testified for more than one hour, supporting A. J. Ellis's report of "usurious brokerage" in the hiring system. He, too, accused the Leyland and Harrison Lines of a conscious speed-up policy through racial competition. Screwmen had, by necessity, responded with half-and-half, Black and white working abreast in the same hatch.[17]

From the Horse's Mouth

Management witnesses began testifying several days later, on March 17. Cotton merchant William Mason Smith accused the Board of Trade of laxity in cotton inspection: More substandard cotton passed through New Orleans than through other ports. Shippers thus diverted much freight to Mobile, Galveston, and Savannah. Former South Atlantic Line agent Alfred Clement alleged that the Illinois Central had fixed lower freight rates for cotton destined for export aboard Harrison and Leyland ships, giving those lines a monopoly.[18]

Key testimony opened on March 19 with the remarks of Leyland Line agent M. J. Sanders, the heavy hitter among employers. So crucial was his appearance that Mayor Behrman attended the proceedings.

Sanders conceded that the Leyland and Harrison Lines enjoyed cheaper freight rates for railroad shipments of cotton headed for Liverpool. The commission, however, focused inquiries upon white-Black labor relations.

Sanders recalled that he had once employed only Black screwmen. Back in 1894, whites had burned his wharf to protest this exclusive hiring. After the levee race riots, he had employed whites as well, and by 1900 had consented to hire whites and Blacks on a 50-50 basis. But the screwmen's 1902 half-and-half agreement had surprised him and other agents, for it entailed "a secret agreement by which they would stow only 120 bales a day." Having been used to screwmen's work loads of 230 to 250 bales daily, with "no limits placed on what they would do," the shipping lines lost heavily.

Rebuking the charge of widespread loansharking, Sanders also denied firing A. J. Ellis for promoting interracial solidarity. Significantly, however, Sanders "opposed the amalgamation" of the Black and white screwmen because he "wanted to keep the peace, and knew that could best be done by keeping the races apart." Trade unionism as such did not trouble him, but he did "not favor whites and negroes working side by side."

He offered the faster-working Galveston screwmen as a model for local labor. In continuing testimony on March 20, Sanders insisted that neither the current 180-bale work load nor a projected accord at 200 bales amounted to the necessary parity with Galveston.[19]

The investigation continued on March 23 with the interrogation of William P. Ross, agent for two lines and chairman of the Joint Conference of Steamship Agents and Stevedores. Ross believed screwmen's labor was not so taxing, for the workers "were a fine body of men physically." Galveston men stowed 200 to 250 bales, easily. Local levee problems originated with half-and-half. Ross vehemently denied having invited half-and-half by the speed-up policy. "They simply found that by pulling together they would have us under better control."

A revealing exchange then ensued between Ross, Senator Cordill, and commissioner T. C. Barret:

> *Barret*: Is there any way they could be worked separately and their rights protected?
>
> *Ross*: I don't see why not. I think it's a bad condition; too near social equality.
>
> *Cordill*: It doesn't elevate the negro, and it degrades the white man.
>
> *Ross*: I think the whites will be run off the levee entirely, or be degraded to the level of the negro. Every man prefers dealing with his own color, and as far as I have known, the white man has always been given the preference on the levee.
>
> *Barret*: In other ports they work on different ships.
>
> *Ross*: And I don't see why it can't be done here.[20]

The commission next called upon Harrison Line agent Alfred Le Blanc. He reiterated previous assertions: the half-and-half agreement had damaged commerce, the two races held to a "secret understanding" to limit stowage, and "usury" on the docks did not exist. Before 1902, he reminisced, "when the whites and blacks were being worked separately on the ships, the whites hand stowed 225 bales a day and the negroes 275 bales."

Le Blanc testified that he had totally eliminated whites from his employ in the late 1890s, relenting only after the 1900 Robert Charles race riot, during which the mayor had warned him against "endangering the peace of the city by employing negroes to the exclusion of the whites." To commission attorney Samuel Gilmore's query, "Do you know anything about the system of playing the whites off against the negroes, telling each side that the other was doing more work, and making threats of dismissals," Le Blanc answered, "That's the imagination of Mr. A. J. Ellis."

The half-and-half system paralyzed his business. It forced him to delay work assignments until equal numbers of whites and Blacks showed up for work, for gangs labored only on a 50-50 basis. The "costly" disruptions proved that dockworkers cared nothing for the port's commercial interests. They "deliberately rob us," Le Blanc concluded emotionally: "This is the worst labor-ridden city in the country."[21]

The testimony of steamship agents touched a responsive chord in the commission and the press. At the same time, it tapped and mined a local deposit of resentment. Many had long suspected the British-owned powerhouse Leyland and Harrison firms of monopolistic tendencies and arbitrary practices. Indeed, Covington Hall pointed out "the general hostility" of Orleanians to the local influence of foreign shipping corporations and major railroads.

Confirmation of the long-rumored cheaper freight rates provided Leyland and Harrison by the Illinois Central fortified popular displeasure. Thus, the *Picayune*, while concurring with the agents' racial attitudes, condemned at the same time the "selfish interests" behind the discriminatory "combination" of key railroad and steamship lines.[22]

This foreshadowed the astounding testimony of stevedore John B. Honor. As labor contractor for several lines, Honor had become prominent in levee management, well known for attempts to sue striking unions. Appearing on March 27, Honor tore into the half-and-half concept and agreements, but he placed sole blame for the levee's Black-white configuration upon the Leyland and Harrison Lines. Driven by an "insane desire for power and ambition," certain agents had pitted Blacks against whites in order to lower wages and crush unionism. An employer of impeccable white supremacist reputation, Honor charged openly "that the whites and blacks had been pitted against each other by M. J. Sanders" of the Leyland Line.

The agents had brought disaster upon the port with their racial manipulation, Honor testified. Interracial solidarity in the unions would never have developed but for the agents' ill-considered policy of replacing whites with Blacks, fostering racial enmity and precipitating riot. The problem began when "the negroes were being worked in to put the white men out," a practice continued by Leyland's Sanders until "he was promised the mayoralty if he would take back the whites."

The humiliation of both white and Black had thrown the two groups into each other's arms, resulting in the half-and-half position that endangered port commerce.

Honor gave highmarks to the labor of New Orleans dockworkers. "The Screwmen have always kept their promise to me," he reflected, and "the Longshoremen are the best class of workmen I have ever seen." Unlike the steamship agents, Honor supported the signing, then and there, of a three-year screwmen's contract at 180 bales per gang, far below the heralded parity with Galveston.

But he unalterably opposed half-and-half and deeply resented white-Black cooperation in the screwmen's joint conference, "composed of twelve whites and twelve negroes," which "raises all the hell it can in as short a time as possible." The joint screwmen's conference "practically controls things and fines the foremen when the latter don't suit."

Due to past experience, Blacks no longer trusted certain employers; this was unfortunate and problematic, for essentially "the black man has all the characteristics of a child, and he believes in the white man."

The session ended with a cadenza of racism. Asked his opinion of whites and Blacks working together, Honor declared, "I'm a Southern man; you don't have to ask me about that. I believe in white supremacy." And Senator Cordill repeated: "It doesn't elevate the negro and it degrades the white man."

And the commission members "were of one accord in saying that such equality of the races as exists today on the Levee was a disgrace to a Southern city."[23]

Honor was a difficult witness to follow, but stevedore William Kearney's testimony added a visual dimension to the investigation. He was labor contractor for the Harrison Line and utilized his appearance to reveal that levee laborers, screwmen especially, worked far below capability. Kearney brought to the witness table a small wooden box, meant to represent the hold of a ship, and "five tiny bales of cotton."

He demonstrated how cotton was hand stowed. With his model, he showed how screwmen "married" two bales together (see Chapter II) by tilting them on edge against each other and pressing down on top to squeezed them into tight spaces. Fascinated, members of the commission watched Kearney prove how, through proper stowage, "the vessel could economize space."

After show and tell, Kearney charged that screwmen had not worked up to par ever since the 1902 "amalgamation of the races." Rather, they "just put the bales in loosely." Before "amalgamation," screwmen had stored 280 bales a day and "did not go for whiskey at 3 o'clock as now." The 280-bale average, Kearney recalled, prevailed between 1900 (when the major lines had rehired whites and deployed the two races in separate holds) and 1902. Kearney did not join John Honor's denunciation of the Leyland/Harrison tandem. As far as he could remember, the agents had employed more Blacks than whites in the 1890s only "because there were so few white men" to hire. Inexplicably, then, more whites had appeared on the levee in 1900.

Kearney attacked the power of the levee unions. They dominated the docks, ignored the stevedores, and "governed and tyrannized over" the foremen. No one could control the unions nor check their influence. He recalled being insulted and kicked out of Screwmen's Hall during the recent levee strike. In stowage, the most decisive realm, the screwmen's joint Black-white committee held sway. Senator Cordill interrupted: "Do I understand you to say that twelve white men and twelve negroes dominate the commerce of this port?" Kearney responded, "Yes, sir." Cordill commented: "Well, we are practically under negro government."[24]

After a lengthy Easter recess, employers from other spheres of the labor process took the stand. Several alleged that union leaders dominated the workers. According to merchant E. F. Kohnke, management's proposals during the 1907 strike fell on deaf ears because "a negro longshoremen named Jim Porter would not even let the laboring men consider the proposition." A boss draymen complained that the cotton teamsters' union, all-Black, stood ready at moment's notice to engage in sympathy actions: "The negroes will haul no freight that is unloaded by nonunion men . . . " The union had itself won demands with Dock and Cotton Council backing. Often, charged drayman Peter Fabacher, teamsters quit work early, leaving the wharves blocked with cotton.

Other employers attested to the burden of labor solidarity. One remembered that a dispute with union scalemen, all–Black, had brought a Dock and Cotton Council delegation to his office door: "In three minutes," it "forced him to submit to the scalemen." But, incomprehensibly, the council delegation had included white union men James Byrnes and Chris Scully, and the employer "thought it rather hard that white men should force another white man to submit to the unjust exactions of a gang of negroes."[25]

Cotton factor Adam Lorch, an employer of cotton yardmen, found the steamship agents inflexible. The current 180-bale screwmen's work load, he told the commission, was fair. Laborers were honest and law-abiding, while certain agents pursued selfish interests at the expense of the port. Like stevedore John Honor, he blamed the agents for the tough, united stance of white and Black levee laborers.

Lorch's testimony broke Senator C. C. Cordill loose of all restraints. In a voice that hushed the crowded, bustling hearing room, the sugar planter asked the witness: "Who Africanized the labor on the river front; the British ship agents, wasn't it?"

Lorch: I think so.

Cordill: That was the beginning of your downfall?

Lorch: Yes sir.

Cordill: It's rather a hard condition when a nigger like E. S. Swan can say he'll get a white man up against the Blue Ridge Mountains and fix him up, don't you think so, Mr. Lorch?

Lorch: Yes sir.

Cordill: This is the worst nigger-ridden city in the South, and when niggers like Swan and Ellis have more power than Governor San-Blanchard, I should say, and Mayor Behrman, well it's time for the white man to take some action.

Lorch informed Cordill that even Black union delegates tied up his cotton presses in various labor disputes: "It's a pity that I have to sit here and admit that such a condition exists." Lorch described how Black yardmen and teamsters dragged cotton "ruthlessly" along the ground, through the mud. This information touched Cordill personally: "That was my sister's cotton, and I'm glad we weep over it; I guess she wept too, as she lost $15 on every bale."

Juices flowing, commission lawyer Parkerson now gave the hearing a more physical tone: "How long would Swan last up in your parish, Senator?" To which Cordill replied "I don't think Swan would find it very healthy where I live. In this town there are five white men to every nigger, and yet the nigger is the boss. It's the only town in the South where they'd stand for it."

Only the vigorously pursued subordination of Blacks would solve this problem. Cordill warned: "You'll have to talk to those niggers as a nigger talks to a mule, with a single-tree."[26]

A New Contract

The investigation wound down. On April 29, the commission solicited employer opinions on a new screwmen's pact. Leyland's M. J. Sanders, still smarting from critical testimony against him, called for a five-year contract. He joined the commissioners in urging the renewal of segregation on the job. He proposed restoration of pre-half-and-half conditions, under which shoot-the-chute and high productivity prevailed. At the same time, he termed the charge of setting white workers against Blacks "an absolute and unqualified untruth."[27]

Appearing the next day, the Port Investigation Commission's final witness was popular white screwman Thomas Harrison. He ignored Sander's denial and asserted that before half-and-half the races indeed "were pitted against each other . . . they did more work than they could stand." The agents *forced* white and Black screwmen to cooperate for mutual protection. Whites had no choice. Hovering above was the old management option of racially exclusive hiring: " . . . The whites had to amalgamate with the negroes or lose everything."[28]

The commission retired to draw up its official report, bidding screwmen and agents to meet while promising to assist if necessary. Agents soon invited the white and Black locals to negotiate; this after refusing to treat with Blacks the previous November. Hence, the screwmen sent Black and white delegates, five of each race (including James Byrnes, Thomas Harrison, T. P. Woodland, Edward Gray, and Nelson Shepard). Labor offered to stow 180 bales at $26 daily per gang ($5 per man, $6 for the foreman) — as at present — or 200 bales at $31 daily (with a wage increase). Agents felt neither offer a guarantee or parity with Galveston and proposed 200 bales at the old wage, $26 dollars per gang. The sides failed to agree.[29]

The screwmen, Black and white, meeting jointly on May 5, voted to ask the commission to intervene; nearly one-third of the screwmen present, however, opposed the motion, fearing the imposition of an unfavorable work load. Thomas Harrison pleaded with the men and threatened to resign, over contrary shouts of "No, no!": "Gentlemen we must let them arbitrate, we have just on our side and we will be treated fairly."

Amid reports that it opposed management's intransigence, the commission stepped in and recommended, in binding arbitration, that screwmen stow 187 bales by hand (and 90 by screw as agreed in 1903) at $26 per gang: more work at the old wages. Agents of course, had hoped for much more, but none dissented. As for the unions, "neither President Byrnes nor Mr. Harrison would express an opinion on the finding. The laborers were, however, not very pleased." But they could do nothing about it. The settlement appeared to close the book "on what proved to be one of the most disastrous strikes in the history of the city of New Orleans."[30]

Agents and screwmen signed the new five-year contract on May 12. It was indeed a spring contract as Senator Cordill intended, guaranteed not to seriously disrupt commerce upon expiration. The spring signing, observed steamship agent William P. Ross, would "obviate the dread of labor troubles during the early part of the cotton season . . . " Ross expected "an era of good feeling" on the levee.

Now, no labor leader, even the critical Thomas Harrison, dissented from the signing of the contract in the spring. In Covington Hall's judgement, the spring signing and the heavier work load (at the old wage) constituted a serious setback for levee labor. It was indeed. It filed down union power. Later, during the World War I, the screwmen would demand and win the return of busy season contracts. Hence, the decisive clashes of the early 1920s would take place in autumn.[31]

But the levee unions were not crushed. The powerful Dock and Cotton Council still operated. The commission had imposed a wage-cutting solution which nonetheless fell far short of management's goals. Agents favored 250, 240, 225, or at least 200 bales stowed per gang; the contract called for 187. Agents had hoped openly to eliminate the screwmen's locals and afterward to reduce the strength of other levee unions. Their statements in October 1907 suggest that they neither favored nor foresaw the continued existence of organization among the white and Black screwmen.

It was perhaps in this light that the labor leaders signed the contract in May, a pact requiring more work for the same pay. Considering the agents' designs, one may conclude that in maintaining organizational integrity and unity, in keeping working conditions from deteriorating to parity with Galveston and other open shop ports where the races worked separately, the New Orleans screwmen won the 1907–1908 levee war.

The new contract carried over certain prior achievements. Choosing of gangs remained in union hands, directed by member foremen overseen by stevedores. Division of labor between screwmen and longshoremen, in spite of agents' efforts to have the latter do the former's work, remained. The contract continued to recognize loading of ships at downriver wharves as overtime work.

Above all, despite the fierce attacks by agents, stevedores, newspapers, and port investigators, half-and-half survived the contest. The contract signed by labor and management in May 1908 retained the previous accord's 50-50 clause verbatim: "The steamship agents agree that their stevedores and superintendents shall employ . . . half white and half colored men, and the walking foreman shall distribute them equally abreast of each other in each hatch."[32]

The Necessity of Segregation

On May 28, the Port Investigation Commission published its conclusions. In measured, optimistic tones, it summarized five months of proceedings, drawing particularly on the 52 sessions in New Orleans.

A deep harbor, easy access to the sea, a matrix of railroads, and a vast potential for growth gave New Orleans a clear advantage over other ports. No Gulf port could compare with or in any way rival the Crescent City.

New Orleans was in the forefront of cotton, coffee, and fruit commerce. But the commission stated frankly that it would be shut out of the lumber trade entirely unless viable storage facilities could be quickly constructed on the levee. To fund the comprehensive improvement and expansion of wharves and sheds, the commission recommended that the state legislature draw up a constitutional amendment providing for the sale of $3.5 million in bonds by the Dock Board. The crucial measure would liberate the Dock Board from borrowing money "from the several steamship lines doing business at the port." (See Chapter II.) Publicly supervised wharves distinguished New Orleans from other Southern ports, but only better funding could lend real power and effectiveness to that supervision.

The commission condemned the Illinois Central-Harrison Line-Leyland Line monopoly on cotton exported to Britain. It held that monopolization was "injurious to the port" though the two shipping lines rendered "a splendid service" to New Orleans commerce overall. The commission's report called upon the legislature to take active steps against "discrimination."

Hence, "natural advantages" alone could not ensure the port's preeminence. If the state took concrete steps to improve the port, if decent men united their efforts, New Orleans would reach greatness. The report chastized commercial hypochondriacs: "Cease croaking." If all Orleanians pulled together and unfurled "the banner of good will, industry and prosperity," then New Orleans had "nothing to fear" and would soon enter "the foremost ranks of the cities of the earth."

But one intangible remained: the labor problem. At other ports, the commission witnessed nothing resembling the Crescent City levee: "There was no hostility between employer and employed at Galveston; none at Savannah; none at Pensacola, and none at Mobile."

"Capital and labor" worked elsewhere for the interests of commerce "and the common welfare of both," never hesitating to have "a "heart-to-heart" talk when "differences arose." They "thrashed out the whole subject and settled it amongst themselves without stopping work or resorting to strikes or lockouts."

Not so in New Orleans, where "hostility, distrust and suspicion" prevailed between unions employers. Which side was right? The laborer felt the employers "gave him no consideration" and "exacted more onerous service of him," while the steamship agent "complained that he could not get dispatch because the laborer would not stow enough cotton," and the union gave him "no latitude."

Between them, labor and management crushed the 350,000 citizens of New Orleans, holding hostage the city's economic life. But the commission expressed confidence that the new contract, buttressed by renewed faith and general concern, would change things. Perhaps all sides would learn from the 1907 strike. If hopes for "marked improvement in the relations between the parties" bore fruit in the next five years, then "peace is an assured fact for an indefinite period."

Ultimately, however, true labor peace demanded a solution to the "race question" on the levee. This involved morality as well as economics. In order to advance, the port required a labor arrangement of another kind, in keeping with essential values. The commission examined the unfortunate status quo:

One of the greatest drawbacks to New Orleans is the working of the white and negro races on terms of equality. It drags down the white man; it does not uplift the negro; and so we find white men working hopelessly for existence under these intolerable surroundings.

These conditions do not exist in any other port. Elsewhere if the two races work in the same ship they load in different hatches. In New Orleans they work in the same hatch, abreast of each other, and often a negro foreman directs the white gangs.

The commission believes that this has been the fruitful source of most of the trouble on the New Orleans levee.

Thus concluded the Port Investigation Commission. The report capped a careful, business-like investigation designed to ensure prosperity through labor peace. Sifting through mountains of testimony "on every possible phase of the subjects to which its attention had been directed," the commission set forth, in sober tones befitting a public body, all the preconditions of commercial expansion: wharf improvements, abolition of railroad rebates, subsidization of the Dock Board, new storage sheds, universal goodwill, and racial segregation on the levee.[33]

The 1908 Strikes

In spite of the commission's recommendations and management's hopes, two united dock strikes broke out within a month of the Port Investigation Commission's report. These involved freight handlers and longshoremen, with sympathetic involvement of other levee trades. Cooperation between white and Black dockworkers sustained the walkouts.

The spring and summer of 1908 witnessed another trend, however. While levee organizations held to half-and-half agreements, white dock locals joined the newly formed state Federation of Labor in May, an organization which excluded Black levee and other unions. Black unions may have hoped that recent experiences in the United Labor Council, the 1907 strike, and the 1908 investigation, might ease entry into the new Federation of Labor. But the Federation's convention turned away Black delegates. The organization inserted "white" into the constitutional clause on affiliation.[34]

A second segregated body arose after the investigation, in July, in the midst of the freight handlers' and longshoremen's strikes. This was the state Board of Arbitration, a permanent institution initiated by Governor Jared Sanders. Sanders discussed the idea in Baton Rouge with levee men James Byrnes, John Higgins, Chris Scully, and E. S. Swan. He planned to solicit representation from labor and management. The arbitrators would "all be white men," reported the *Picayune*: Black workers would "have to content themselves with leaving their case in the hands of the white labor representatives on the Commission." White unions, including dock locals, nominated seven workers to the Board, of whom Governor Sanders chose two, including longshoreman Rufus Ruiz.[35]

Sanders initiated the Board of Arbitration amid fiercely contested levee strikes in spring and summer, disputes so bitter that the Port Investigation Commission came close to reconvening. Neither the disputes, nor their attendants' sympathetic actions, however, hurt agents to the extent of strikes in September or October during the busy season.

At the end of May, as the Port Investigation Commission issued its warning against interracial labor cooperation, white and Black longshoremen struck. Walking off several ships, they complained they could not keep pace with the screwmen in the holds. They insisted that employers hire additional men. Other levee workers boycotted affected ships.

At a conference with white (Scully, Keegan, and others) and Black (E. S. Swan "and half a dozen negroes") leaders on May 30, steamship agents promised to consider the demand. Time elapsed and the locals met jointly on June 3 to threaten a full strike unless extra men were supplied. Further complicating matters, the Illinois Central freight handlers, Black and white, issued a demand on June 3 for higher wages. Their contract expired on June 30: They would strike if necessary.[36]

Although it was the off season, agents had hardly expected disputes that soon after the Port Investigation Commission's findings. Determined to prevail, they dug in and charged the longshoremen with breaking contract stipulations against work rules changes. They called upon the Port Investigation Commission to intervene and arbitrate, further notifying presidents Swan and Scully that the unions' power to affect trade and labor was intolerable. The disbanded Port Investigation Commission, however, could reconvene only with the consent of all concerned parties. The situation deteriorated.

To management's surprise, the Joint Conference of Exchanges supported labor's call for hiring additional longshoremen to accommodate the heavier workload accruing to the screwmen's contract.[37] Anticipating that this pressure would induce accord, Mayor Behrman invited the parties to negotiate. Agents demurred. Extra labor aside, they felt a deeper problem was involved. The very prerogative of unions to influence work, the power of Scully, Swan, and other walking delegates to "watch the work and give instruction as to what shall be done," impeded settlement. Armed with the Joint Conference of Exchanges' endorsement, the white and Black locals refused to discuss the matter. Cotton backed up on the levee.[38]

This was not a general strike. Several agents and stevedores did agree to expand longshoremen's work teams. The loading and unloading of products customarily stowed by longshoremen alone continued: sugar, coffee, grain, and molasses kept moving. Laborers in jobs preliminary to longshoremen's stowage — union teamsters and scalemen — continued working.

But when the Illinois Central freight handlers struck as promised on June 30, the levee situation altered. The Black and white freight handlers received and unloaded from railroad cars all manner of cargo, including products then being stowed aboard ship without dispute. If the railroad ignored their demands for a pay raise to $2.50 per day (from $1.80) and hired strikebreakers, the impact on dock labor would be great. The Port Investigation Commission, impressed with the inspired testimony of boss draymen, cotton factors, public weighers, and steamship agents, had hoped to avoid this situation. But, on July 1, the *Picayune* pronounced the levee outlook "gloomy."

Insisting that rising "house rents," costs of "provisions" and "general living" expenses necessitated higher wages, the Illinois Central freight handlers watched as strikebreakers took their jobs. The railroad hired both white and Black ("plantation negroes out of employment") nonunion men, assigning them to segregated work teams and sleeping quarters.

Amid the festering longshoremen's controversy, the Dock and Cotton Council debated the necessity of a general strike. As in 1903, member unions tacitly agreed not to load or touch freight handled by nonunionists, without declaring a dockwide walkout. Council sentiment seemed "to be strong for peace" and the implicit boycott unfolded inconsistently. But, on Independence Day, the longshoremen's locals struck in sympathy with the freight handlers.

Rumors abounded of racial dissension among the freight handlers, hinting that Blacks resisted, while whites supported, the strike's prosecution. As in the past, the *Picayune* attributed the walkout to the pressures of the whites, claiming also that "in the big strike last year the negroes were largely opposed to the trouble."

But when the railroad announced that strikebreakers would be permanent and would thereafter be paid according to the amount of work performed (not by the hour), the Black and white freight handlers' unions issued a joint blast, branding the move "unjust." White leader Ethan Duffy declared angrily, "I don't think the unions will stand for it."[39]

Contrary to reports, the Black and white freight handlers stood together for the duration of the strike. The Dock and Cotton Council support, however, appeared to ebb. The longshoremen's achievement of their extra labor demand in mid-July (without reducing the power of union delegates to delay work) significantly lightened the atmosphere. Most Dock and Cotton Council unions, themselves recovering slowly from the general strike of the year before and "taking into consideration the recent financial panic and the present money stringency," strove to alleviate the material pressures by asking the freight handlers to lower their wage demands (several council unions opposed this concession, however). The strikers grudgingly agreed and the Dock and Cotton Council then intervened on their behalf with the railroad.[40]

But the freight handlers remained united and on strike, despite new reports of white-Black discord. Moreover, the Council's majority decision notwithstanding, screwmen and longshoremen continued to boycott "scab freight" at several ships. A steamship agent observed:

> The men may be working and doing their best, but when any of the radicals appear on the Levee everything stops and the men leave their jobs. I can't say just how the order is given, or who gives it, but as I said before, it strikes me as being a very peculiar situation.[41]

Pressure on the freight handlers mounted, however. As the strike persisted, it lost the support of its previous backers within the Dock and Cotton Council. By a great majority, the council then threatened the two locals with expulsion. The sporadic boycotts came to an end. The cargo logjam on the docks began to loosen. At the end of the strike's third week, white and Black freight handlers jointly agreed to sign a five-year accord at the old pay scale.[42]

In the immediate wake of the Port Investigation Commission, two strikes therefore developed. Black and white longshoremen won their case; Black and white freight handlers were defeated. As the latter experience bore more comprehensively on the other fields of levee labor, it carried for a time the potential of a general strike. In all likelihood, the freight handlers could not have won without active sympathy, and this latter lagged or evolved unevenly because dock unions felt unequipped to go the mat again, at least so soon. Dock and Cotton Council solidarity traditions forced other unions to consider the implications of each union's dispute.

Reports to the contrary, however, racial antipathy between Black and white strikers did not develop. Striking longshoremen and freight handlers struck, met, settled, and returned on the basis of the half-and-half principle which the Port Investigation Commission had explicitly condemned. Again, strikers stayed out in the confidence that neither Blacks not whites would abandon the cause. The longshoremen won the hiring of additional men and defended the on-the-spot stoppage of work by union delegates in case of grievances, a prerogative strenuously fought by employers. In the freight handlers' strike, however, material hardship appears to have forced other dock unions to forego solidarity, although not without strong contrary boycotts.

There were different trends. Unions sought to find their bearings after sacrifices during a long period of decisive battle. Still, employers could not have been too pleased at so quick a renewal of levee union struggles, so rapid a reaffirmation of interracial cooperation. Essential issues of trade union power persisted, were fought out in the summer of 1908, and would be contested again. The postinvestigation period witnessed victory and defeat, but half-and-half remained. The Port Investigation Commission's injunction echoed in the ears of employers in the summer of 1908: Through the disruption of solidarity lay the path to levee peace. But that path would have to be blazed.

Aftermath

A glance forward indicates that levee unionism suffered slow erosion after 1908. Efforts by employers to speed up the process, however, evoked resistance. Sustained by white-Black cooperation, dock unionism persisted beyond World War I, succumbing over time to the open shop and the tightening noose of segregation. These pressures fused during the Great Depression in a white supremacist proposal of uncommon invention, a city ordinance requiring longshore workers to be registered voters.

Several prominent levee unionists passed from the scene within a short time of the 1907 — 1908 dock wars. Screwman James Byrnes resigned as president of the white local in September 1908, apparently to accept a government job: He returned to union service during World War I. Barred from riverfront employment after his forthright testimony before the Port Investigation Commission, Black longshoreman and screwman A. J. Ellis became a night watchman. White longshoremen's president Chris Scully died in 1910; the day of his funeral, the white and Black locals announced: "All work on steamships . . . will cease this noon in respect to the memory of our esteemed president, Christopher Scully."[43]

A number of key leaders remained, most notably Thomas Harrison, who replaced James Byrnes as white screwmen's president in 1908 and held that position for 15 years. Harry Keegan assumed the leadership of the white longshoremen after Chris Scully's death; he, too, would be around for quite a while. Black dockworkers retaining union posts in the 1910s included James Porter (Longshoremen), T. P. Woodland (Screwmen), and J. C. Coats (Cotton Teamsters), an associate of Covington Hall. Black leadership would soon include screwman John Granderson (one of the proposed negotiators rebuffed by steamship agents in 1907) and Albert Workman of the longshoremen. With Keegan and Harrison, these men led the dock unions on the eve of the fatal 1923 strike, outlined below.[44]

The Black and white screwmen, whose unions were strongest and character of labor most disputed, kept their half-and-half agreement in effect for a decade after the 1907–1908 encounters. The 1909 work rules reiterated verbatim the half-and-half rule established earlier in the decade. As late as 1917, the half-and-half principle could still be found in the cooperative agreement of white and Black screwmen. It involved not only a 50-50 division of work, but also, at least in theory, joint leadership, Black-white juries, regular consultations, and a generally united approach to management. Half-and-half also prevailed among the longshoremen, whose 1917 rules committed union foremen to 50-50 hiring and distribution of workers, adding identical numbers of extra men when needed, and ending the day by "discharging the men . . . equally."

Significantly, screwmen succeeded in keeping cotton stowage rates well below the demands of management for parity with Galveston. Contracts during the ten years after the general levee strike were almost identical to that arbitrated in 1908. According to the 1917 contract, 187 bales stowed by hand and 90 by screw constituted a day's work for a five-man gang. Work rates for tobacco loading remained the same as in 1908. In 1917, the men received $6 per day, an increase of $1 from 1908. The 1917 contract, like its predecessors, also recognized the right to strike sympathetically with other recognized dock unions. Likewise, contemporary freight handlers' and longshoremen's contracts sanctioned solidarity on the waterfront.[45]

But business and technology assaulted the screwmen. The employers' old cry that improvement in shipbuilding and cotton pressing made a separate category of skilled cotton stowers unnecessary was not farfetched. It made more sense as time went on.

During the early twentieth century, cotton commerce experienced a technological revolution which, over time, divested cotton stowage of the last remnants of skill. Faster, larger steamers emerged from the shipyards, with a capacity of 20,000 bales by World War I: three times the 1900 capacity. The new, high-density cotton press, appearing shortly before the war, reduced the size of the "standard" bale by more than 30%.

The largest presses operated in the great Cotton Warehouse and Terminal Plant, proposed in 1914 and completed during the war by the Dock Board. Covering five waterfront blocks, with an annual storage capacity of two million bales, the concrete plant featured the latest cranes, grapples, and conveyors, showcasing an automatic "bale puller" permitting a worker to pull any particular shippers' bales out of a tier — regardless of how high — in a matter of minutes. Everything moved smoothly, the cranes and conveyors powered by purring motors, hoisting 500-pound bales and depositing them upon swiftly moving trucks bound for the wharf. Encouraged by the steamship lines, the Dock Board also built a Public Grain Elevator during the war. Designed to store, condition, and blend grain, the facility included a drying plant, every manner of trucking vehicle, a sophisticated system of conveyors, and passages leading directly to the ships.

Backed by all of organized dock labor, the screwmen meanwhile held on through the second decade of the century, but they would not long keep their grip. Clearly, mechanization brought the posibilities of wider, more profitable port commerce. Not surprisingly, the commercial confinement threatened by the longstanding 187-bale stowage (prevailing despite the new potential), convinced employers of the urgency of the open shop.[46]

Complicating matters further for the screwmen was the wartime establishment of the U. S. Shipping Board which was empowered to purchase, lease, build, and operate government merchant marine vessels by arrangement with private shipping companies. Four of the smaller steamship lines doing business in New Orleans contracted with the Shipping Board. But its involvement with New Orleans dock labor extended beyond the connection with particular shippers. During the war years, it became an agency of overall mediation in the shipping industry. Structured along the lines projected (unsuccessfully) by Mayor Martin Behrman in 1907, with representatives of labor, management, and government, the Shipping Board was, in fact, part of a network of wartime authorities (headed by the War Labor Board) overseeing labor relations. In this capacity, the Shipping Board and its National Adjustment Commission (NAC) investigated the New Orleans dockworkers during and after the war. NAC documents reveal the persistence of interracial cooperation and union strength on the Crescent City levee.

Like other government bodies in the period, the Shipping Board promoted mutual respect between labor and management. The Council of National Defense had declared in April 1917 that "neither employees nor employers shall endeavor to take advantage of the country's necessities to change existing standards." The National Industrial Conference Board's warning to employers not to undermine union shops and to open shop workers not to seek unionization "for the duration of the war," were echoed in the work of the Shipping Board.[47]

Created in August 1917 to resolve dock labor issues, the NAC gave tripartite representation to labor, government, and management delegates. In New Orleans, as in other ports, the NAC helped create a Local Adjustment Commission (LAC). Together the NAC and the New Orleans LAC endeavored to adjust longshoremen's disputes during and just after the war. And there were plenty in New Orleans.[48]

Crescent City unionism made an instant impression on LAC chairman Pierce T. Murphy, a U. S. Army Reserve captain: "Conditions in this port are most peculiar," he wrote NAC chairman R. B. Stevens. Murphy reported that white and Black locals were found in the dock trades, most affiliated with the ILA. All belonged to "a body which is known as the Dock and Cotton Council, and of which Mr. Thomas Harrison is President and Alexander Paul (a colored man), President of the Car Loaders and Unloaders [freight handlers] Local is Vice-President." Dock labor seemed exceptionally well organized; again he mentioned the curious organization "known as the Dock and Cotton Council," which functioned as a "clearing house" embracing "all the organized labor along the river front . . . "[49]

Although participating in the LAC (represented by such men as Thomas Harrison and James Byrnes of the white Screwmen) and being aware of government warnings against wartime strikes, levee men showed no disposition to bite the bullet. In view of the port's mechanization, expansion, and new role as embarkation point for Allied supplies, both employers and government put a premium on expeditious labor. Dockworkers, however, felt the pinch and resisted the pressures.

Two freight handlers' strikes broke out during the war, in September 1917 and July 1918. P. T. Murphy was convinced that longshoremen incited the second strike, and urged federal action to break it: the government demurred. Longshoremen and screwmen supported the wartime walkouts and a 1920 freight handlers' strike as well, which found the wharves, as earlier in the century, "filled with inward cargo than cannot be moved."[50] Of greater significance, a longshoremen's dispute broke out during the war over the number of flour sacks carried to the ships by a two-man truck. The usual number was eight, but longshoremen cut back to seven, openly resisting the stress of faster and otherwise heavier wartime loading. The contention endured throughout the fall and winter of 1917–1918. At bottom, P. T. Murphy opined, the longshoremen must have had "some influence, inimical to the Government's interest, at work among them." Indeed, shipping agents termed the white and Black longshoremen's stance "both unpatriotic and a distinct aid to the Nation's enemies." The flour in question was bound for the Allies.[51]

Promising to continue working pending resolution of the issue, Harry Keegan and Albert Workman assured Murphy of labor's loyalty and willingness "to co-operate with you and the National Government in bringing the war to a successful close." Controversy persisted though, after the white and Black locals defied the LAC's recommendation (in which screwman-LAC member Thomas Harrison concurred) that eight 140-pound sacks were indeed the normal load; labor ignored management's order to work "as formerly." The frustrated Murphy asked his superiors to give the LAC "such legal power as would compel respect of its decisions." The Army Reserve captain and LAC chairman pleaded for a mandate of force:

> . . . The best remedy . . . is a battalion of stevedore regiment encamped at Camp Nicholls, just in the suburbs of New Orleans.
>
> With such a unit there would be no question as to what the Longshoremen would do and this mulish obstinacy and procrastination on their part would instantly disappear.[52]

Disputes of this type recurred during and after the war, evading true solution. Freight handlers and longshoremen, asked for higher wages, continuing to send Black-white committees to deliberate with employers; screwmen continued to handstow 187 cotton bales per day per gang, a fact that must have been particularly irksome to levee employers in the expanding port.

Under these circumstances, the NAC and LAC held a series of investigations into labor conditions on the New Orleans levee toward the end of 1918. Here again were several labor participants from the 1908 Port Investigation Commission which had put half-and-half on trial: James Byrnes, T. P. Woodland, and Harry Keegan. Longshoremen were entitled to higher wages, Keegan now testified, "for the simple reason that the members of our organizations, both white and colored, are drifting away from the levee because they have other jobs, or are getting other jobs which pay them steady pay." The war notwithstanding, he continued, work remained irregular and workers needed "some inducements" to stay on the levee: "You must give these men something." He joined with Black longshoremen's president Albert Workman in noting the greater occupational hazards attendant to wartime handling of steel and railroad iron.

Freight handlers gave testimony in support of a pay increase. Said one: "We have never been getting . . . enough wages for the work performed." A government official engaged the witness in dialogue: Was not their work easier than that of longshoremen? Or more regular? Or safer? Or, involving unloading of railroad cars under protective sheds, less affected by weather? The witness answered "no" to all queries; resolution of the grievance was deferred.[53]

Understandably, the hearings dealt with that historically most controversial local levee problem: the stowage of cotton by screwmen. New Orleans steamship agents endeavored to obtain NAC backing for their demand that screwmen's gangs handstow 225 bales per day. Again, that magic word "Galveston" appeared, now, as before, synonymous with faster work and weaker unions. Galveston steamship representatives spoke before the NAC in New Orleans. In their city, one stated, 225 bales was in fact considered a *minimum* day's work; rather 270 bales was a more realistic workload for a screwmen's gang. Galveston labor, another contended, could easily handle 300 bales per gang on a daily basis. But the New Orleans screwmen's leader James Byrnes informed the NAC — to the incredulity of Galveston employers present — that Crescent City screwmen were in fact at that moment asking a higher wage for stowing the same number of bales as they had stowed since 1908: 187.[54]

Small wonder then that the debates of ten years earlier were revived. "To put New Orleans on a par with Galveston," employers asserted, local screwmen had to stow 225 bales. Parity was the issue once more. As the NAC sought to calculate a standard day's work for screwmen, New Orleans shippers asked the NAC to keep in mind "the greatly increased cost of operating ships during [the] past few years" and the "scarcity and marked decreased efficiency of labor . . . ." Pressured to take a stand, the NAC recommended that New Orleans screwmen continue to hand stow 187 bales, then confessed an inability to determine a fair day's work and asked for more time.[55] The question went unresolved. Shipping interests bombarded the NAC with information: 225, 250, 270 bales — all were possible to stow in a day. In his experience, a Galveston shipping agent wrote the NAC, 225 bales was by no means a day's work: it was a half day's work. But the NAC failed to reach a conclusion.

In fact, noted a businessmen's publication, despite its expansion, New Orleans had lost its share of national commerce during World War I, dropping from second to sixth among the leading ports between 1911 and 1918. Although Atlantic and Pacific ports had enjoyed strategic superiority during the war, Crescent City shippers might well have wondered about the role of the labor unions in retarding the pace of commercial development.

Disgusted with federal inaction in the screwmen's case, the New Orleans Steamship Association declared that it would no longer cooperate with the NAC.[56]

By the early 1920s, the U. S. Shipping Board, through contracts with four shipping lines, controlled 30% of the port's tonnage. While dockworkers at private lines still labored under the same conditions as those employed by the Shipping Board, the New Orleans Steamship Association was under no obligation to match the labor standards prevailing at the Shipping Board's docks. This state of affairs fertilized the soil of levee union disaster. When the private and public employers of dock labor parted company, taking different approaches to the 1923 dock strike, common conditions of labor no longer obtained and the work force was split.[57]

The trend toward Black majority in the labor force had meanwhile quickened during the 1910s.

While more than one-half of the 1907 strikers were Black, and scholars Spero and Harris found levee labor "about evenly divided" in the early 1910s, the century's second decade witnessed a dramatic rise in the ratio of Black dockworkers to whites. World War I spurred the process. Whites were able to take advantage of expanding opportunities in new fields of employment more reliable than casual dock work. Port activity boomed during wartime, attracting a great many new workers — predominantly Black — to the docks. According to one source, the Black longshoremen's union in 1923 comprised 4,400 members, its white counterpart 1,400. Another found the Black-white longshoremen's ratio that year to be more disproportionate than the government-estimated 65:35 in 1920. Clearly, by the early 1920s, Black men constituted the great majority of dockworkers.[58]

The trend complicated half-and-half. Although joint bodies, meetings, and decisions — organizational operations — continued to resist Jim Crow proscriptions, half-and-half in the division of jobs became increasingly discriminatory. Even under the circumstances of decisive Black majority, Black unions never won parity of foremen. As the constituency of Black locals rose sharply during the war, half-and-half increasingly operated at the expense of interracial cooperation.

This was not unrelated to the continuing procession of Jim Crow in the city. Despite protest meetings, organizations, and activities, the restrictions proliferated and deepened. A greater number of facilities, events, and outlets became off-limits to Blacks. As late as February 1916, Black youth could not attend high school. In 1911, the City Council banned Black participation in the Mardi Gras.[59]

Charity Hospital opened an inferior facility for Blacks in the summer of 1911, inspiring other health care institutions to follow suit. The Board of Health reported an increase in the Black death rate during the 1910s, attributable in part to tuberculosis. With a decline in living standards generally, drug addiction, especially to cocaine, became a serious problem. Among the emerging trends which posed responses to Jim Crow, the Marcus Garvey movement began to attract a following in New Orleans. By the early 1920s, its mass meetings were held at the hall of the Black longshoremen.[60]

Dawn of the Open Shop

Under conditions of industrial change, advancing segregation, and developing intraunion inequality, a less cohesive levee labor movement confronted the steamship agents at the end of the second decade of the twentieth century. But the employers had also changed, committed now as never before to the vision of a levee free of unions. In 1921, they recorded an important gain against the screwmen, whose elimination as a category and an organized force, was so basic to antiunionism. For the first time, local cotton stowage reached the 200-bale per day per gang figure.[61]

Employers seemed determined to maintain the momentum, for in November of that year, they proposed that more bales be stowed. Over 1,500 screwmen walked off the job. On November 24, the Dock and Cotton Council called a general strike of the 12,000–15,000 men organized in its 24 member organizations. When strikers confronted nonunionists at the foot of Canal Street on November 24, a massive disturbance followed: 250 policemen with riot guns subdued the combatants.

The strike endured for eight days. But the levee unions were weaker and the Dock and Cotton Council less effective than before. Settlement brought parity with Galveston. The agents' quest was realized: 225 bales were to be stowed daily per gang, at piece-rate wages.

When the strike ended, the United Fruit Company broke with organized labor, making its strikebreakers permanent. The Southern Pacific and two other firms abandoned union contracts in 1922. Thus, on several piers the open shop prevailed even before the 1923 encounter which marked the "end of an era of powerful domination by the unions of the Dock and Cotton Council." The levee confrontation of 1923 dispatched the screwmen "to that oblivion which their outworn economic function made eventually inevitable."[62]

The last of the major New Orleans levee wars before the Great Depression opened in September 1923. It involved at first the Black and white locals of the longshoremen and the screwmen. Contracts for both of these units of dock labor expired then. Longshoremen's leaders Albert Workman and Harry Keegan put forth demands for a pay increase, hiring extra men to transfer cotton to the burdened screwmen in the holds, and the restoration of a grievance committee.

When employers promised to concede the pay raise while rejecting the additional hiring demand, Workman and Keegan denounced their stance as "not fair, just or right, either to yourself or us or the community at large." After the Black (led by John Granderson) and white (headed by Thomas Harrison) screwmen submitted their own appeal for higher wages and promised to support the longshoremen, the lines were drawn.

Granderson, Keegan, Workman, and Harrison all hailed from the period of dock union power, the first decade of the century. But it was clear now that interracial cooperation had eroded. Joint statements and resolutions now were few and far between. Labor's spokesmen here were Keegan and Harrison: both had supported the selection of Granderson to the proposed Black-white screwmen's negotiating team in 1907. In 1923, however, Granderson took little part in decision making. Spero and Harris indicate that Black dock locals in fact opposed a strike in 1923; so, too, did many whites, but all walked out when a strike was declared.

Clearly steamship agents had had enough of the screwmen and levee unionism. Within hours after the screwmen struck sympathetically with the longshoremen on September 16, employers stated officially: "The question of open shop has been touched upon. We propose to keep the ships working, unions or no unions." Unless the four striking locals returned, observed the *Picayune*, "the open shop rule will prevail."[63]

To the employers, the screwmen's very existence in New Orleans now posed a "disadvantage in competition with other Gulf ports." The "artificial differentiation" between screwmen and longshoremen was "the root of the incessant agitations and turmoils" troubling the port. Technology, they stressed, made screwmen redundant: nowhere else did those responsible for the now simple task of cotton stowage still constitute a separate class of laborers with "special privileges and greater pay." "Cotton is no longer crowded" into the holds, declared the president of the New Orleans Steamship Association on September 25: The claim that "stowing cotton still requires greater skill and harder work than stowing general cargo" had "not been true for many years." Screwmen's unions were "small, select exclusive organizations," representing a "falsely privileged caste on the docks," "the Brahmins of our riverfront. Brahmins are out of date."

The screwmen were finished. The agents were serious, refusing to negotiate with striking longshoremen until they agreed to replace the screwmen from then on, until they accepted "consolidation" into "one class of labor with one wage scale."

Times had changed, warned the employers. Management would prevent the exercise of power by levee unions. Employers would not answer the longshoremen's appeal for a new grievance committee, branding the demand an "absurdity," an "impracticability." They had bitter memories:

> Prior to and during the war, the application or interpretation of union labor rules, always susceptible to dispute by the men themselves, was the cause of grave delays. The work would be stopped while the point for or against would be argued out before a 'grievance committee.'[64]

Despite Thomas Harrison's vow that "the strike can never end as long as the agents demand the destruction of the two screwmen's organizations," management fully prevailed. Nonunion men already worked permanently at several wharves, and other strikebreakers were brought in. In contrast to the composition of levee labor, most of the strikebreakers were white. On September 21, a predominantly Black group of strikers clashed with nonunion workers on Canal Street. Shipping lines attempting to use crews to load vessels found their efforts temporarily but effectively blocked by an IWW appeal to marine workers for solidarity. Still, even after Illinois Central freight handlers left their jobs (and cotton teamsters threatened the same) in sympathy with the longshoremen and screwmen, commerce proceeded close to the norm. The other levee unions did not register their solidarity consistently or for long. Returning after a while, they cooperated with strikebreakers in forwarding cotton and other items to the ships. The pace of business quickened.[65]

As before, agents housed strikebreakers aboard hotel ships anchored in the river. Finding the increased police squads inadequate to protect the nonunion men from angry strikers at dockside — armed Black and white strikers fired upon strikebreakers on September 24 — shipping agents obtained an unprecedented court order. Handed down by Judge Foster of the Federal District Court, the injunction Vs. Harry Keegan, Et. Als charged the unions with having "conspired with other and others unknown to strike." Accusing the men of "injuring the business of complainants" and "impending and delaying . . . interstate and foreign commerce," the order banned the "use of threats or personal injury, intimidation, suggestion of danger or threats of violence of any kind," "in any way or manner whatsoever," by dock unionists. It barred strikers from the docks, wharves, grain elevators, and vessels.

Pronouncing the order the "most drastic . . . ever made effective along the waterfront" and particularly noting the sweeping proscriptions upon any "suggestion" of danger, the longshoremen appealed for redress. They obtained an injunction, effective upon the posting $5,000 by the locals, blocking the Foster decision. The new order recognized workers' right to strike ("if the conditions of employment or their wages are unsatisfactory") as well as their right to "observe the situation" on the levee, "to communicate" peacefully with "those who have taken their places and to endeavor to persuade them to cease work."

But the longshoremen's locals could not post bond, the original restrictions stood and were in fact upheld by the state Supreme Court in mid-October. "Under very distinct handicaps," the striking unions now faced the end.[66]

The press soon announced that the port had registered an unparalleled volume of trade during September, had broken all one-month records despite the strike. The news whetted further the antiunion bent of the steamship agents. The agents, reported the *Picayune* on October 19, "are going to run an open shop."[67]

The downfall of levee unionism came with the innocuous announcement on October 18 by the U. S. Shipping Board that it would grant the longshoremen's demands and continue to recognize the screwmen at its piers. The private shipping lines refused to follow suit and closed their doors to organized labor, leaving union men the only alternative of contracting with the Shipping Board, which controlled no more than 30% of port commerce. Because the private lines would not alter their decision, the unions pursued this option and signed with the Shipping Board. Five thousand union screwmen and longshoremen therefore came into exclusive possession of only a fraction of port jobs. Only one-third could hope to find work.[68]

Matters became worse within days. "Weakened terrifically," the unions faced exclusion not only from the bulk of levee jobs, but also from contact with other dockworkers. On October 21, the Shipping Board moved to concentrate the trade of its four contracting lines at one dock, thus segregating union longshoremen and screwmen in a corner of the riverfront. And now, wrote Arthur R. Pearce,

> the waterfront was definitely split — and the screwmen were dead. Even for the Shipping Board they retained the exclusive right to handle cotton and tobacco only when they were in large lots. Small lots mixed in with other cargo would be handled by the longshoremen.

The Shipping Board would soon lease its lines to private operators who would lock out the union longshoremen.

In the meantime, the private shipping lines proclaimed their interest in starting a new union, "modelled along lines to avert squabbling among the workmen and assure reasonable continuous work without interruption." They wanted an "independent" union, for they had never opposed the right to organize. "What we objected to was the arbitrary, intolerable aggressions of the leaders of the unions that walked out. We do not mind dealing with any sort of association reasonably managed."[69]

In keeping with these sentiments, steamship agents kept out workers suspected of affiliation to or preference for the old unions. Toward that end, they introduced a system of fingerprinting, photo-identification, and identification badges during the 1920s.

Although a majority of the 1923 strikebreakers had been white, agents quickly discharged them; for a period they only hired Black workers. These workers did form a union, though a weak one. The "Africanization" of the port frightened certain powerful white politicians who made it an electoral issue in the late 1920s. They encouraged white ex-dockworkers to form an organization to demand reinstatement in dock jobs. Subsequently, agents hired a number of whites.

But black predominance remained. How to evict Black workers from a field where they had constituted so basic a component for so long became a ticklish question. Employers and city fathers alike bore the scars of battle with a united interracial labor force: they were determined not to live through that again. But perhaps a need for diplomacy and sophistication plagued their collective conscience. Jim Crow was in the saddle, but could thousands of Black workers, at once and together, simply be driven from the waterfront?

Such considerations apparently motivated men of influence. A pretext had to be found. Differences between the white and Black unions arose over the conduct of strikes in 1927 and 1931, for which mutual support did not materialize. In 1931, the head of the white union (himself a political influential) demanded that the Black organization — as a precondition of its continuation — resolve that only "certified registered voters should be employed in loading and unloading" ships, trucks, and freight cars on the waterfront "within the territorial limits of the city."

Great pressure forced the Black union to adopt the resolution, which then became a city ordinance. Few Black longshoremen met the new criteria. The rule needed only to be enforced. A thorny problem had apparently been solved.[70]

Conclusion

Under the shadow of white supremacy, an effective interracial dockworkers' movement developed in New Orleans during the early twentieth century. A resurrected levee unionism affirmed labor's right to shape the work process. In its own behalf, it managed for a period to impose limits on the amount and pace of work — cotton handling, above all — that thwarted the commercial aspirations of powerful railroad and steamship corporations. In the great 1907 dock strike, more than 10,000 Black and white dockworkers held off and defeated the concerted antiunion efforts of those corporations.

Industrially amalgamated and interracially cooperative in contrast to the contemporary policies of the AFL, New Orleans dockworkers created mechanisms of interracial solidarity that became traditional in the first decade of the century. Unions adopted and abided by statutes of cooperation. The ways and means of solidarity — from joint representation to the alternate Black-white speaking rotation during meetings — endured throughout the period. Solidarity became almost *de rigueur*. It therefore became possible for Black dockworkers to play an active role in unionism, a role defended and affirmed by white unionists.

The evidence shows that Black levee men did not abandon unionism after the riots of the mid-1890s, that they did not become an accommodating source of cheap labor. On the contrary, they built strong unions in the early twentieth century and fought for joint policies and action. Together with whites, they developed an industrywide, interracial approach to trade unionism.

Crescent city dock unionism derived its power from interracial unity. Black-white cooperation gave levee men some measure of control over working conditions. Their consequent strength stymied commercial interests, to whose anger the 1908 Port Investigation Commission gave full expression. Senator C. C. Cordill, chairman of the Commission, spoke on behalf of others when he decried the shameful white "alliance with a band of negroes," which purported to "tie up this port." Employers felt that "twelve white men and twelve negroes [the joint screwmen's committee] dominate the commerce of this port." The workers, alleged a steamship agent, "deliberately rob us." Cordill told the unions, "You run things to suit yourself. You are the czar and it isn't fair."[1]

Even though such charges tended to distort the realities of class relations beyond all recognition, shippings interests were indeed frustrated. The only other American port that appears to have witnessed anything remotely similar to the Dock and Cotton Council during the early twentieth century was

Philadelphia. Under IWW leadership in the early 1910s longshoremen in that city regularly elected both white and Black delegates to union posts and adopted a rotating, white-Black, system of chairmen.[2]

Half-and-half experienced some rough going in New Orleans. Under cooperative agreements, union locals remained segregated. Joint meetings were segregated in the same hall. At no point did Black dockers achieve parity of foremen. In fact, half-and-half tended to connote separate (though complementary) parts, not components of a single whole.

White supremacist, antilabor, antiimmigrant, and antiunion views suffused the New Orleans press, including the newspaper that provided the most comprehensive chronicle of half-and-half. Consequently, its portrayal of the experience of solidarity must be regarded with care. But the omnipresent inequality of foremen and the active involvement of many white dockworkers in the political campaigns of white supremacists (in whose wards union men often held a balance of votes, compelling political support for levee labor) would suggest that egalitarian sentiment among the whites was never all-encompassing. Still, in their firm adherence to such half-and-half essentials as joint representation, equal division of work, interracial juries, Black-white leadership, and consultation at every step, white dockworkers swerved directly from and broke with the basic pattern of Southern race relations. Levee unionism in New Orleans was less segregated and allowed for less discriminatory Black-white relationships — not to mention joint action — than other areas of social and economic life during the nadir.

Black dockworkers, steadily increasing in number and by World War I, a decisive majority, supported half-and-half with special vigor, pursuing its fuller application, particularly in the foreman dispute. As the latter indicated, they felt entitled to a more equitable half-and-half system. Many Black dockworkers challenged the exigencies of segregation while engaging in joint action with white fellow workers. In the labor-led Equal Rights League, Black levee men appealed for political representation and voting rights. Such Black unionists as A. J. Ellis and cotton yardman I. G. Wynn expressed especially strong convictions about segregation, views which contrasted with both the antilabor white supremacy of employers and the views of many white dockworkers.

Why did white-Black cooperation develop in New Orleans? What accounts for its endurance in the decidedly inhospitable surroundings of the nadir in American race relations?

Spanish-French settlement had left its mark in an unusually complex set of relations, yielding a tradition of contact. Antebellum race relations were multifold, rooted in slavery and inequality while white men rubbed shoulders with Blacks in many arenas, crowded the Black Creole-owned "grog shops," and engaged in liaisons with Black women. But they held no assumptions of Black integrity or dignity. Miscegenation acquired antebellum distinction and formed (in historian John Blassingame's words) the city's "most unique feature," giving the domination by upper-class white men its fabled flair.[3]

Still, customs of common white-Black association, residential proximity, and the assertive presence of a large free Black community may well have facilitated a tradition in which cooperation on the docks might grow after the Civil War. Having fought slavery and actively experiencing the Civil War as Union soldiers, defenders of fugitives, and enemies of bondage, New Orleans's Black Creoles emerged as vocal supporters of the freedmen's efforts, as leaders of the struggle for equality. The city had swelled with thousands of plantation refugees, including future longshoremen E. S. Swan and James E. Porter. The milieu played a role in the freedmen's struggles. Even though other Southern cities witnessed activity for postbellum justice, historians have suggested that in the battle against Jim Crow, Crescent City Blacks enjoyed the advantage of a particularly well-organized Creole community and a Black "rank-and-file sufficiently unterrified to support such an endeavor." They created a "highly promising environment for protest," knocked down segregation in many local schools, on railroads and streetcars, and in many other accommodations, all to a degree unknown elsewhere. That experience may well have touched turn-of-the-century New Orleans dockworkers, many of whom had grown up in the atmosphere it generated. In no sense and at no point did New Orleans' institutions become completely or mainly integrated in the Reconstruction years. But the city had "more integration of public resort" than any other city in the south, more than many Northern cities.[4]

In a city where there were, as nowhere else, "many cracks in the color line," local and state bodies filled in the spaces in the late nineteenth century with official exclusion and segregation. The Black electorate was virtually destroyed. Notwithstanding the victories under Reconstruction, local patterns of occasional integration and interaction staggered out of the nineteenth century. By the early twentieth century, segregation held sway. Inferior, separate conditions prevailed for Blacks. Racial animosity and labor strife merged in a wave of fatal attacks on Black dockworkers in 1894 and 1895. Disfranchisement rode the crest and kept white supremacy in the saddle.[5]

That the older, complex tradition of race relations, while giving way before the inexorable advance of white supremacy in law and deed, may yet have exerted a force is not impossible. That integrated housing patterns persisted suggests that the customs of interracial contact were not dead. No other major Southern city witnessed side-by-side habitation of Black and white in the early twentieth century.[6] But the older Spanish-French customs and the antebellum tradition of interracial association presupposed inequality, not mutual concern; aside from the aspect of contact itself, these traditions — even had they not weakened before contemporary encroachments of white supremacy — would have contributed little to notions of working-class solidarity.

The older tradition does not satisfactorily explain the cooperation between white and Black dockworkers during the nadir in New Orleans. Taken together with other factors, however, the tradition of contact — as well as the city's cosmopolitan environment — may be considered among the potential agents of labor cooperation on the levee. Significantly, cotton commerce brought seamen from all over the world to the port, many of whom were organized in strong unions. Irish, British, and Swedish sailors pledged and practiced solidarity with striking levee men in 1907 and at other times by refusing to replace them. Prominent Black unionist A. J. Ellis first experienced trade unionism as a member of the socialist-leaning German seamen's union: he had worked on German ships for a time.[7]

The exchange of union cards, induced by seasonality of labor, enabled dockworkers to seek jobs in other unionized fields, such as brewing, construction, and music. It promoted the notion of mutual support underlying the fraternal bedrock of levee unionism. Confronting the hazards of dock labor, levee men developed a belief in labor's interdependence. Thus, they took the lead in supporting the brewery strike and the United Labor Council in 1907. That numbers of dockworkers found off season employment in the brewery industry and thus held membership in the industrially oriented Brewery Workers, had a significant impact on local labor, on and off the levee.

The very organization of dock work influenced solidarity. The importance of the cotton trade in New Orleans gave early centrality to that most crucial of levee components, the skilled screwmen. This small body of workers became the first to organize. Skill distinguished them from the other dockworkers. Strategically located, the screwmen were organized enough to sustain the unionization of the evolving differentiated categories of cotton handlers whose tasks preceded theirs in the labor process: teamsters, yardmen, and longshoremen.

Cotton commerce linked the levee trades and unions, making them reliant on one another. But the screwmen, skilled and decisively placed, were central. Their unions were older, stronger, their labor most respected, their backing most essential to other locals. As the strong force at the end of a cotton-based work process, the screwmen affected that process significantly. They could cripple the port. Even as technology eroded skill and status, the Black and white screwmen's locals remained the backbone of levee labor. The dock wars of the early twentieth century, particularly the 1907 general levee walkout, were led by the screwmen, revolved around them, and concluded with their extinction. Solidarity on the levee became, in the first place, solidarity with the screwmen.

But dock labor and levee unions were segregated. Above all, segregation hindered the unifying potential of collective work, limiting the horizons of dedicated unionists and curtailing the power of the locals. The last decade of the nineteenth century found the multiracial, cosmopolitan, collectively working, interdependent work force split along racial lines. Exclusion by employers of either race from the levee, or the alternate policy of working Black and white work gangs on separate ships (or opposite sides) led to the race riots of the 1890s. Longshore unions were at the mercy of management. It was then, remembered steamship agents and workers alike, that shoot-the-chute came into its own and cotton stowage broke all records.

The experience of violent racial confrontation and intensified exploitation led to profound reevaluation by dockworkers. Half-and-half became the mechanism through which the solidarity-inducing, union-empowering factors of levee labor became realized. Half-and-half, particularly among the white and Black screwmen — who chose to perform their crucial end of the work process in gangs of both races working abreast — enabled workers to rein in the pace of work. It saved the screwmen, preserving and strengthening their locals as the buttress of levee unionism despite the exactions of technology.

Workers declared that half-and-half stemmed from experiences on the levee. When the races decided to "go together," to amalgamate, they thought seriously about their actions. A. J. Ellis, the Black screwman, reasoned " . . . We were tired of being used as an instrument to starve our brother workmen, the white men . . . ." Black and white longshoremen, affirmed white leader Harry Keegan, would stand together "for mutual protection." Wherever Black and white remained separate — in labor and in organization — "starvation wages would be the rule," according to white Central Trades and Labor Council leader Robert E. Lee. Half-and-half brought a halt to the alternate hiring of the races; otherwise, exclusion of either loomed as a constant threat. White screwman Thomas Harrison exclaimed: "The whites had to amalgamate with the negroes or lose everything."

A veritable open shop prevailed in the other Southern ports, with higher stowage rates wherever Black-white cooperation did not exist. "The white and colored screwmen are fighting each other" in Galveston, charged Black leader T. P. Woodland, "and to that circumstance is largely due the conditions that prevail there." Black longshoreman E. S. Swan knew the days when the employers used racial enmity to stimulate productivity: "The agents wanted to break up the unions." So, indeed, a white dockworker stressed, "in the white supremacy strike some years ago, we learned the lesson that the white and negro workers had to go together . . . ."[8]

Thus amalgamated, New Orleans dockworkers created a potent union movement that achieved significant strength between 1901 and World War I. Levee labor as a whole, including the unorganized roustabouts, held tenaciously to conviction of solidarity. In an analysis of lower-class interracial cooperation in the period, an economist suggests several factors, among them "the degree of commonality in black and white economic positions," the degree of government hostility, and the overall economic scene. Noting that white alliances with Blacks on the New Orleans levee owed much to "the similarity of their class positions," he maintains that such ties seemed stronger "when unemployment was low." This indeed coincided with the solidarity experiences of the 1880s and the revival of solidarity in the early twentieth century following the depression of the 1890s.

However, common class positions and relatively healthy economy did not usually lead to labor solidarity in the South. Did New Orleans local government manifest greater tolerance for interracial labor cooperation? Perhaps, if older traditions of interracial contact yet exerted a force by 1900; but the cooperation in question was *labor* solidarity in the basic Crescent City industry during the nadir, a cooperation which purported to and did affect the city's political economy. Moreover, examples of the callousness of official local Jim Crow abounded in segregation, lower living standards, race riots, deprivation of education, a Black illiteracy rate of 14% by 1900. Again one should explore other contributing factors to interracial solidarity on the levee.[9]

The levee labor movement included a radical presence that cannot be ignored. Indeed, the Port Investigation Commission in 1908, as well as employers and the press, regarded the half-and-half principle as subversive of the status quo. A probing student of New Orleans labor, Arthur R. Pearce, wondered: "Was all this radicalism merely another manifestation of Populism, even at that late date?"[10] But if there were memories in New Orleans of Populism's interracial alliances, they were probably not as tangible as those in the rural, timber parishes of Louisiana, where Populism, socialism, and the IWW developed in succession between the late nineteenth century and World War I. New Orleans, in fact, gave birth to its own radical trend: homegrown, urban, Black and white. While not responsible for the half-and-half approach, local radicals aided its application, working concertedly to strengthen levee solidarity in the early twentieth century.

To the ingredients of the city's dock labor movement, one must then add the radical dockworkers and propagandists who spoke for unity and industrial unionism as the levee disputes deepened. The *Labor World* and the *Daily News's* "World of Labor" column provided popular expression of dock labor's views during the 1907 upheaval and general levee strike; they were widely distributed and read. The radical group included Covington Hall, editor Oscar Ameringer (the only non-Orleanian), Black teamster Joseph Coats, and white screwman Thomas Gannon, among others. These men built harmonious, cooperative relations with dockworkers and worked closely with the Dock and Cotton Council, particularly during 1907.

Radicalism also embraced the brewery worker's union, an organization that included Thomas Gannon and many other dockworkers. The 1907 brewery strike, assisted by local radicals and actively supported by white and Black dock unions, gave rise to an unprecedented levee militancy, precipitating a break within the Central Trades and Labor Council. Such council stalwarts as longshoreman Rufus Ruiz and screwman Thomas Harrison quit the body they had helped to found, left their roots behind, turned their backs on labor colleagues in Democratic politics, and moved, with the dockworkers of both races, into the United Labor Council.

That council was the largest radical undertaking theretofore attempted in New Orleans. By statute, it promoted industrial unionism and sympathetic strikes. It brought Black and white together at the level of a city central. It advocated a "more just system . . . in which each shall enjoy the full product of his toil."

Buttressed by local radicalism, the council rested upon the traditions of levee cooperation. It represented more than a split within local labor: its constituent unions defied AFL custom to the "inconceivable" extent of creating an industrial-unionist interracial central body.[11]

In an atmosphere of inspired labor militancy, matters came to a head on the docks. If moods are indicative, then 1907 was the most inopportune moment for employers to insist upon parity with Galveston in working conditions and output on the Crescent City levee. The dock unions stood ready to help the screwmen resist the imposition of said parity. Black-white cooperation had attained new levels in the founding of the new United Labor Council. But steamship agents locked out the screwmen in October. Dockworkers launched the general strike and forestalled parity with Galveston.

Again, the dispute aligned dockworkers behind the mainstays of unionism, the screwmen. But the stakes were higher: employers hoped to abolish the screwmen's locals for good, and thereby weaken the other unions. Management fought harder, longer, and with greater coordination than earlier in the decade over what had become a perennial problem: the limits imposed upon stowage by labor through interracial cooperation. Employers threw all resources against the dockworkers: armed guards, trainloads of strikebreakers, and the reliable instrument of old, race-baiting; they considered reviving the infamous White League. Nevertheless, the white and Black dockworkers prevailed, not only standing together, but becoming closer; they were, in E. S. Swan's words, "never before so strongly cemented in a common bond . . . ."[12] The 1907 strike marked the high point of levee unionism in the early twentieth century.

In its immediate aftermath, interracial cooperation deepened. Great pressures were exerted upon the screwmen to withdraw the Black nominees from the original investigating committee. Officials and media administered a concentrated dose of hysteria to the public at large and to the dock unions in particular to induce a split between white and black. But none resulted.

Unity was the outstanding discovery of the poststrike investigation. Management and commission members alike hurled every white supremacist phrase and image at the united labor movement on the New Orleans docks.

Upholding the open shop conditions under which racially split work forces labored in most Southern ports, the Port Investigation Commission condemned the "equality of the races as exists today on the Levee" as "a disgrace to a Southern city." Commissioners lectured the levee labor movement on the elementary principles of Southern civilization. Yet no labor witness repudiated solidarity.[13] Ultimately, the Commission openly appealed to employers to divide the races on the levee. For Black-white cooperation had been "the fruitful source of most of the trouble . . . ."[14]

Over time, after 1907, interracial labor cooperation weakened: so too, and not coincidentally, did dock unionism as a whole. Black-white solidarity had kept trade unionism alive and kicking long after levee employers had determined to suppress it. But other factors entered the picture during the century's second decade. These struck at the coherence of dock unionism.

Technological progress assaulted the screwmen and destroyed them forever. The best-organized and strongest levee organizations, the white and Black screwmen's locals, had long been the mainstay of levee labor. But they could not long curb the events which eroded skill in the stowage of cotton into ships. They became increasingly redundant: the larger ships, modern warehouses, new conveyors, and more efficient cotton presses deprived even hand stowing of the last remnants of craft. As dock organizations continued to support the viability of a truly obsolete trade, they occupied shakier ground. The levee's fundamental productivity issues had always concerned the screwmen's crucial work; labor's most important expressions of solidarity had emerged during screwmen's controversies. The point came, however, when the developing obsolescence of the screwmen's craft and the growing determination of employers outpaced the ability of dockworkers to prevent, through solidarity, the demise of the screwmen themselves.

World War I witnessed the departure of many whites from the levee and the acceleration of the process of Black majority that had operated for some time. Where half-and-half had reflected the rough parity in actual numbers at the turn of the century, its by-the-book application now allocated jobs disproportionately to whites, for they were no longer half, by any means. Forms of solidarity did persist, however, and Black-white juries and negotiating teams continued to meet. But increasingly, white leaders alone spoke for levee labor, unlike the times when Black leaders E. S. Swan, T. P. Woodland, and A. J. Ellis might also have spoken for the labor movement.

Key problems of half-and-half resurfaced in the 1910s and early 1920s. Solidarity had developed between ostensible "halves" on the levee that were not at all equal in society. The loss by the Black component of basic rights during the late nineteenth and early twentieth centuries had been largely ignored by the white "half." Refusal to adopt parity of Black and white foremen, a source of contention before, became now a much greater indication of trade union inequality. Despite the permanence of joint working bodies, half-and-half had perhaps at times tasted of expediency. That employers had given Black and white "no choice" but to "amalgamate," that labor had been goaded and driven by management toward half-and-half became a common answer of white union leaders pressured to explain their "blasphemy"; this suggested that if other avenues of self-preservation opened, these might be pursued. White workers occasionally responded to employer race-baiting by saying, in effect: Don't blame us; this half-and-half business is your fault!

All the while, segregation became more entrenched, its practice more embracing, its laws more elaborate, and its propagation in all media more considered and intensive. Local radicalism, whose adherents had so aided dock labor, ebbed after the 1907–1908 upsurge. Oscar Ameringer went to Oklahoma as a Socialist organizer. Screwman Thomas Gannon grew disillusioned with and later abandoned the labor movement, telling Covington Hall, " . . . You are crazy to keep at it. The working class will never do anything but beg for a little more wages." Hall however did keep "at it." but not in New Orleans. By the early 1910s he was organizing Black and white timber workers in the piney woods parishes.[15]

In streamlined and well-directed coordination, steamship companies and railroad corporations could confidently announce in the early 1920s that they would wipe out the screwmen and their locals and destroy levee unionism as then constituted. They made no secret of their open-shop aims. And thus, amid weakening solidarity, the increasing difficulty of Black-white cooperation and the undermining of the levee's pivotal screwmen's unions, the employers of dock labor fulfilled their vow.

The nadir witnessed the summoning of every state device and instrument of physical coercion to institutionalize segregation in the South. White supremacy acquired the legal sanction of all branches of government; the new laws, observes C. Vann Woodward, did not assign Blacks a "fixed status," but rather pushed them "further down."[16] Propaganda in every medium trumpeted white superiority, buttressed by an avalanche of "scientific" findings.

But despite the immediacy of promulgation and enforcement, segregation did not spring to actual life in one piece, at one time; it evolved. Of course, the practice — and the very envisioning — of interracial labor solidarity became far more difficult. Moreover, the labor movement generally, particularly the craft unions, practiced segregation in this period: the AFL abandoned the promotion of interracial solidarity and, after 1900, did little to support white-Black cooperation.

Nevertheless, solidarity developed across the color bar in the early twentieth century. Despite great pressure, laborers in Southern mines, tobacco factories, timber forests, construction trades, and iron plants practiced interracial cooperation. The experience of New Orleans dockworkers and the dogged persistence of this pattern in many Southern localities suggest that in the early twentieth century the South was not "solid."[17]

For a time, New Orleans dockworkers made solidarity a principle. There were problems and disruptions, due in no small measure to the broader state of affairs, but clearly, dockworkers made race relations in New Orleans far more complex than "white over Black." Tradition, the multiethnic labor force, a legacy of militant Black struggles, reflections upon the consequences of racial splitting, the prominence of radicalism, and decades of work and union experience merged to create a levee labor movement of great vitality and durability. These features do not isolate New Orleans dockworkers from Southern history, but rather put them at the forefront of a certain trend.

Fissure along class lines was nothing new in the history of white attitudes to race. Surely, New Orleans dockworkers could recall the interracial 1892 general strike. A provocative essay on post-Civil War racism suggests that "what might appear from a distance to be a single ideology cannot hold the same meaning for everyone"; for example, " to people having different social experiences." Allegations of white uniformity "betray the illusion that beliefs about race are a biological product rather than the creation of men and women in society."[18]

In New Orleans, class considerations remained a part of working-class and trade union activity and policy. Interracial unity enabled dock unions to improve conditions and to create a more humane work experience and environment. For a period, dockworkers withstood both the pressures of technology — which management would use to help destroy union power — and regional competition between shipping centers, although this, too, would work against their achievements.

With interracial cooperation the status quo on the waterfront, therefore, segregation and white supremacy on the docks had to be dinned into the ears of the labor force, pushed and imposed. City officials, cotton merchants, steamship agents — "men of affairs" — expended much time and effort to hinder, disrupt, and break labor solidarity, to convince dockworkers that racial differences superseded their common interests. But for a generation, those dockworkers and their unions held the protagonists of segregation at bay.

Notes

Introduction

1. *New Orleans Daily Picayune*, November 2, 1907; *New Orleans Times-Democrat*, November 1, 1907; Oscar Ameringer, *If You Don't Weaken*, New York, 1940, 216–217.

2. Joe Gray Taylor, *Negro Slavery in Louisiana*, Baton Rouge, 22, 195–196; Frank Tannenbaum, *Slave and Citizen*, New York, 1946, 42–65; Thomas Marc Fiehrer, "The African Presence in Colonial Louisiana: An Essay on the Continuity of Caribbean Culture," in Robert R. Macdonald, John R. Kemp, and Edward F. Haas, eds., *Louisiana's Black Heritage*, New Orleans, 1979, 30; Richard C. Wade, *Slavery in the Cities*, New York, 1964, 17, 38, 48–49; Howard N. Rabinowitz, *Race Relations in the Urban South 1865–1890*, New York, 1978, xv.

3. Taylor, 8, 168; H. Hoetink, *The Two Variants in Caribbean Race Relations*, London, 1967, 120–177, *passim*; Gabriel Debien, "Marronage in the French Caribbean," in Richard Price, ed., *Maroon Societies*, Baltimore, 1979, 108–134; Marvin Harris, "The Myth of the Friendly Master," in Laura Foner and Eugene D. Genovese, eds., *Slavery in the New World*, Englewood Cliffs, 1969, 38–47; Herbert S. Klein, *Slavery in the Americas: A Comparative Study of Virginia and Cuba*, Chicago, 1967, 80–85, 90, 104–105; Philip S. Foner, *A History of Cuba and its Relations with the United States*, Vol. II, New York, 1963, 34–35, 54, 90, 108, 293.

4. Winthrop Jordan, *White Over Black*, Baltimore, 1968, 3–43, *passim*; Peter H. Wood, *Black Majority*, New York, 1975, 106, 229; James Hugo Johnston, *Race Relations in Virginia and Miscegenation in the South, 1776–1860*, Amherst, 1970, 186, 188; Edmund S. Morgan, *American Slavery, American Freedom*, New York, 1975, 328, 316–337 *passim*.

Perceptive arguments making the same point can be found in, among others, Herbert Aptheker, "The History of Anti-Racism in the United States: An Introduction," *The Black Scholar*, VI, January–February 1975, 16–22; George Frederickson, *White Supremacy*, New York, 1981, 68–79; and Oscar Handlin, *Race and Nationality in American Life*, New York, 1957, 4–22 *passim*.

5. John W. Blassingame, *Black New Orleans: 1860–1880*, Chicago, 1973, 15, 210; Blassingame, 20; Blassingame, 15.

6. Taylor, 195–196; Rudolph Lucien Desdunes, *Our People and Our History*, Baton Rouge (1911) 1973, 109–112; Ira Berlin, *Slaves Without Masters*, New York, 1974, xiv.

7. Blassingame, 180–197; Roger A. Fischer, *The Segregation Struggle in Louisiana, 1867–1877*, Urbana, 1974, 29, 39, 86, 115, 131; Blassingame, 217; Blassingame, 206, 208–209; George E. Cunningham, "The Italian: A Hindrance to White Solidarity in Louisiana," *Journal of Negro History*, L, No. 1 (January 1965), 24, 25, 22; Paul Worthman, "Black Workers and Labor Unions in Birmingham, Alabama, 1897–1904," *Labor History*, 10, No. 3 (Summer 1969), 379; John R. Commons, "Types of American Trade Unions: The Longshoremen of the Great Lakes," *Quarterly Journal of Economics*, 20, No. 1 (November 1905), 64.

8. See, for example, Rabinowitz, *Race Relations in the Urban South, 1865–1890* and Fischer, *The Segregation Struggle in Louisiana, 1867–1877*.

9. Henry C. Dethloff and Robert R. Jones, "Race Relations in Louisiana, 1877–1898," *Louisiana History*, IX, No. 4 (Fall 1968), 301–323; Germaine A. Reed, "Race Legislation in Louisiana, 1864–1920," *Louisiana History*, VI, No. 4 (Fall 1965), 379–392; C. Vann Woodward, *The Strange Career of Jim Crow*, New York, 1966, 44.

Woodward includes a discussion of the development of Jim Crow, in light of the criticism made of his own work, in *Thinking Back: The Perils of Writing History*, Baton Rouge, 1986, 81–83, 94–99.

10. J. Morgan Kousser, *The Shaping of Southern Politics*, New Haven, 1974, 261; Kousser, 107; Woodward, *Strange Career*, 64, Kousser, 262–263.

11. Leon Fink, "Irrespective of Party, Class or Social Standing: The Knights of Labor and Opposition Politics in Richmond," *Labor History*, 19, No. 3 (Summer 1978), 325–349; Melton A. McLaurin, *The Knights of Labor in the South*, Westport, 1978, 135–148; William Ivey Hair, *Bourbonism and Agrarian Protest*, Baton Rouge, 1969; Woodward, *Origins of the New South*, Baton Rouge, 1971, 252, 255–263; Roger W. Shugg, "The New Orleans General Strike of 1892," *Louisiana Historical Quarterly*, 21 (April 1938), 547–560; David Paul Bennetts, *Black and White Workers: New Orleans, 1880–1900*, doctoral dissertation, Urbana, 1972.

12. McLaurin, 146; Bennetts, 559.

13. Woodward, *Strange Career*, 55–57; Bennetts, 479.

14. Herbert G. Gutman, *Work, Culture, and Society in Industrializing America*, New York, 1976, 121–208; James R. Green, *Grass-Roots Socialism*, Baton Rouge, 1978, 204–222; Melvyn Dubofsky, *We Shall Be All*, Chicago, 1969, 210–220; W. E. B. DuBois, *The Negro Artisan*, Atlanta, 1902, 111–112, 114–115, 127–128, 162–163; Worthman, "Black Workers and Labor Unions in Birmingham, Alabama, 1897–1904," *Labor History*, 10, No. 3 (Summer 1969), 375–407.

15. Hair, 186.

16. *Picayune*, September 7, 1907.

17. David Montgomery, *Workers' Control in America*, New York, 1979, 83.

18. Philip S. Foner, *History of the Labor Movement in the United States, Vol. 3*, New York, 1964, 253.

19. *New Orleans Daily News*, October 25, 1907.

20. Roger W. Shugg, *Origins of Class Struggle in Louisiana*, Baton Rouge, 1939, 30.

Chapter One

Abbreviations

Central Trades and Labor Council   CT&LC
Screwmen's Benevolent Association   SBA

1. *American Federationist*, September 1905, 636.

2. Rayford W. Logan, *The Betrayal of the Negro*, New York, 1967, 9.

3. August Meier, *Negro Thought in America, 1880-1915*, Ann Arbor, 1964, 22; Logan, 220–221, 225, 297–300, 98.

4. C. Vann Woodward, *Origins of the New South*, Baton Rouge, 1971, 121, 125; J. Morgan Kousser, *The Shaping of Southern Politics*, New Haven, 1974, 8, 34–38; Kousser, *passim*; Howard N. Rabinowitz, *Race Relations in the Urban South: 1865-1890*, New York, 1978; Kousser, 262, Woodward, *Origins*, 321–322, 327, 350. See the pioneering article by Herbert Aptheker, "American Imperialism and White Chauvinism" (1950) in Aptheker, *Afro-American History*, New York, 1971, 100-108.

5. Woodward, *Origins*, 350–351; Walter White, *Rope and Faggot*, New York, 1929, 230–237; Logan, 100.

6. Rabinowitz, *passim*; Kousser, 39–72, 139–191, 257–258; Germaine A. Reed, "Race Legislation in Louisiana, 1864–1920," *Louisiana History*, VI, No. 4 (Fall 1965), 392; Richard Hofstadter, ed., *Great Issues in American History, Vol. 2*, New York, 1958, 54–56; Otto H. Olson, "Reflections on the *Plessy v. Ferguson* Decision of 1896," in Edward F. Haas, ed., *Louisiana's Legal Heritage*, Pensacola, 1983, 164–168, 182. See also Logan, 114–121.

7. Logan, 147–148; Louis L. Lorwin, *The American Federation of Labor*, Washington, 1933, 488; Philip S. Foner, *History of the Labor Movement in the United States, Vol. 3*, New York, 1964, 27; Leo Wolman, *Ebb and Flow in Trade Unionism*, New York, 1936, 184–185; James O. Morris, *Conflict Within the AFL*, Ithaca, 1958, 15.

8. David Brody, *Workers in Industrial America*, New York, 1980, 24; Foner, *History, Vol. 3*, 28; Foner, *History, Vol. 3*, 26–27; Foster Rhea Dulles, *Labor in America*, New York, 1949, 154–155; Foner, *History, Vol. 3*, 33, 41–42; David Montgomery, *Workers' Control in America*, New York, 1979, 60–61; Brody, 24–28; Foner, *History, Vol. 3*, 32–60.

9. Melton A. McLaurin, "The Racial Policies of the Knights of Labor and the Organization of Southern Black Workers," *Labor History*, 17, No. 4 (Fall 1976), 572, 577, 581, 585; McLaurin, *The Knights of Labor in the South*, Westport, 1978, 147–148.

See also Sidney Kessler, "The Organization of Negroes in the Knights of Labor," *Journal of Negro History*, XXXVII, No. 3 (July 1952), 262–265, 272–275.

10. Bernard Mandel, "Samuel Gompers and the Negro Workers, 1886–1914," *Journal of Negro History*, XL, No. 1 (January 1955), 40–41; Charles Wesley, *Negro Labor in the United States*, New York, 192, 257; Sterling D. Spero and Abram L. Harris, *The Black Worker*, New York, 1974, 87; Foner, *History, Vol. 2*, New York, 1955, 196–197.

11. Foner, *History, Vol. 3*, 203; Mandel, 46; Foner, *History, Vol. 2*, 204; Spero and Harris, 87–89; Foner, *History, Vol. 3*, 233, 238; Wesley, 259; Foner, *History, Vol. 3*, 235; Foner, *History, Vol. 3*, 242.

12. T. W. Campbell, *Manual of the City Council for 1900–1904*, New Orleans, 1900, 35, 37; Campbell, *Municipal Manual of the City of New Orleans*, New Orleans, 1901, 48; Campbell, *Municipal Manual of the City of New Orleans*, New Orleans, 1903, 77.

13. Joy J. Jackson, *New Orleans in the Gilded Age*, Baton Rouge, 1969, 221; Andrew Morrison, New Orleans and the New South, New Orleans, 1888, 57–58, 62; *New Orleans Daily Picayune*, December 2, 1903; *Picayune*, December 4, 1903; *Picayune*, December 26, 1904.

14. Earl F. Niehaus, *The Irish in New Orleans, 1800–1860*, Baton Rouge, 1965, 48; John F. Nau, *The German People of New Orleans, 1850–1900*, Leiden, 1958, 65–67.

15. Jackson, 22; John W. Blassingame, *Black New Orleans: 1860–1880*, Chicago, 1973, 62, W. E. B. DuBois, *Crisis*, 2, No. 6 (October 1911), 229: Jack Buerkle and Danny Barker, *Bourbon Street Black*, New York, 1973, 10.

16. Henry G. Dethloff and Robert R. Jones, "Race Relations in Louisiana, 1877–1898," *Louisiana History*, IX, No. 4 (Fall 1968), 314–315; Alan Lomax, *Mister Jelly Roll*, New York, 1950, 289; Reed, "Race Legislation," 383; Dale A. Somers, *The Rise of Sports in New Orleans, 1850–1900*, Baton Rouge, 1972, 289; Charles B. Rousseve, *The Negro in Louisiana*, New Orleans, 1937, 139.

17. Blassingame, 208; U. S. Bureau for the Census, *Twelfth Census of the United States*, Schedule No. 1 — Population, 1900; Rabinowitz, 97–106; *Picayune*, August 25, 1904; *Picayune* September 18, 1906; Pops Foster, *The Autobiography of a New Orleans Jazz Musician*, Berkeley, 1971, 61.

18. *Crisis*, 2, No. 5 (September 1911) 184; *Crisis*, 1, No. 6 (April 1911), 9; *Crisis*, 1, No. 5 (March 1911), 8; 126 La. 300, *State v. Treadway* in Theodore Cotonio, ann., *Constitution of the State of Louisiana*, 1898–1912, New Orleans, 1913, 349–350; *Southwestern Christian Advocate*, March 14, 1907; City Council of New Orleans, Official Minutes, 1907–1908, March 12, 1907.

19. Jackson, 183; *Biennial Report of the Board of Health of the City of New Orleans, 1906-1907*, New Orleans, 1908, 120, 23-29.

20. *Southwestern Christian Advocate*, April 25, 1907; *Southwestern Christian Advocate*, January 9, 1908; *Picayune*, December 14, 1901; *Southwestern Christian Advocate*, May 24, 1906; *Picayune*, May 21, 1905; *Picayune*, March 14, 1907.

21. Herbert Aptheker, ed., *A Documentary History of the Negro People in the United States*, Vol. 2, Secaucus, 1951, 907; *Picayune*, August 23, 1906; *Picayune*, June 7, 1906; *Picayune*, August 23, 1906; *Picayune*, January 25, 1906.

22. Kousser, 152-165; *Official Journal of Proceedings of the Constitutional Convention of the State of Louisiana Held in New Orleans*, February 8-May 12, 1898, New Orleans, 1898, 10, 9; Dethloff/Jones, "Race Relations in Louisiana, 1877-1898," 317; Rousseve, 132; *Picayune*, November 29, 1903, January 14, 1904; Woodward, *Origins*, 328-343.

23. George M. Reynold, *Machine Politics in New Orleans: 1897-1926*, New York, 1936, 32-33, 109; *Louisiana Convention Proceedings*, 1898, Delegates; Reynolds, 139, 152-153, 230, 212, 158.

24. *Picayune*, July 28, 1905, April 17, 1906; Gustavus Myers, *History of the Great American Fortunes*, New York, 1936, 530-531, 607, 614.

25. David Brown, *A History of Who's Who in Louisiana Poitics in 1916*, Baton Rouge, 1916, 32-33; Works Progress Administration, *Adminstrations of the Mayors of New Orleans*, New Orleans, 1940, 210.

26. *Union Advocate*, June 1, 1903; *Times-Picayune*, February 29, 1916; Convington Hall, *Labor Struggles in the Deep South*, unpublished ms., n.d., 64.

27. *Who's Who in Louisiana and Mississippi*, New Orleans, 1918.

28. William M. Deacon, *Martin Behrman Administration Biography*, New Orleans, 1917, 5-6; WPA, *Administrations of the Mayors of New Orleans*, 1940, 219-221; John R. Kemp, ed., *Martin Behrman of New Orleans: Memoirs of a City Boss*, Baton Rouge, 1977, xxii-xxiii, 12-13, 71-78; Patrick Welsh to Martin Behrman, August 17, 1906, New Orleans, Mayor's Office, *Letters, 1906-1908; Picayune*, February 15, 1908; Kemp, 51, 55, 52, 102-104.

29. *Union Advocate*, January 12, 1903; *Picayune*, January 28, 1903; *Union Advocate*, February 9, 1903; *Union Advocate*, November 9, 1903.

30. *Picayune*, February 4, 1903; *Picayune*, August 16, 1903.

31. *Picayune*, February 5, 1903.

32. *Picayune*, October 29, 1903, October 12, 1903.

33. *Picayune*, October 30, 1903; *Picayune*, November 4, 1903; *Picayune*, November 14, 1903; *Picayune*, December 6, 1903; *Picayune*, December 23, 1903; *Picayune*, January 1, 1904.

34. *Picayune*, September 20, 1904; *Picayune*, October 10, 1904; *Picayune*, October 12, 1904; *Picayune*, September 28, 1904; *Picayune*, September 29, 1904; *Picayune*, October 3, 1904; *Picayune*, October 12, 1904; *Picayune*, November 4, 1904.

35. *Picayune*, September 25, 1905; *Picayune*, October 14, 1905; *Picayune*, October 24, 1905; *Picayune*, October 28, 1905.

36. *Picayune*, March 9, 1907; *Cleveland Citizen*, May 4, 1907; *Picayune*, January 27, 1908.

37. *Conference Rules of the Stevedores and Longshoremen's Benevolent Association and Longshoremen's Protective Union Benevolent Association*, New Orleans, 1892, *SBA Records*, Folder 31, Special Collections, Louisiana State University Libraries; *Picayune*, September 8, 1903.

38. *Picayune*, December 18, 1905, January 9, 1906; Oscar Ameringer, *If You Don't Weaken*, New York, 1940, 217; Ameringer, 219; *Picayune*, October 29, 1903, June 9, 1908, September 6, 1904; *Picayune*, November 16, 1910.

39. *Picayune*, January 27, 1908; CT&LC, *Minutes*, June 10, 1900; *Memorandum of Agreement Between SBA and SBA No. 1 (Colored) and the Steamship Agents and Stevedores*, New Orleans, 1917, 8, *SBA Records*, Folder 31; *Picayune*, August 13, 1904; *Picayune*, September 5, 1905; *United Labor Journal*, January 5, 1908.

40. *Picayune*, October 10, 1903, May 18, 1904; *Picayune*, June 5, 1907, July 17, 1907; Covington Hall, *Labor Struggles in the Deep South*, 63, 68, 70, 97.

41. Rudolphe L. Desdunes, *Our People and Our History*, Baton Rouge (1911), 1973, 130–131, 135; Rousseve, 128–132; Louis A. Martinet, ed., *The Violation of a Constitutional Right*, New Orleans, 1893, 2; *Report of Proceedings of the Citizen's Committee for the Annulment of Act No. 111, Commonly Known as the Separate Car Act of 1890* (circa 1897) (in *A. P. Tureaud Papers*, Amistad Research Center, New Orleans), 10–11; Martinet, 16.

42. *Southwestern Christian Advocate*, February 8, 1906; *Southwestern Christian Advocate*, May 31, 1906; *Southwestern Christian Advocate*, February 21, 1907; *Southwestern Christian Advocate*, February 6, 1908; *Southwestern Christian Advocate*, April 19, 1906; *Southwestern Christian Advocate*, January 23, 1908.

43. Meier, 175; *Southwestern Christian Advocate*, July 12, 1906; *Picayune*, February 19, 1904.

44. *Southwestern Christian Advocate*, March 14, 1907; *Southwestern Christian Advocate*, April 26, 1907; *Southwestern Christian Advocate*, March 5, 1908; Meier, 234; *Southwestern Christian Advocate*, August 30, 1906; *Crisis*, 11, No. 4 (February 1916), 169.

45. William Ivey Hair, *Carnival of Fury*, Baton Rouge, 1976, 100–106, 108, 111; *Jelly Roll Morton: The Library of Congress Recordings* (May–June 1938), Vol. 5, Riverside, RLP 9005; Hair, 145, 150–155, 176–178, 180; Morton, *Recordings*, Vol. 5.

46. Louis R. Harlan and Raymond W. Smock, eds., *The Booker T. Washington Papers*, Vol. 6, Urbana, 1977, 304–305; *Picayune*, November 1, 1902; *Crisis*, 11, No. 4, (February 1916), 190.

47. *Picayune*, February 21, 1904, February 19, 1904; *Picayune*, May 3, 1904, May 4, 1904, May 11, 1904. See also Woodward, *Origins*, 219, 256, 276, 324, 461–464; Louis Harlan, *Booker T. Washington: The Wizard of Tuskegee 1901–1915*, New York, 1983; Harlan and Raymond W. Smock, eds., *The Booker T. Washington Papers*, Vol. 8, Urbana, 1979; Paul Casdorph, *Republicans, Negroes and Progressives in the South, 1912–1916*, University [Alabama], 1981.

48. *Picayune*, February 21, 1904.

49. *Picayune*, March 11, 1904; *Picayune*, May 28, 1904; *Picayune*, June 22, 1904; *Picayune*, June 30, 1904.

50. *Picayune*, January 5, 1905; *Picayune*, August 27, 1905; *Republican Liberator*, September 9, 1905.

51. *Republican Liberator*, September 9, 1905; *Republican Liberator*, January 4, 1908.

52. David Paul Bennetts, *Blacks and White Workers: New Orleans, 1880–1900*, doctoral dissertation, Urbana, 1972, 561, 369, 525, 551; International Longshoremen, Marine and Transportworkers' Association, *Proceedings of the Eleventh Convention* (1902), 73–74; ILA, 1903 *Proceedings*, 236; *Picayune*, February 19, 1904, February 21, 1904; *Picayune*, July 3, 1903.

53. *Picayune*, August 23, 1903; Ameringer, 217; *Picayune*, February 21, 1904; *Picayune*, March 12, 1908; *Soards' New Orleans City Directory for 1911*, New Orleans, 1911, 400; *Times-Picayune*, June 18, 1951.

54. Bennetts, 561, 369; *Picayune*, September 9, 1903; *Picayune*, September 17, 1903; *Picayune*, July 3, 1903; *Picayune*, May 25, 1904; *Picayune*, May 1, 1906, May 7, 1906, May 21, 1907; *Picayune*, February 21, 1904; *Picayune*, August 24, 1907.

55. *Picayune*, September 8, 1903, January 25, 1904; Allen T. Woods, *Woods Directory*, New Orleans, 1913, 11; *Picayune*, October 27, 1902, October 30, 1902, November 4, 1903; *Crusader*, July 19, 1890, *Picayune*, January 20, 1906; U. S. Census Bureau, *Twelfth Census*, Schedule No. 1 — Population, 1900, Enumeration District 123, Twelfth Ward, Seventh Precinct, 7; *Picayune*, February 19, 1904, March 11, 1904, May 28, 1904, June 30, 1904, January 5, 1905.

56. Roger W. Shugg, "The New Orleans General Strike of 1892," *Louisiana Historical Quarterly*, 21 (April 1938), 548; Shugg, *Origins of Class Struggle in Louisiana*, Baton Rouge, 1939, 304; Arthur Raymond Pearce, *The Rise and Decline of Labor in New Orleans*, master's thesis, New Orleans, 1938, 2; Bennetts, 326; Blassingame, 64–65; Jackson, 223–230.

57. Shugg, "The New Orleans General Strike," 550; Bennetts, 336, 351–355.

58. Bennetts, 326; Jackson, 226.

59. Aptheker, *Documentary History*, 552, 554–559; Shugg, "New Orleans General Strike," 549; Blassingame, 65; Bennetts, 322; Jackson, 228, 226.

60. Jackson, 226; Shugg, "New Orleans General Strike," 550.

61. Bennetts, 290–302, 303.

62. Bennetts, 369, 372, 373, 375.

63. Bennetts, 377.

64. Shugg, "New Orleans General Strike," 551–552.

65. Bennetts, 397; *Conference Rules of the Stevedores and Longshoremen's Benevolent Association and Longshoremen's Protective Union Benevolent Association*, New Orleans, Rule II, SBA Records, Folder 31.

66. Shugg, "New Orleans General Strike," 552–552; Bennetts, 400.

67. Shugg, "New Orleans General Strike," 553–554; Foner, *History, Vol. 2*, 200–201; *New Orleans Times-Democrat*, November 1, 1892; *Times-Democrat*, November 4, 1892.

68. Bennetts, 415; Shugg, "New Orleans General Strike," 555; *Picayune*, November 5, 1892.

69. John Callaghan to Samuel Gompers, November 7, 1892, in Phillip S. Foner and Ronald L. Lewis, eds., *The Black Worker*, Vol. 4, Philadelphia, 1979, 20–21.

70. Bennetts, 415; Bennetts, 417; *Picayune*, November 10, 1892, Shugg, "New Orleans General Strike," 555.

71. Foner, *History, Vol. 2*. 206–209; Bennetts, 419–420; Shugg, "New Orleans General Strike," 556-559; Bennetts, 427-428.

72. Bennetts, 430, 428, 435; Shugg, "New Orleans General Strike," 559; Gompers to Callaghan, November 21, 1892 in Foner-Lewis, *Vol. 4*, 23; Foner, *History, Vol. 2*, 203; Callaghan to Gompers, November 13, 1892, in Foner-Lewis, *Vol. 4*, 22; Foner, *History, Vol. 2*, 203.

73. Jackson, 229–230; Bennetts, 449.

74. Bennetts, 462–468; *Picayune*, October 27, 1894; *Picayune*, October 28, 1894; Bennetts, 473–474.

The white SBA local's resolution against the race riot can be found in English and French in *SBA Records*, Folder 27.

75. Bennetts, 476–479; *Picayune*, March 15, 1895.

76. Bennetts, 515, 531; United Labor Council, *Directory of New Orleans, La.*, New Orleans, 1894.

77. Central Trades and Labor Council, New Orleans, *Minutes*, October 8, 1899, October 22, 1899, November 26, 1899, January 11, 1901, December 9, 1900, Stoddard Labor Collection, University of New Orleans.

78. Foner, *History, Vol. 3*, 235; James E. Porter to Samuel Gompers, April 20, 1900, Foner-Lewis, ed., *The Black Worker, Vol. 5*, Phila., 1980, 119; James Leonard to Gompers, May 19, 1900, Foner/Lewis, *Vol. 5*, 120; Porter to Gompers, June 15, 1900, Foner-Lewis, *Vol. 5*, 120; CT&LC, *Minutes*, July 22, 1900.

79. CT&LC, *Minutes*, February 22, 1901; Frank Morrison to L. B. Landry, March 16, 1901, CT&LC, *Correspondence*, Stoddard Labor Collection, University of New Orleans; *Picayune*, September 8, 1903, September 6, 1904, September 4, 1906, September 3, 1907.

80. *Picayune*, November 14, 1902; *Picayune*, November 4, 1903; American Federation of Labor, *Report of Proceedings of the Twenty-fourth Convention* (1904), Washington, 1904, 77–78; AFL *1906 Proceedings*, 27–29; AFL *1905 Proceedings*, v, x; AFL, *1906 Proceedings*, 233.

81. Spero and Harris, 182–183; W. E. B. DuBois, *The Negro Artisan* Atlanta, 1902, 128, 160; ILA, *1902 Proceedings*, 73–74; ILA *1902 Proceedings*, 27-29; *Picayune*, April 26, 1903, April 28, 1903, May 1903.

82. ILA, *1903 Proceedings*, 188; *Picayune*, August 4, 1903; *Picayune*, August 4, 1903. See also *Union Advocate*, July 13, 1903, July 20, 1903.

83. *Picayune*, November 22, 1901; *Picayune*, April 30, 1904.

84. *Picayune*, September 9, 1902; June 13, 1903; *Picayune*, June 28, 1903; *Picayune*, July 26, 1903; *Picayune*, July 28, 1903; *Republican Liberator*, September 9, 1905.

85. *Picayune*, August 11, 1906; *Picayune*, August 26, 1907; *Picayune*, July 27, 1907; *Daily News*, July 27, 1907; *Picayune*, July 30, 1907.

Chapter Two

Abbreviations: Screwmen's Benevolent Association (SBA)

1. Louisiana Chamber of Commerce, *The City of New Orleans*, New Orleans, 1894, 89; Charles H. Hillcoat, *Notes on the Stowage of Ships*, New York, 1919, 219; SBA, *Constitution and By-Laws,*, Article VII, New Orleans, 1877, SBA Records, Folder 31, Louisiana State University.

2. T. W. Campbell, *Municipal Manual of the City of New Orleans*, New Orleans, 1901, 48–49; David Paul Bennetts, *Blacks and White Workers: New Orleans, 1880-1900*, doctoral dissertation, Urbana, 1972, 20.

3. Peirce Lewis, *New Orleans: The Making of an Urban Landscape*, Cambridge, 1976, 20–27.

4. *Union Advocate*, November 30, 1903.

5. Pops Foster, *The Autobiography of a New Orleans Jazz Musician*, Berkeley, 1971, 12–13; Harry P. Letton, *Rat Proofing the Public Docks of New Orleans*, 1915, Washington, 4–5.

6. Raymond J. Martinez, *The Story of the Riverfront at New Orleans*, New Orleans, 1948, 42–46; James P. Baughman, "Gateway to the Americas," in Hodding Carter, ed., *The Past as Prelude: New Orleans 1718–1968*, New Orleans, 1968, 275.

7. U. S. Industrial Commission, *Report*, Vol. IX, Washington, 1901, clxxxii; *Who's Who in Louisiana and Mississippi*, New Orleans, 1918, 145; Martinez, 111–113; *New Orleans Daily Picayune*, March 6, 1904.

8. *Picayune*, February 9, 1906; *Picayune*, January 5, 1904.

9. Gilson Willetts et. al, *Workers of the Nation, Vol. II*, New York, 1903, 512–513; John Chase, *Frenchman, Desire Good Children*, New York, 1979, 161; Martinez, *The Story of the Riverfront at New Orleans*, 1955 edition, 233.

10. Martinez (1948), 152–153; *Picayune*, September–October 1903, October–November 1905, March 28, 1908.

11. Oscar Ameringer, *If You Don't Weaken*, New York, 1940, 195; U. S. Bureau of the Census, *Twelfth Census of the United States*, Schedule No. 1 — Population, Washington, 1900.

For dockworkers belonging to more than one dock union, see obituaries in the *Picayune* for Edward Paul (April 24, 1904), Joseph Brown (October 16, 1906), Charles Hale (August 31, 1905), and Edward Ryan (September 20, 1905).

See also Pops Foster, *The Autobiography of a New Orleans Jazz Musician*, Berkeley, 1971, 27, 61, for recollections of a longshoreman-cotton teamster.

For dockworkers working in nonlevee occupations, see *Colored Men in the Customs Service District of New Orleans, and in the Internal Revenue Service, Department of Justice, and the Post Office*, New Orleans, c. 1900, for listing of screwman Victor Joychin; see also the designation of leading cotton yardman Frederick Grosz as a court clerk in the *Office Journal of the Proceedings of the Constitutional Convention of the State of Louisiana*, New Orleans, 1898, 50.

See also obituaries in the *Picayune* for Harry Whelege (June 25, 1904: fireman), John Gillespie (June 9, 1906: pile driver), and Mrs. Alonzo J. Ellis (June 18, 1951) and the listing for Alonzo J. Ellis in *Soards' New Orleans City for Directory for 1911*, New Orleans, 1911, 400: watchman and sleeping car porter.

The former screwman Thomas Gannon was a leading brewery worker in 1907: See Covington Hall, *Labor Struggles in the Deep South*, unpublished ms., n.d., 63, 77; and *Picayune*, June–August 1907.

12. *Picayune*, April 9, 1903, May 1, 1903; *Union Advocate*, May 3, 1903; *Picayune*, April 6, 1903, April 7, 1903, April 9, 1903; *Picayune*, October 5, 1905, *Daily News*, October 5, 1907, *Item*, October 4, 1907; *Picayune*, March 11, 1908, *Picayune*, March 12, 1908; Sterling D. Spero and Abram L. Harris, *The Black Worker*, New York, 1974, 186.

13. Jelly Roll Morton, quoted in Martin Williams, *Jazz Masters of New Orleans*, New York, 1967, 44; U. S. Industrial Commission, *Report*, Vol. IX, 1901, 395; Willetts, *Workers of the Nation, Vol. II*, 603.

14. *Picayune*, December 9, 1902, September 3, 1907; *Picayune*, September 3, 1904; Foster, *New Orleans Jazz Musician*, 27; *Times-Democrat*, October 1907; *Picayune*, September 1904, September 1905.

15. Sterling D. Spero and Abram L. Harris, *The Black Worker*, New York, 1974, 184–185; *Picayune*, September 3, 1907; *Picayune*, November 10, 1904; Theodore R. Taylor, *Stowage of Ship Cargoes*, Washington, 1920, 39, 45; Hillcoat, *Notes on the Stowage of Ships*, 72; Taylor, 42–43.

16. Taylor, *Stowage of Ship Cargoes*, 22–26; *Picayune*, July 10, 1903.

17. *Picayune*, September 20, 1905; *Picayune*, October 31, 1903; *Picayune*, January 31, 1904; *Picayune*, August 31, 1904.

18. *Conference Rules of the Stevedores and Longshoremen's Benevolent Association and Longshoremen's Protective Union Benevolent Association*, New Orleans, 1892, *SBA Records*, Folder 31, Special Collections, Louisiana State University Libraries; Foster, *New Orleans Jazz Musician*, 61; U. S. Industrial Relations Commission, *Industrial Relations*, Vol. III, Washington, 1916, 2128, 2055.

19. *Picayune*, April 22, 1903, July 10, 1903, July 11, 1903; *Picayune*, September 14, 1903; *Picayune*, September 11, 1903; *Picayune*, September 17, 1903; *Picayune*, September 13, 1903, September 14, 1903; *Picayune*, August 26, 1906, August 31, 1906.

20. *Picayune, August 26, 1906, August 27, 1906, September 1907, Picayune*, September 15–19, 1903; *Picayune*, August 31, 1906.

21. *Picayune*, October 22, 1903, April 19, 1903, March 12, 1908; Lester Rubin, *The Negro in the Longshore Industry*, Philadelphia, 1974, 15–16; Morton, quoted in Williams, *Jazz Masters of New Orleans*, 44; *Union Advocate*, June 15, 1903.

22. Hall, *Labor Struggles in the Deep South*, 77; Taylor, *Stowage of Ship Cargoes*, 36–45; Roy S. MacElwee and Thomas R. Taylor, *Wharf Management*, New York, 1921, 199; *Picayune*, November 4, 1902.

23. *Picayune*, March 30, 1905, April 14, 1905; *Picayune*, October 6, 1903, October 8, 1903; *Picayune*, November 3, 1902; *Picayune*, November 5, 1902.

24. *Picayune*, April 24, 1903; *Picayune*, April 12, 1903; *Picayune*, April 21, 1903; *Picayune*, October 4, 1903.

25. *Picayune*, April 7, 1903.

26. *Picayune*, April 12, 1903.

27. *Picayune*, October 30, 1902; *Picayune*, October 22, 1902, April 5, 1903.

28. *Picayune*, November 3, 1902.

29. Ameringer, 195–196.

30. Hall, *Labor Struggles in the Deep South*, 50; *Picayune*, October 19, 1903; Arthur R. Pearce, *The Rise and Decline of Labor in New Orleans*, master's thesis, New Orleans, 1938, 49; F. Ray Marshall, *Labor in the South*, Cambridge, 1957, 63.

31. *Union Advocate*, June 15, 1903; Carroll George Miller, *A Study of the New Orleans Longshoremen's Union from 1850 to 1962*, master's thesis, Baton Rouge, 1969, 223; Marshall, *Labor in the South*, 61.

32. John W. Blassingame, *Black New Orleans: 1860–1880*, Chicago, 1973, 64–65; Jackson, *New Orleans in the Gilded Age*, 224.

33. *Picayune*, July 13, 1903. See also *Picayune*, July 9–31, 1903.

34. *Picayune*, September 3–19, 1903; *Picayune*, April 1, 1904, April 1904, *Picayune*, November 11, 1902; *Picayune*, September 1905.

35. SBA, *1867 Constitution*, Article XV, *SBA Records*, Folder 31; SBA, *1877 By-Laws*; SBA, *Correspondence — Membership applications*, 1870s and 1880s, *SBA Records*, Folder 23 and 25; SBA, *1887 By-Laws*, Article I, *SBA Records*, Folder 31; SBA, *1894 By-Laws*, *SBA Records*, Folder 31.

36. SBA, *1867 Constitution*, Article XVI; SBA, *1877 By-Laws*; SBA *1887 By-Laws*, Article II; SBA, *Correspondence*, 1905-1911, *SBA Records*, Folder 29.

37. SBA, *Bills and Receipts*, 1897–1898, *SBA Records*, Folder 28; SBA *Correspondence*, 1905–1911.

38. International Longshoremen's Association, Local 1419, "Story of Progress" (1951), in Charles Ortique, *A Study of the Longshore Industry in New Orleans, with Emphasis on Negro Longshoremen*, master's thesis, Urbana, 1956, 37; SBA, *1867 Constitution*, Article XII; SBA, *1867 Constitution*, Article XVII; *1887 By-Laws*; SBA, *1877 By-Laws*, Article III; SBA, *1894 By-Laws*, Article III; SBA, *1897 By-Laws*, Article III.

39. SBA, *1877 By-Laws*, Article XVII; SBA, *1894 By-Laws*, Article III; Lower District Relief Committee to SBA, April 8, 1878, and Upper District Relief Committee to SBA, April 8, 1878, *SBA Records* Folder 23; Dr. D. M. Lines to John Davilla, February 1892 and Louisiana Retreat to SBA, March 1892, *SBA Records*, Folder 26; Hotel Dieu to SBA, *Bills*, 1894, *SBA Records*, Folder 27.

40. SBA, *membership card*, SBA Records, Folder 30; SBA, *1877 By-Laws*, Article VII, and *1877 Constitution*, Article XIV; *Conference Rules of the Stevedores and Longshoremen's Benevolent Association and Longshoremen's Protective Union Benevolent Association*, Rule III; *Memorandum of Agreement Between SBA and SBA*

No. 1 (Colored) and The Steamship Agents, Rules 1 and 2, New Orleans 1908, *SBA Records*, Folder 31; *Memorandum of Agreement Between SBA and SBA No. 1 (Colored) and The Steamship Agents and Stevedores*, Rule 3, New Orleans, 1917, *SBA Records*, Folder 31.

41. Allen T. Woods, *Woods Directory*, New Orleans. 1912, 9–10; SBA, *1867 By-Laws*, Article VII; *Picayune*, August 26, 1903, September 10, 1905, September 9, 1903; Ameringer, *If You Don't Weaken*, 199; *Picayune*, September 9, 1903.

42. SBA, *1867 By-Laws*, Article V; SBA *1877 By-Laws*, Article VII; *Contract and Rules of SBA and SBA No. 1 (Colored): Rules of the Screwmen's Joint Conference*, Rules XVIII, XIX, XXV, New Orleans, 1909, *SBA Records*, Folder 31; SBA, *1867 Constitution and By Laws*; *Picayune*, March 22, 1908.

43. SBA, *Bills and Receipts*, 1897–1898; *Picayune*, December 24, 1902; SBA, *1887 By-Laws*, Article IV; SBA, *1867 By-Laws*, Article IV; SBA, *1877 By-Laws*, Article IV; John A. Betat to SBA, October 19, 1875, *SBA Records*, Folder 23; *Picayune*, November 27, 1905.

44. *Picayune*, April 17, 1904; *Picayune*, November 15, 1910, November 16, 1910; Donald M. Marquis, *In Search of Buddy Bolden*, New York, 1980, 33; Danny Barker in Nat Shapiro and Nat Hentoff, *Hear Me Talking' To Ya*, New York, 1955, 16; Johnny St. Cyr in Alan Lomax, *Mister Jelly Roll*, New York, 1950, 101.

45. *Picayune*, August 27, 1905; *Southern Republican*, February 15, 1900, April 14, 1900; Marquis, *In Search of Buddy Bolden*, 53, 68; Foster, *New Orleans Jazz Musician*, 61; *Union Advocate*, June 1, 1903; Foster, *New Orleans Jazz Musician*, 64; *Picayune*, October 11, 1903.

46. Jackson, *New Orleans in the Gilded Age*, 224, 226; SBA, *1877 By-Laws*; John A. Betat to SBA, October 19, 1875, *SBA Records*, Folder 23; *Picayune*, September 4, 1906, September 6, 1904, September 3, 1907; *Picayune*, September 6, 1904, September 2, 1906, September 3, 1907; *Picayune*, September 6, 1903.

47. *Picayune*, August 8, 1903, August 9, 1903, September 4, 1906; Marquis, *In Search of Buddy Bolden*, 116; *Picayune*, September 4, 1906; Frederick Turner, *Remembering Song*, New York, 1982, 36.

48. *Picayune*, September 6, 1903, September 3, 1904, September 5, 1904; *Picayune*, September 6, 1903; *Picayune*, September 3, 1905; Woods, *Woods Directory*, 1912, 13; *Woods Directory*, 1913, 11, 13.

49. *Morning Star*, June 6, 1908; *Picayune*, November 15, 1910, *Times-Picayune*, October 22, 1925; *Picayune*, April 24, 1904, February 1, 1905, September 20, 1905, August 30, 1903.

50. August Meier, *Negro Thought in America, 1880–1915*, Ann Arbor, 1964, 130; W. E. B. DuBois, ed., *Economic Cooperation Among Negro Americans*, Atlanta, 1907, 25, 121–122; *History and Manual of the Colored Knights of Pythias*, Nashville, 1917, 586; *The Crusader*, July 19, 1890; *Southern Republican*, September 9, 1899, *Picayune*,

February 19, 1904; Woods, *Woods Directory*, 1913, 23; *Picayune*, January 20, 1906; *Picayune*, December 24, 1902.

51. *Times-Picayune*, December 22, 1925; *Picayune*, October 20, 1905, April 1, 1906, February 23, 1904; *Morning Star*, May 23, 1908; *Times-Picayune*, November 17, 1953, *Picayune*, February 24, 1905, November 22, 1904, August 24, 1905.

52. *Morning Star*, July 18, 1918; *Morning Star*, July 25, 1908; *Morning Star*, February 22, 1908, February 8, 1908.

53. *Morning Star*, May 2, 1908, August 29, 1908, December 19, 1908; Charles B. Rousseve, *The Negro in Louisiana*, New Orleans, 1937, 109, 129, 139; Du Bois, *Economic Cooperation Among Negro Americans*, 24; Du Bois, *Some Efforts of American Negroes For Their Own Social Betterment*, Atlanta, 1898, 4; *Republican Courier*, December 2, 1899; *Southwestern Christian Advocate*, June 7, 1906, August 30, 1906, June 6, 1907.

54. *The Crisis*, February 1916 (Vol. 11, No. 4), 169; *Southwestern Christian Advocate*, June 11, 1908, April 5, 1906, April 12, 1906.

Chapter Three

Abbreviations: Screwmen's Benevolent Association (SBA)

1. *Picayune*, May 1, 1908; *Picayune*, May 4, 1903; *Picayune*, November 1, 1902.

2. David Paul Bennetts, *Black and White Workers: New Orleans, 1880-1900*, doctoral dissertation, Urbana, 1972, 554, 553, 558, 559, 552; W. E. B. Du Bois, *The Negro Artisan*, Atlanta, 1902, 160.

3. Lester Rubin, *The Negro in the Longshore Industry*, Philadelphia, 1974, 98; F. Ray Marshall, *Labor in the South*, Cambridge, 1957, 61, 63; Oscar Ameringer, *If You Don't Weaken*, New York, 1904, 196–197.

4. Bennetts, 476–477; *Conference Rules of the Stevedores and Longshoremen's Benevolent Association and Longshoremen's Protective Union Benevolent*, New Orleans, 1892, Rule II, *SBA Records*, Folder 31, Special Collections, Louisiana State University Libraries; *Longshoremen's Rules*, Rule VIII; *Longshoremen's Rules*, Rule XXVII; Bennetts, 476–479.

5. Bennetts, 479.

6. *Picayune*, September 11, 1901; *Picayune*, September 13, 1901; *Picayune*, September 14, 1901; *Picayune*, September 17, 1901; *Picayune*, September 21, 1901; *Picayune*, September 17, 1901; *Picayune*, September 12, 1901; *Picayune*, September 20, 1901; *Picayune*, September 21, 1901.

7. *Picayune*, October 6, 1901; *Picayune*, October 8, 1901; Ameringer, 214; *Picayune*, October 6, 1901; *Picayune*, May 1, 1903; *Picayune*, April 29, 1904; *Picayune*, February 15, 1908; *Picayune*, May 4, 1903.

8. *Picayune*, May 24, 1903; *Picayune*, May 20, 1903; *Picayune*, May 23, 1903; *Picayune*, May 24, 1903; *Picayune*, May 20, 1903; *Picayune*, May 19, 1903.

9. *Picayune*, December 14, 1902.

10. *Picayune*, September 11, 1903; *Picayune*, August 31, 1903; *Picayune*, September 4, 1903; *Picayune*, September 5, 1903; *Picayune*, September 9, 1903; *Picayune*, September 10, 1903.

11. *Picayune*, September 10, 1903; *Picayune*, September 9, 1903; *Picayune*, September 9, 1903; *Picayune*, September 11, 1903.

12. *Picayune*, September 13, 1903; *Picayune*, September 14, 1903; *Picayune*, September 13, 1903.

13. *Picayune*, September 11, 1903; *Picayune*, April 1, 1904; *Picayune*, April 11, 1904; *Picayune*, May 14, 1904.

14. *Picayune*, March 16, 1904; *Picayune*, March 18, 1904; *Picayune*, March 21, 1904; *Picayune*, April 1, 1904; *Picayune*, April 6, 1904.

15. *Picayune*, September 2, 1906; *Picayune*, September 11, 1906; *Picayune*, September 12, 1906; *Picayune*, September 13, 1906; *Picayune*, September 27, 1906; *Picayune*, September 29, 1906.

16. *Picayune*, September 9, 1905; *Picayune*, September 4, 1905; *Picayune*, September 8, 1905; *Picayune*, September 9, 1905; *Picayune*, September 10, 1905; *Picayune*, September 11, 1905.

17. *Picayune*, September 12, 1905; *Picayune*, September 13, 1905; *Picayune*, September 16, 1905; *Picayune*, September 17, 1905; *Picayune*, September 22, 1905; *Picayune*, September 23, 1905.

18. *Picayune*, November 9, 1902; *Picayune*, December 13, 1902; *Picayune*, December 14, 1902; *Picayune*, December 18, 1902; *Picayune*, December 22, 1902.

19. *Picayune*, December 13, 1902; *Picayune*, December 20, 1902; *Picayune*, December 23, 1902; *Picayune*, December 17, 1902; *Picayune*, December 23, 1902; *Picayune*, December 24, 1902.

20. *Picayune*, August 25, 1903; *Picayune*, September 2, 1903; *Picayune*, May 14, 1903; *Picayune*, August 25, 1903; *Picayune*, September 2, 1903; *Picayune*, September 12, 1902; Works Progress Administration of Louisiana, *Wreck Reports, U. S. Custom District, Port of New Orleans, 1873–1924*, Baton Rouge, 1939, 68–69 (copy at Louisiana Historical Center, New Orleans).

21. *Picayune*, September 9, 1903; *Picayune*, September 5, 1903; *Picayune*, September 7, 1903; *Picayune*, September 15, 1903; *Picayune*, September 6, 1903; *Picayune*, September 17, 1903.

22. *Picayune*, July 7, 1906; *Picayune*, July 7, 1906.

23. *Picayune,* July 8, 1906; *Picayune,* July 10, 1906; *Picayune,* July 8, 1906; *Picayune,* July 9, 1906; *Picayune,* July 10, 1906; *Picayune,* July 11, 1906, *Picayune,* July 12, 1906.

24. Cotton Yardmen: *Picayune,* August 29, 1903, September 21, 1903; Freight Handlers: *Picayune,* August 25, 1903, September 3, 1903, September 17, 1903; Longshoremen: *Picayune,* August 31, 1903, September 1, 1903, September 14, 1903; *Picayune,* September 2, 1906; *Picayune,* September 6, 1907, September 15, 1907.

25. *Picayune,* November 6, 1902.

26. *Constitution and By-Laws of the Screwmen's Benevolent Association,* New Orleans, 1894, By-Laws, Art. VIII, Sec. 4, *SBA Records,* Folder 31, Louisiana State University; SBA, *1887 By-Laws,* Article VIII, Folder 31, *SBA Records; Picayune,* April 12, 1903; *Picayune,* November 4, 1902.

27. *Picayune,* April 12, 1903; *Picayune,* November 6, 1902.

28. *Picayune,* April 24, 1903; *Picayune,* October 22, 1902.

29. *Picayune,* October 22, 1902; *Picayune,* October 30, 1902; *Picayune,* October 27, 1902; *Picayune,* October 30, 1902.

30. *Picayune,* November 1, 1902; *Picayune,* November 2, 1902; *Picayune,* November 3, 1902; *Picayune,* November 4, 1902; *Picayune,* November 5, 1902.

31. *Picayune,* November 6, 1902; *Picayune,* November 7, 1902; *Picayune,* May 4, 1903.

32. *Picayune,* December 25, 1902; *Picayune,* December 26, 1902.

33. *Picayune,* April 5, 1903; *Picayune,* April 6, 1903; *Picayune,* April 7, 1903; *Picayune,* April 10, 1903.

34. *Picayune,* April 12, 1903.

35. *Picayune,* April 14, 1903; *Picayune,* May 10, 1903; *Picayune,* April 19, 1903; *Picayune,* April 20, 1903; *Picayune,* April 21, 1903.

36. *Picayune,* May 1, 1903; *Picayune,* April 26, 1903; *Picayune,* May 5, 1903; *Picayune,* May 7, 1903; *Picayune,* May 9, 1903; *Picayune,* May 8, 1903; *Union Advocate,* April 13, 1903; *Union Advocate,* April 27, 1903; *Union Advocate,* May 11, 1903.

37. *Picayune,* June 25, 1903; *Picayune,* July 18, 1903; *Picayune,* August 11, 1903; *Picayune,* August 26, 1903; *Picayune,* August 23, 1903; *Picayune,* August 29, 1903.

38. *Picayune,* September 11, 1903; *Picayune,* September 11, 1903; *Picayune,* September 21, 1903; *Picayune,* September 28, 1903; *Picayune,* September 30, 1903.

39. *Picayune,* October 2, 1903; *Picayune,* October 2, 1903; *Picayune,* October 4, 1903; *Picayune,* October 5, 1903; *Picayune,* October 11, 1903; *Picayune,* October 7, 1903; *Picayune,* October 9, 1903.

40. *Picayune*, October 10, 1903; *Picayune*, October 12, 1903; *Picayune*, October 13, 1903.

41. *Picayune*, October 19, 1903; *Union Advocate*, October 26, 1903.

42. *Picayune*, March 10, 1904; *Picayune*, March 15, 1904; *Picayune*, March 23, 1904; *Picayune*, March 26, 1904; *Picayune*, May 18, 1904; *Picayune*, August 13, 1904; *Picayune*, October 29, 1904.

43. *Contract and Rules of SBA and SBA No. 1 (Colored): Rules of the Screwmen's Joint Conference*, New Orleans, 1909, Rule XXXII, 20, *SBA Records*, Folder 31.

Chapter Four

Abbreviations: Central Trades and Labor Council (CT&LC)

1. *Picayune*, June 5, 1907; *Daily News*, August 11, 1907.

2. *Machinists Monthly Journal*, May 1907, 481; *Picayune*, March 29, 1907, April 1, 1907, April 8, 1907, April 25, 1907, July 10, 1907.

3. *Picayune*, June 4, 1907; *Picayune*, June 5, 1907.

4. *Picayune*, February 11, 1907, February 14, 1907, March 8, 1907; *Picayune*, June 28, 1907; *Picayune*, August 10, 1907, August 11, 1907.

5. *Picayune*, August 11, 1907; *Brauer-Zeitung*, August 17, 1907; *Picayune*, August 21, 1907; Covington Hall, *Labor Struggles in the Deep South*, manuscript in Howard-Tilton Library, Tulane University, New Orleans, n. d., 74.

6. *Picayune*, January 27, 1906, February 24, 1906, January 26, 1907.

7. Hall, 51; Philip S. Foner, *History of the Labor Movement in the United States, Vol. 4*, New York, 1965, 40, 45, 52–53; *Picayune*, March 30, 1906; *Picayune*, April 24, 1906; Hall, 51–53.

8. *Picayune*, October 17, 1903; *Union Advocate*, February 2, 1903; *Union Advocate*, February 16, 1903; *Union Advocate*, March 30, 1903.

9. Joyce L. Kornbluh, ed., *Rebel Voices*, Ann Arbor, 1968, 259–260; *Picayune*, June 17, 1903; *Picayune*, August 12, 1903; *Picayune*, January 3, 1904; *Picayune*, September 15, 1904; *Picayune*, December 14, 1905.

10. *Picayune*, June 11, 1904; *Picayune*, August 20, 1906, November 9, 1906, November 16, 1906; Oscar Ameringer, *If You Don't Weaken*, New York, 1940, 209; *Picayune*, February 24, 1905; Ameringer, 209. See also Joseph Robert Conlin, *Bread and Roses Too: Studies of the Wobblies*, Westport, 1969, 35.

11. *Picayune*, September 19, 1903; Philip S. Foner, *American Socialism and Black Americans*, Westport, 1977, 131–138.

12. Hall, 54–57.

13. Hall, 94; Ameringer, 193; James R. Green, *Grass-Roots Socialism*, Baton Rouge, 1978, 36–37; Len De Caux, *Labor Radical*, Boston, 1970, 130; Hall, 47, 64, 73–74, 92–94.

14. Green, 35, 64, 76–77, 225, 247; Grady McWhiney, "Louisiana Socialists in the Early Twentieth Century: A Study of Rustic Radicalism," *Journal of Southern History*, XX, No. 3 (August 1954), 315-336, *passim*.

15. Paul F. Brissenden, *The IWW*, New York, (1919), 1957, 38.

16. John R. Commons and Associates, *History of Labour in the United States, Vol. II*, New York, 1921, 487–488; Philip Taft, *The AFL in the Time of Gompers*, New York, 1957, 189; Louis Lorwin, *The American Federation of Labor*, Washington, 1933, 85.

17. Brauer-Zeitung, June 8, 1907; *Labor World*, March 2, 1907; *Picayune*, June 25, 1903; *Picayune*, March 12, 1907.

18. CT&LC, *Minutes*, July 8, 1900, Stoddard Labor Collection, University of New Orleans; CT&LC, *Minutes*, November 25, 1900; CT&LC, *Minutes*, January 11, 1901; CT&LC, *Minutes*, April 12, 1901; CT&LC, *Minutes*, April 26, 1901.

19. *Picayune*, December 2, 1901, December 15, 1901; *Union Advocate*, August 17, 1903; *Union Advocate*, August 24, 1901; *Picayune*, June 15, 1903, June 17, 1903; *Picayune*, September 10, 1903; *Union Advocate*, October 5, 1903; *Picayune*, October 20, 1903; *Picayune*, September 6, 1903.

20. *Picayune*, June 18, 1904; *Brauer-Zeitung*, January 5, 1907; *Brauer-Zeitung*, January 12, 1907.

21. *Picayune*, August 18, 1905; *Picayune*, September 18, 1905, October 6, 1905; October 12, 1905, November 4, 1905.

22. Taft, 192.

23. American Federation of Labor, *Report of Proceedings of the Twenty-Sixth Annual Convention of the American Federation of Labor* (1906), Washington, 1907, 51; Hermann Schluter, *The Brewing Industry and the Brewery Workers' Movement in America*, New York, (1910), 1970, 226; *AFL, 1906 Proceedings*, 14; C. L. Stamp to Frank Morrison, January 4, 1907, *John Mitchell Papers*, Reel 11; John Mitchell to Frank Morrison, January 4, 1907, *Mitchell Papers*, Reel 11; Frank Morrison to AFL Executive Council Members, January 11, 1907, *Mitchell Papers*, Reel 11.

24. *Picayune*, June 1, 1907; *Picayune*, June 2, 1907; *Picayune*, June 23, 1907; *Brauer-Zeitung*, August 10, 1907; *Brauer-Zeitung*, February 29, 1908.

25. *Labor World*, January 19, 1907; *Brauer-Zeitung*, January 19, 1907; Gompers to AFL Executive Council members, January 5, 1907, *Mitchell Papers*, Reel 11; Frank Morrison to AFL Executive Council members, January 11, 1907, *Mitchell Papers*, Reel 11; *Labor World*, March 30, 1907; *Labor World*, June 1, 1907.

26. Gompers to Louis Kemper, March 1, 1907, American Federation of Labor, *Letter-Press Copybooks of Samuel Gompers and William Green*; Gompers to Kemper, March 19, 1907, Gompers, *Letters; Brauer-Zeitung*, February 2, 1907; *Brauer-Zeitung*, March 9, 1907.

27. *Labor World*, March 2, 1907; *Labor World*, May 11, 1907; *Brauer-Zeitung*, June 8, 1907, *Labor World*, June 8, 1907; Gompers to Kemper, May 28, 1907, Gompers, *Letters*.

28. *Picayune*, May 24, 1907; *Picayune*, May 25, 1907; *Picayune*, May 28, 1907; Hall, 57; Hall, 58.

29. *Picayune, June 1, 1907; Picayune*, June 2, 1907; Hall, 64; *Picayune*, June 4, 1907; *Picayune*, June 2, 1907; *Picayune*, June 1, 1907; *Picayune*, June 5, 1907; *Picayune*, June 6, 1907; *Picayune*, June 7, 1907.

30. James Leonard to Frank Morrison, June 2, 1907, *Mitchell Papers*, Reel 12; Leonard to Gompers, June 9, 1907, *Mitchell Papers*, Reel 12; *Picayune*, June 7, 1907; *Picayune*, June 8, 1907; *Industrial Union Bulletin*, June 15, 1907.

31. Gompers to Leonard, June 12, 1907, Gompers, *Letters*; Gompers to Leonard, June 19, 1907, Gompers, *Letters*; Gompers to Leonard, June 25, 1907, Gompers, *Letters*.

32. *Picayune*, June 25, 1907; *Picayune*, June 26, 1907; *Picayune*, June 30, 1907; *Daily News*, July 2, 1907.

33. *Picayune*, June 6, 1907. (See also James Leonard to Frank Morrison, July 7, 1907, *Mitchell Papers*, Reel 12); *Picayune*, July 11, 1907; *Daily News*, July 4, 1907; *Picayune*, July 6, 1907; *Daily News*, July 5, 1907 (The entire July 4 cable to Gompers is in *Industrial Union Bulletin* August 31, 1907.) Gompers to Rufus Ruiz, July 5, 1907, Gompers, *Letters*.

34. Leonard to Morrison, July 7, 1907, *Mitchell Papers*, Reel 12; *Daily News*, July 5, 1907; *Picayune*, July 10, 1907; *Picayune*, July 11, 1907; Hall, 64; Hall, 65; *Picayune*, July 12, 1907; *Picayune*, July 13, 1907; *Brauer-Zeitung*, August 8, 1907.

35. *Daily News*, July 17, 1907; *Picayune*, July 26, 1907; *Picayune*, July 21, 1907; *Labor World*, July 13, 1907; *Dallas Laborer*, quoted in *St. Louis Labor*, August 3, 1907; *Appeal to Reason*, quoted in *Brauer-Zeitung*, August 10, 1907; *St. Louis Labor*, July 27, 1907; *Daily News*, July 26, 1907.

36. *Daily News*, July 27, 1907; *Picayune*, July 26, 1907; *Picayune*, July 27, 1907; *Daily News*, July 29, 1907; *Picayune*, July 30, 1907.

37. Gompers to Robert E. Lee, August 8, 1907, Gompers, *Letters*; Robert Lee Guard to Robert E. Lee, August 20, 1907, Gompers, *Letters*; James Leonard to Frank Morrison, September 1, 1907, *Mitchell Papers*, Reel 12; Gompers to Lee, August 17, 1907, Gompers, *Letters*; Gompers to Ruiz, August 26, 1907, Gompers, *Letters*; Gompers to Ruiz, September 12, 1907, Gompers, *Letters*.

38. *Brauer-Zeitung*, August 10, 1907; Leonard to Morrison, September 29, 1907, *Mitchell Papers*, Reel 12; *Daily News*, August 20, 1907; *Brauer-Zeitung*, September 7, 1907; *Brauer-Zeitung*, August 31, 1907.

39. *Brauer-Zeitung*, August 10, 1907; *Picayune*, August 12, 1907; *Picayune*, September 11, 1907; *Picayune*, February 22, 1908.

40. *Picayune*, August 27, 1907; Gompers to Robert E. Lee, September 13, 1907, Gompers, *Letters*; Leonard to Morrison, September 1, 1907, *Mitchell Papers*, Reel 12; Leonard to Morrison, September 1, 1907, *Mitchell Papers*, Reel 12.

41. *Picayune*, September 24, 1907; *Brauer-Zeitung*, December 7, 1907; AFL, *Report of Proceedings of the Twenty-Seventh Convention* (1907), Washington, 1907, 159, 317, 277, 20, 44; Gompers to Leonard, December 8, 1907, Gompers, *Letters; Brauer-Zeitung*, February 1, 1908, March 21, 1908; Gompers to Louis Kemper, March 11, 1908, Gompers, *Letters*; Gompers to American Brewing Company of New Orleans, March 26, 1908, and to the Columbia, Jackson, Louisiana, Pelican, Security, New Orleans and Standard Brewing Companies, same date, Gompers, *Letters; Picayune*, June 5, 1908; *Picayune*, June 24, 1908.

42. *Daily News*, August 11, 1907.

43. *Daily News*, August 15, 1907; *Picayune*, August 16, 1907.

44. *Daily News*, August 17, 1907; *Picayune*, August 17, 1907; *Picayune*, August 18, 1907; *Picayune*, August 24, 1907; Hall, 70; *Picayune*, August 24, 1907.

45. Hall, 67; Gompers to Leonard, September 11, 1907, Gompers, *Letters*; Leonard to Morrison, September 29, 1907, *Mitchell Papers*, Reel 12; *Brauer-Zeitung*, August 31, 1907; *Picayune*, August 31, 1907.

46. *United Labor Journal*, August 31, 1907; *Picayune*, September 3, 1907; CT&LC, letter to organized labor, September 14, 1907, in *Brauer-Zeitung*, October 12, 1907.

47. *Picayune*, June 5, 1908; *Brauer-Zeitung*, June 20, 1908.

Chapter Five

1. *Picayune*, October 9, 1907; *Times-Democrat*, November 1, 1907.

2. David Montgomery, *Workers' Control in America*, New York, 1979, 93; Philip S. Foner, *History of the Labor Movement in the United States, Vol. 3*, New York, 1964, 253; *Cleveland Citizen*, November 9, 1907; Covington Hall, *Labor Struggles in the Deep South*, ms. in Howard-Tilton Library, Tulane University, New Orleans, n.d., 80.

3. New Orleans Cotton Exchange, *Thirty-Sixth Annual Report, Year Ending October 31, 1906*, New Orleans, 1906, 10; Cotton Exchange, *Thirty-Seventh Annual Report*, 1907, 10–11.

4. *Picayune*, July 28, 1907; *Picayune*, August 18, 1907; *Picayune*, August 25, 1907; *Picayune*, August 22, 1907; *Picayune*, August 23, 1907.

5. *Picayune*, August 27, 1907; *Picayune*, August 28, 1907; *Picayune*, August 29, 1907; *Picayune*, August 30, 1907; *Picayune*, August 31, 1907; Hall, 78.

6. *Picayune*, August 29, 1907, *Picayune*, September 1, 1907; *Picayune*, September 4, 1907; *Picayune*, September 6, 1907; *Picayune*, September 10, 1907; *Picayune*, September 6, 1907.

7. *Picayune*, September 7, 1907.

8. *Picayune*, September 9, 1907; *Picayune*, September 11, 1907; *Picayune*, September 14, 1907; *Picayune*, September 16, 1907.

9. *Picayune*, September 17, 1907; *Picayune*, September 10, 1907; *Picayune*, September 12, 1907; *Picayune*, September 13, 1907.

10. *Picayune*, September 11, 1907; *Picayune*, September 19, 1907; September 27, 1907; Hall, 79; *Picayune*, September 24, 1907; *Picayune*, September 27, 1907.

11. Philip S. Foner and Ronald L. Lewis, eds., *The Black Worker, Vol. 4*, Philadelphia, 1970, 67, 62–70 *passim*; *Picayune*, October 24, 1903, October 25, 1903, October 26, 1903; *Galveston City-Times*, January 7, 1905; *City-Times*, June 17, 1905, June 15, 1907; *City-Times*, January 7, 1905, May 12, 1906, May 19, 1906; *Picayune*, January 10, 1908; *Picayune*, January 11, 1908.

12. Hall, 83.

13. *Picayune*, September 25, 1907; *Picayune*, September 26, 1907; *Picayune*, September 27, 1907; *Picayune*, September 28, 1907; *Picayune*, September 29, 1907; *Picayune*, September 30, 1907.

14. *Picayune*, September 30, 1907; *Picayune*, October 2, 1907; Hall, 80; *Picayune*, October 2, 1907; Martin Behrman to James Byrnes, October 2, 1907, Mayor's Office, New Orleans, *Letters*; *Picayune*, October 3, 1907.

15. *Picayune*, October 5, 1907, *Times-Democrat*, October 6, 1907; *Picayune*, October 5, 1907; *Daily News*, October 5, 1907.

16. Hall, 83; Rayford Logan, *The Betrayal of the Negro*, New York, 1967, 296–300; John Wilds, *Afternoon Story*, Baton Rouge, 1976, 65–67; *Picayune*, October 5, 1907; *Times-Democrat*, October 5, 1907; *Times-Democrat*, October 5, 1907; *Times-Democrat*, October 8, 1907; *Times-Democrat*, October 5, 1907, October 6, 1907; *New Orleans Item*, October 5, 1907; *Times-Democrat*, October 11, 1907; *Picayune*, October 6, 1907; *Picayune*, October 7, 1907.

17. *Picayune*, October 7, 1907; *Picayune*, October 9, 1907; *Times-Democrat*, October 10, 1907; *Daily News*, October 7, 1907; Hall, 92; *Daily News*, October 5, 1907; *Times-Democrat*, October 5, 1907, *Times-Democrat*, October 7, 1907, *Times-Democrat*, October 11, 1907, *Picayune*, October 11, 1907; *Times-Democrat*, October 6, 1907.

18. Oscar Ameringer, *If You Don't Weaken*, New York, 1940, 198; *Times-Democrat*, October 6, 1907.

19. *Picayune*, October 7, 1907, October 8, 1907, *Times-Democrat*, October 7, 1907, October 8, 1907; *Times-Democrat*, October 6, 1907; *Picayune*, October 8, 1907; *Picayune*, October 11, 1907; *Picayune*, October 10, 1907, *Times-Democrat*, October 10, 1907; *Item*, October 9, 1907; Ameringer, 200.

20. *Picayune*, October 9, 1907, October 10, 1907; *Picayune*, October 5, 1907; *Times-Democrat*, October 5, 1907; *Picayune*, October 9, 1907; *Picayune*, October 10, 1907.

21. *Times-Democrat*, October 8, 1907, October 10, 1907, October 11, 1907, *Picayune*, October 7, 1907, *Picayune*, October 10, 1907, *Times-Democrat*, October 10, 1907, October 11, 1907; *Times-Democrat*, October 9, 1907, October 9, 1907, Hall, 81–82; Ameringer, 200; *Picayune*, October 11, 1907.

22. *Times-Democrat*, October 8, 1907, October 10, 1907, October 11, 1907, *Picayune*, October 11, 1907; Hall, 81–82; Ameringer, 201; *Picayune*, October 7, 1907; *Picayune*, October 10, 1907, *Times-Democrat*, October 10, 1907, October 11, 1907; *Times-Democrat*, October 9, 1907, October 9, 1907, Hall, 81–82; Ameringer, 200; *Picayune*, October 11, 1907.

23. *Daily News*, October 10, 1907; Behrman to Captain O. M. Dunn, Superintendent, Illinois Central Railroad, New Orleans, October 8, 1907, *Behrman Letters*; Behrman to Martin A. Knapp, Chairman, Interstate Commerce Commission, October 9, 1907, October 10, 1907, *Behrman Letters*; Behrman to E. S. Whitaker, Inspector of Police, October 10, 1907, *Behrman Letters*.

24. *Picayune*, October 9, 1907; Behrman to E. F. Kohnke, Chairman, Conference of Exchanges, October 11, 1907; *Times-Democrat*, October 12, 1907.

25. Ameringer, 201; *Picayune*, October 16, 1907.

26. *Daily States*, October 17, 1907; *Daily News*, October 12, 1907.

27. Behrman to E. F. Kohnke, October 11, 1907, *Behrman Letters*; *Times-Democrat*, October 12, 1907; *Daily States*, October 12, 1907; *Picayune*, October 12, 1907; *Daily States*, October 12, 1907; *Picayune*, October 12, 1907; *Times-Democrat*, October 13, 1907, *Picayune*, October 13, 1907; *Times-Democrat*, October 14, 1907; *Picayune*, October 14, 1907.

28. *Picayune*, October 15, 1907, *Times-Democrat*, October 15, 1907; *Times-Democrat*, October 14, 1907; *Picayune*, October 15, 1907; Ameringer, 198–199.

29. *Times-Democrat*, October 18, 1907, *Picayune*, October 18, 1907; *Times-Democrat*, October 19, 1907, *Daily News*, October 18, 1907; *Picayune*, October 19, 1907; *Times-Democrat*, October 18, 1907.

30. *Picayune*, October 12, 1907, *Times-Democrat*, October 15, 1907; *Times-Democrat*, October 14, 1907, October 15, 1907.

31. *Times-Democrat*, October 15, 1907, October 18, 1907; ·*Times-Democrat*, October 17, 1907; *Picayune*, October 15, 1907, October 19, 1907; Behrman to O. M. Dunn, October 12, 1907, *Behrman Letters*; *Picayune*, October 13, 1907; W. P. Ball (Behrman's secretary) to E. S. Whitaker, Inspector of Police, October 15, 1907, *Behrman Letters*.

32. *Times-Democrat*, October 12, 1907, October 13, 1907, October 14, 1907; Julius Weiss, Chairman, Cotton Factors Committee, to Behrman, October 17, 1907, *Behrman Letters*; Weiss to Behrman, October 17, 1907, *Behrman Letters*; Hall, 83.

33. Ameringer, 198.

34. *Times-Democrat*, October 16, 1907, October 17, 1907, *Picayune*, October 16, 1907, October 17, 1907; *Picayune*, October 18, 1907, *Times-Democrat*, October 17, 1907, October 19, 1907.

Such assaults on strikebreakers were not unprecedented. During a 1902 round freight teamsters' walkout, the union president noted: "Two . . . scab drivers were run off their floats at the corner of Poydras and Liberty Streets this forenoon by women and children. No men took part." See *Picayune*, December 16, 1902.

35. *Times-Democrat*, October 22, 1907; Behrman to William P. Ross and members of Ship Agents Committee, October 18, 1907, *Behrman Letters*; *Picayune*, October 19, 1907; *Picayune*, October 20, 1907; *Times-Democrat*, October 20, 1907.

36. *Picayune*, October 20, 1907; *Picayune*, October 23, 1907; *Appeal to Reason*, October 26, 1907; *Times-Democrat*, October 20, 1907; *Times-Democrat*, October 21, 1907; *Picayune*, October 21, 1907, *Times-Democrat*, October 21, 1907.

37. Behrman to Ross, October 21, 1907, *Behrman Letters*; *Picayune*, October 22, 1907; *Times-Democrat*, October 22, 1907; *Times-Democrat*, October 22, 1907.

38. *Picayune*, October 22, 1907; *Daily States*, October 22, 1907; *Daily News*, October 22, 1907; *Times-Democrat*, October 23, 1907; *Picayune*, October 23, 1907; *Times-Democrat*, October 23, 1907; *Picayune*, October 24, 1907; *Times-Democrat*, October 24, 1907; *Picayune*, October 25, 1907.

39. On the Southern Pacific strike, see *Picayune*, October 29–November 5, 1907; for the Illinois Central freight handlers, see *Picayune*, October 26, 1907, *Times-Democrat*, October 26, 1907.

Picayune, October 25, 1907, *Item*, October 25, 1907, *Times-Democrat*, October 25, 1907, *Daily News*, October 25, 1907, *Daily States*, October 24, 1907; *Brauer-Zeitung*, November 2, 1907, *Cleveland Citizen*, November 9, 1907; *Mobile Register*, October 26, 1907, in W. J. Ennis to Behrman, November 3, 1907, *Behrman Letters*.

40. William P. Ross to Behrman, in Behrman to James Byrnes, November 9, 1907, *Behrman Letters*; *Daily News*, October 27, 1907.

41. *Picayune*, October 29, 1907; *Times-Democrat*, October 29, 1907; *Times-Democrat*, October 30, 1907; *Item*, October 29, 1907; *Picayune*, October 30, 1907.

42. Behrman to Ross, October 31, 1907, *Behrman Letters*; *Picayune*, November 1, 1907.

43. *Times-Democrat*, November 1, 1907; *Picayune*, November 2, 1907; *Times-Democrat*, November 1, 1907; *Item*, November 2, 1907, November 4, 1907; Ameringer, 215.

44. *Times-Democrat*, November 1, 1907; *Picayune*, November 1, 1907, Ameringer, 216–217; *Times-Democrat*, November 1, 1907.

45. *Picayune*, November 2, 1907; *Picayune*, November 3, 1907, November 9, 1907; *Item*, November 3, 1907; *Item*, November 3, 1907.

46. *Picayune*, November 5, 1907, *Times-Democrat*, November 5, 1907, Behrman to Ross, November 16, 1907, *Behrman Letters*; *Picayune*, November 5, 1907; *Picayune*, November 14, 1907, November 22, 1907.

Chapter Six

Abbreviations: National Adjustment Commission (NAC); Local Adjustment Commission (LAC); Screwmen's Benevolent Association (SBA).

1. *Picayune*, May 29, 1908.

2. *Picayune*, November 22, 1907; Covington Hall, *Labor Troubles in the Deep South*, ms. in Howard-Tilton Library, Tulane University, New Orleans, n.d., 87.

3. William Ivey Hair, *Bourbonism and Agrarian Protest*, Baton Rouge, 1969, 72, 78; Grady McWhiney, "Louisiana Socialists in the Early Twentieth Century: A Study of Rustic Radicalism," *Journal of Southern History*, XX, No. 3 (August 1954), 315–336; *Picayune*, March 4, 1904, March 5, 1904, April 12, 1905; Oscar Ameringer, *If You Don't Weaken*, New York, 1940, 218.

4. Picayune, January 10, 1908; McWhiney, 317–138; *Who's Who in Louisiana and Mississippi*, New Orleans, 1918, 146; James R. Green, *Grass-Roots Socialism*, Baton Rouge, 1978, 250, 204–222.

5. *Appeal to Reason*, December 21, 1907; Martin Behrman to George B. McLellan, February 25, 1908, Behrman to Rolla Wells, February 24, 1908, Mayor's Office, New Orleans, *Behrman Letters*.

6. *Picayune*, January 10, 1908, January 11, 1908, January 12, 1908, January 13, 1908.

7. *Picayune*, February 5, 1908, February 6, 1908; *Savannah Tribune*, January 12, 1907, March 9, 1907, March 23, 1907, May 4, 1907, July 20, 1907; *Picayune*, February 5, 1908, February 8, 1908; *Savannah Tribune*, February 9, 1907; *Picayune*, February 6, 1908.

8. *Picayune*, February 7, 1908; *Picayune*, February 8, 1908; *Picayune*, February 9, 1908; *Picayune*, October 24, 1903, October 26, 1903, October 17, 1903, October 30, 1903, November 3, 1903; *Picayune*, February 9, 1908.

9. *Picayune*, November 22, 1907.

10. *Picayune*, February 11, 1908; *Picayune*, February 15, 1908; *Picayune*, February 15, 1908; *Picayune*, April 21, 1908.

11. *Picayune*, March 11, 1908.

12. *Picayune*, March 25, 1908.

13. *Picayune*, March 12, 1908.

14. *Picayune*, April 19, 1903.

15. *Picayune*, March 12, 1908; Hall, 88–89.

16. *Picayune*, March 14, 1908.

Parkerson's role in the 1891 lynching of Italians in New Orleans is described in Richard Gambino, *Vendetta*, Garden City, 1977, 78–86.

17. *Picayune*, March 14, 1908.

18. *Picayune*, March 18, 1908; Hall, 89.

19. *Picayune*, March 20, 1908.

20. *Picayune*, March 24, 1908.

21. *Picayune*, March 25, 1908.

22. Hall, 83; *Picayune*, March 27, 1908.

23. *Picayune*, March 28, 1908.

24. *Picayune*, March 28, 1908.

25. *Picayune*, April 26, 1908; *Picayune*, April 24, 1908; *Picayune*, April 25, 1908.

26. *Picayune*, April 25, 1908.

A single-tree is the pivoted swinging bar to which the traces of a harness are fastened and by which a vehicle is drawn.

27. *Picayune*, April 30, 1908.

28. *Picayune*, May 1, 1908.

29. *Picayune*, May 2, 1908, *Picayune*, May 3, 1908.

30. *Picayune*, May 6, 1908, *Times-Democrat*, May 6, 1908; *Picayune*, May 5, 1908; *Picayune*, May 6, 1908.

31. *Picayune*, May 12, 1908, May 13, 1908; *Times-Democrat*, May 15, 1908; Hall, 90–91; *Memorandum of Agreement Between SBA and SBA No. 1 (Colored) and the Steamship Agents and Stevedores*, New Orleans, 1917, Folder 31, *SBA Records*, Special Collections, Louisiana State University Libraries.

32. *Times-Democrat*, May 15, 1908.

33. *Picayune*, May 29, 1908.

34. *Picayune*, May 12, 1908, May 13, 1908.

35. *Picayune*, July 8, 1908; *Picayune*, July 9, 1908, July 10, 1908, July 15, 1908, July 17, 1908, July 19, 1908.

36. *Picayune*, May 27, 1908, May 28, 1908; *Picayune*, May 31, 1908; *Picayune*, June 4, 1908; *Picayune*, June 4, 1908.

37. *Picayune*, June 10, 1908; *Picayune*, June 12, 1908; *Picayune*, June 27, 1908, *Picayune*, June 16, 1908.

38. W. P. Ball to Chris Scully, and to W. P. Ross, June 15, 1908, *Behrman Letters*; *Picayune*, June 17, 1908; *Picayune*, June 27, 1908.

39. *Picayune*, July 1, 1908; *Picayune*, July 2, 1908; *Picayune*, July 5, 1908; *Picayune*, July 6, 1908; *Picayune*, July 10, 1908; *Picayune*, July 8, 1908.

40. *Picayune*, July 12, 1908; *Picayune*, July 20, 1908, July 21, 1908; *Picayune*, July 13, 1908; *Picayune*, July 14, 1908.

41. *Picayune*, July 14, 1908, July 17, 1908; *Picayune*, July 22, 1908.

42. *Picayune*, July 23, 1908; *Picayune*, July 24, 1908; *Picayune*, July 25, 1908.

43. *United Labor Journal*, September 5, 1908, September 19, 1908; SBA, *1917 Memorandum*, 8; *Soards' New Orleans City Directory*, 1911, 400; *Picayune*, November 15, 1910, November 16, 1910.

44. *United Labor Journal*, September 5, 1908; *Times-Picayune*, December 22, 1925; Allen T. Woods, *Woods Directory*, New Orleans, 1913, 11, 17, 19.

45. Contract and Rules of SBA and SBA No. 1 (Colored), New Orleans, 1909, 3; SBA, *1917 Memorandum*, 1; *Agreement and Rules of Stevedores and Longshoremen's Benevolent Society and Longshoremen's Protective Union Benevolent Association*, New Orleans, 1917, 8, in Adjustment Case Files, *Records of the NAC*, Gulf Coast, Cotton Screwmen's Folder; SBA, *1917 Memorandum*; SBA, *1917 Memorandum*; *Working Rules, Dock Loaders and Unloaders, Freight Car Loaders Union # 854*, New Orleans, 1917, in General Records, *NAC Records*, Load of Flour Controversy Folder; *1917 Longshoremen's* Rules, 3.

46. Sterling D. Spero and Abram L. Harris, *The Black Worker*, New York, 1974, 188–189; Charles Frederick Ortique, *A Study of the Longshore Industry in New Orleans with Emphasis on Negro Longshoremen*, master's thesis, Urbana, 1956, 39; William

von Phul, *Mechanical Equipment Used in the Port of New Orleans*, New Orleans, 1916, 5, 16, 17; von Phul, *Physical Characteristics of Cotton Warehouses*, New Orleans, 1915, map; von Phul, *Mechanical Equipment*, 10–11; von Phul, *Mechanical Equipment*, 11, 12, 40–41; von Phul, *Mechanical Equipment*, 6.

47. Harry A. Millis and Royal E. Montgomery, *Organized Labor*, New York, 1945, 138–139; U. S. Shipping Board, Emergency Fleet Corporation, Industrial Relations, *Divisional Bulletin*, No. 5, 1918, 1, 5, 3.

48. U. S. Shipping Board, *Marine and Dock Labor*, Washington, D.C., 1919, 27–28; Rules and Regulations, *NAC Records*.

49. P. T. Murphy to R. B. Stevens, September 27, 1917, Adjustment Case Files, *NAC Records*, Gulf Coast — Cotton Rollers folder; P. T. Murphy to Robert P. Bass, March 9, 1918, General Records — New Orleans, *NAC Records*, Load of Flour Controversy folder.

50. P. T. Murphy to R. B. Stevens, September 25, 1917, Adjustment Case Files *NAC Records*, Gulf Coast — Cotton Rollers folder; Murphy to Chairman, NAC, July 15, 1918, General Records - New Orleans, *NAC Records*, Southern Pacific Docks folder; Robert P. Bass to Murphy, July 15, 1918, General Records — New Orleans, *NAC Records*, Southern Pacific Docks folder; T. P. Woodland *et. al* to W. P. Cole, July 19, 1918, General Records — New Orleans, *NAC Records*, Southern Pacific Docks folder; S. T. DeMilt to B. M. Squires, February 9, 1920, Adjustment Case Files, *NAC Records*, Gulf - New Orleans Freight Handlers folder.

51. Transcripts of Hearings, *NAC Records*, Proceedings of NAC, New Orleans, October 30, 1918 — "In the Matter of Wages of Deep Sea Longshoremen" folder, 117–119, 128; P. T. Murphy to R. B. Stevens, November 3, 1917, General Records — New Orleans, *NAC Records*, Load of Flour Controversy folder; New Orleans Steamship Association, *Minutes*, October 25, 1917, General Records — New Orleans, *NAC Records*, Load of Flour Controversy folder; S. T. DeMilt to Murphy, October 16, 1917, General Records — New Orleans, *NAC Records*, Load of Flour Controversy folder.

52. Harry Keegan and Albert Workman to P. T. Murphy, November 13, 1917, General Records — New Orleans, *NAC Records*, M. E. B. A. folder; LAC Opinion, January 11, 1918, General Records — New Orleans, *NAC Records*, Load of Flour Controversy folder; George Plant to Harry Keegan and Albert Workman, January 21, 1918, General Records — New Orleans, *NAC Records*, Load of Flour controversy folder; Murphy to R. B. Stevens, February 6, 1918, General Records — New Orleans, *NAC Records*, Load of Flour controversy folder; Murphy to R. B. Stevens, February 18, 1918, General Records — New Orleans, *NAC Records*, Load of Flour controversy folder.

53. Transcripts of Hearings, *NAC Records*, Proceedings of NAC, New Orleans, October 30, 1918 — "In the Matter of Wages of Deep Sea Longshoremen" folder, 4–5, 17–18, 19, 117–119, 128; Transcripts of Hearings, *NAC Records*, Proceedings of LAC, New Orleans, November 7, 1918 — "In the Matter of Wages of Freight Handlers" folder, 3–9.

54. Transcripts of Hearings, *NAC Records*, Proceedings of NAC, New Orleans, October 30, 1918 — "In the Matter of Wages of Deep Sea Longshoremen" folder, 54, 62, 51.

55. New Orleans Steamship Association Resolution, November 30, 1918, Adjustment Case Files, *NAC Records*, Gulf - Cotton Screwmen folder; S. T. DeMilt to William Z. Ripley, November 20, 1919, Adjustment Case Files, *NAC Records*, Gulf Ports — Executive Session folder; Awards and Decisions, November 22, 1919, *NAC Records*, Organization and Awards of the NAC and the LAC, September 1919 — folder, 3, 5.

56. Melvin P. Billups to Darragh Delancey, December 23, 1919, Adjustment Case Files, *NAC Records*, Gulf Ports Cotton and Tobacco Handling 1919 Award folder; J. H. Laughen to William Z. Ripley, December 6, 1919, Adjustment Case Files, *NAC Records*, Gulf Ports Cotton and Tobacco Handling 1919 Award folder; Daniel Ripley to B. M. Squires, December 7, 1919, Adjustment Case Files, *NAC Records*, Gulf Ports Cotton and Tobacco Handling 1919 Award folder; *The Book of New Orleans*, New Orleans, 1919, 31; New Orleans Steamship Association to B. M. Squires July 21, 1920, General Records — New Orleans, *NAC Records*, Correspondence — DeMilt folder.

57. *Times-Picayune*, October 18, 1923, Carroll George Miller, *A Study of the New Orleans Longshoremen's Union From 1850 to 1962*, master's thesis, Baton Rouge, 1962, 66; *Times-Picayune*, October 22, 1923.

58. Spero and Harris, 186; Ortique, 42; Miller, 24; Spero and Harris, 186; Miller, 27; Lester Rubin, *The Negro in the Longshore Industry*, Philadelphia, 1974, 34.

59. *Southwestern Christian Advocate*, January 9, 1908, *Crisis*, 2, No. 5 (September 1911), 11, No. 4 (February 1916); *Crisis*, 11, No. 4 (February, 1916); *Crisis*, 1, No. 6 (April 1911).

60. *Crisis*, 2, No. 5 (September 1911); *Crisis*, 11, No. 5 (March 1916); *Southwestern Christian Advocate*, March 19, 1908; Sylvia Woods, "You Have to Fight for Freedom," in Alice and Staughton Lynd, eds., *Rank and File*, Boston, 1974, 116.

61. Arthur R. Pearce, *The Rise and Decline of Labor in New Orleans*, master's thesis, New Orleans, 1938, 74; Miller, 23.

62. Pearce, 75, *Times-Picayune*, November 25, 1921; Pearce, 75, *Times-Picayune*, November 29, 1921; Ortique, 40; Pearce, 75; Miller, 24; Pearce, 80.

63. *Times-Picayune*, September 16, 1923; Spero and Harris, 190; *Times-Picayune*, September 17, 1923.

64. *Times-Picayune*, September 18, 1923; *Times-Picayune*, October 6, 1923; *Times-Picayune*, September 22, 1923; *Times-Picayune*, September 26, 1923; *Times-Picayune*, October 9, 1923; *Times-Picayune*, October 10, 1923; *Times-Picayune*, October 1, 1923.

65. *Times-Picayune*, October 11, 1923; Spero and Harris, 191; *Times-Picayune*, 22, 1923; *Times-Picayune*, September 19, 1923; *Times-Picayune*, September 20, 1923;

Times-Picayune, September 25, 1923; *Times-Picayune*, October 14, 1923, October 17, 1923.

66. *Times-Picayune*, September 25, 1923; *Times-Picayune*, October 6, 1923, October 7, 1923; *Times-Picayune*, October 9, 1923; *Times-Picayune*, October 14, 1923; *Times-Picayune*, October 15, 1923; *Times-Picayune*, October 16, 1923, October 17, 1923.

67. *Times-Picayune*, October 17, 1923; *Times-Picayune*, October 19, 1923.

68. *Times-Picayune*, October 18, 1923; *Times-Picayune*, October 19, 1923; *Times-Picayune*, October 22, 1923.

69. Pearce, 84–85; *Times-Picayune*, October 22, 1923; Pearce, 85; Miller, 26; *Times-Picayune*, October 30, 1923.

70. Ortique, 42, 44, 45, 46.

Conclusion

1. *Picayune*, March 12, 1908; *Picayune*, March 28, 1908; *Picayune*, March 25, 1908.

2. Philip S. Foner, *History of the Labor Movement in the United States, Vol. 4*, New York, 1965, 126.

3. John W. Blassingame, *Black New Orleans: 1860–1880*, Chicago, 1973, 15–17; Richard C. Wade, *Slavery in the Cities*, New York, 1964, 249–253, 258–262; Blassingame, 17–19.

4. Benjamin Quarles, *The Negro in the Civil War*, Boston, 1953, 40, 74–75, 116–118, 214–215, 249; Roger A. Fischer, *The Segregation Struggle in Louisiana, 1862–1877*, Champaign-Urbana, 1974, x, xii, 29; Blassingame, 210.

5. Blassingame, 210; Germaine A. Reed, "Race Legislation in Louisiana, 1864–1920," *Louisiana History*, VI, No. 4 (Fall 1965), 379–392; Henry G. Dethloff and Robert R. Jones, "Race Relations in Louisiana, 1877–1898," *Louisiana History*, IX, No. 4 (Fall 1968), 301–323.

6. Howard N. Rabinowitz, *Race Relations in the Urban South: 1865–1890*, New York, 1978, 97–106.

7. *Picayune*, October 7, 1907; Oscar Ameringer, *If You Don't Weaken*, New York, 1940, 217.

8. *Picayune*, May 4, 1903; *Picayune*, September 7, 1907; *Times-Democrat*, October 6, 1907; *Picayune*, May 1, 1908; *Picayune*, September 27, 1907; *Picayune*, March 14, 1908; *Daily News*, October 27, 1908.

9. Michael Reich, *Racial Inequality*, Princeton, 1981, 218, 244; Joy J. Jackson, *New Orleans in the Gilded Age*, Baton Rouge, 1969, 201.

10. Arthur R. Pearce, *The Rise and Decline of Labor in New Orleans*, master's thesis, New Orleans, 1938, 50.

11. Covington Hall, *Labor Struggles in the Deep South*, unpublished ms. at Tulane University, n.d., 68.

12. *Picayune*, October 19, 1907.

13. *Picayune*, March 28, 1908.

14. *Picayune*, May 29, 1908.

15. Ameringer, 222–223; Hall, 97; James R. Green, *Grass-Roots Socialism*, Baton Rouge, 1978, 210, 219.

16. C. Vann Woodward, *The Strange Career of Jim Crow*, New York, 1966, 108, 67–109; Reed, "Race Legislation in Louisiana," *passim*; Dethloff and Jones, "Race Relations in Louisiana," *passim*.

17. Herbert G. Gutman, *Work, Culture, and Society in Industrializing America*, New York, 1976, 199–202; W. E. B. Du Bois, *The Negro Artisan*, Atlanta, 1902, 114–115, 137, 162–163; Green, 204, 222; Melvyn Dubofsky, *We Shall Be All*, Chicago, 1969, 210–220; Paul Worthman, "Black Workers and Labor Unions in Birmingham, Alabama, 1897–1904," *Labor History*, 10, No. 3 (Summer 1969), 375–407; Foner, *Organized Labor and the Black Worker*, New York, 1982, ix, 93–100, 114–119.

18. Barbara J. Fields, "Ideology and Race in American History," in J. Morgan Kousser and James M. McPherson, eds., *Region, Race, and Reconstruction*, New York, 1982, 155–156.

Bibliography

I. Source Materials

A. Unpublished Sources

SPECIAL COLLECTIONS

Geneological Index, New Orleans Public Library, New Orleans.

Jackson Brewing Company Records. 1907–1908. Howard-Tilton Library, Tulane University, New Orleans.

Records of the National Adjustment Commission. 1917–1920. National Archives, Washington D.C.

Screwmen's Benevolent Association Records. 1850–1917. Special Collections, Louisiana State University Libraries, Baton Rouge.

Records of St. Joseph's Roman Catholic Church. 1907. Archive and Manuscript Department, Earl K. Long Library, University of New Orleans, New Orleans.

Stoddard Labor Collection. Archive and Manuscript Department, Earl K. Long Library, University of New Orleans, New Orleans.

PAPERS

American Federation of Labor. *Letterpress Copybooks of Samuel Gompers and William Green*, 1883–1915. Columbia University.

Nils Douglas Papers. Amistad Research Center. New Orleans.

Letters, 1906–1908. Mayor's Office, New Orleans. New Orleans Public Library.

John Mitchell Papers, 1906–1908. New York Public Library.

A. P. Tureaud Papers. Amistad Research Center, New Orleans.

B. Published Sources

PUBLIC DOCUMENTS

Campbell, T. W. *Manual of the City Council for 1900–1904*. New Orleans; Mauberret's Printing House, 1900.

_____ *Municipal Manual of the City of New Orleans.* New Orleans: n.p., 1901.

_____ *Municipal Manual of the City of New Orleans.* New Orleans: n.p., 1903.

Comptroller's Report, Embracing a Detailed Statement of the Receipts and Expenditures of the City of New Orleans, From January 1st, 1906 to December 31st, 1906. New Orleans, 1906.

_____ *From January 1st, 1907 to December 31st, 1907.* New Orleans, 1907.

City Council of New Orleans. *Official Minutes.* 1907–1908.

Cotonio, Theodore, annotator. *Constitution of the State of Louisiana, 1898–1912.* New Orleans: Louisiana Publishing Company, 1913.

Biennial Report of the Board of Health of the City of New Orleans, 1904–1905. Baton Rouge: The Times, 1906.

_____ *1906–1907.* New Orleans: Brandao Printing Company, 1908.

_____ *1908–1909.* New Orleans: Brandao Printing Company, 1910.

_____ *1910–1911.* New Orleans: Brandao Printing Company, 1912.

Report of New Orleans Playground Commission for 1912–1913.

Annual Report of the Superintendent of the Public Schools of the Parish of New Orleans, 1908–1909. New Orleans: n.p., 1909.

Letton, Harry P. *Rat Proofing the Public Docks of New Orleans.* U. S. Public Health Service. Washington D. C.: Government Printing Office, 1915.

State of Louisiana, *Roster of Labor Organizations.* Baton Rouge: Commissioner of Labor, 1976.

Louisiana State University, Department of Archives. *Directory of Churches and Religious Organizations in New Orleans.* Baton Rouge: Louisiana State University, 1941.

Official Journal of Proceedings of the Constitutional Convention of the State of Louisiana Held in New Orleans. New Orleans: H. J. Hearsey, 1898.

Annual Report of Board of Commissioners of the Police Department and the Inspector of Police Force of the City of New Orleans for the Year 1906. New Orleans: Graham Co., Ltd., 1907.

_____ *1907.* New Orleans: Thomas J. Moran, 1908.

_____ *1908.* Brandau Printing Co., 1909.

Board of Commissioners of the Port of New Orleans. *Port and Terminal Facilities.* New Orleans, 1919.

_____ *Port and Terminal Facilities*. New Orleans, 1920.

Taylor, Theodore R. *Stowage of Ship Cargoes*. Department of Commerce. Washington D. C.: Government Printing Office, 1920.

U. S. Bureau of the Census. *Twelfth Census of the United States*, Schedule No. 1 — Population, 1900.

U. S. Bureau of Labor. *Twenty-First Annual Report of the Commissioner of Labor 1906: Strikes and Lockouts*. Washington D. C.: Government Printing Office, 1907.

U. S. Industrial Commission, *Report*. Vol. IX, XVII. Washington, D. C.: Government Printing Office, 1901.

U. S. Industrial Relations Commission. *Industrial Relations*. Vol. III. Washington, D. C.: Government Printing Office, 1916.

U. S. Shipping Board Emergency Fleet Corporation, Industrial Relations Division. *Divisional Bulletin No. 5*. Philadelphia, 1918.

U. S. Shipping Board, Marine and Dock Industrial Relations Division. *Marine and Dock Labor*. Washington, D. C.: Government Printing Office, 1919.

Wolfe, A. B. *Works Committees and Joint Industrial Councils*. Philadelphia: U. S. Shipping Board Emergency Fleet Corporation, Industrial Relations Division, 1919.

Works Progress Administration. *Administrations of the Mayors of New Orleans, 1803-1936*. New Orleans: Works Progress Administration, 1940.

_____ *Biographies of the Mayors of New Orleans*. New Orleans: Work Progress Administration, 1939.

_____ *Guide to Vital Statistics Records of Church Archives in Louisiana*, Vol. 1 and 2, Baton Rouge: Louisiana State Board of Health, 1942.

PROCEEDINGS AND REPORTS

American Federation of Labor. *Report of Proceedings of the Twenty-Sixth Annual Convention*. (Minneapolis, 1906). Washington, D. C.: National Tribune Co., 1907.

_____ *Twenty-Seventh* . . . (Norfolk), same, 1907.

_____ *Twenty-Fourth* . . . (San Francisco, 1904). Washington, D.C.: Law Printing Co., 1904.

_____ *Twenty-Fifth* . . . (Pittsburgh, 1905), same as latter, 1905.

International Longshoremen, Marine and Transportworkers' Association. *Proceedings of the Eleventh Convention*. (Chicago, 1902). 1902.

_____ *Twelfth Convention* . . . (Bay City, Michigan, 1903), 1903.

New Orleans Cotton Exchange. *Thirty-Sixth Annual Report, Year Ending October 31, 1906*. New Orleans: L. Graham Co., Ltd., 1906.

_____ *Thirty-Seventh* . . . New Orleans: L. Graham Co., Ltd., 1906.

_____ *Thirty-Ninth* . . . New Orleans: L. Graham Co., Ltd., 1907.

_____ *Report of Special Committee* . . . *On Discrimination in Transportation Rates*. New Orleans: New Orleans Cotton Exchange, 1909.

_____ *Reply of the Special Committee* . . . *on Discrimination in Transportation Rates and Others Burdens Upon the Cotton Commerce of the City of New Orleans to the Illinois Central Railroad*. New Orleans: New Orleans Cotton Exchange, 1909.

DIRECTORIES

Soards' Elite Book of New Orleans. New Orleans Soards' Directory Co., Inc., 188?.

Soards' New Orleans City Directory. 1900–1911. New Orleans: Soards' Directory Co., Inc., 1900–1911.

United Labor Council. *Directory of New Orleans, La*. New Orleans: United Labor Council Publishing Committee, 1894.

Allen T. Woods. *Woods Directory: A Classified Colored Business, Professional and Trade Directory*. New Orleans: Allen T. Woods, 1912.

LABOR PUBLICATIONS

Central Trades and Labor Council. *Great Industrial Edition*. New Orleans: n.p., n.d.

_____ *Souvenir Program*. New Orleans: Central Trades and Labor Council, 1936.

PAMPHLETS

Martinet, L. A., ed. *The Violation of a Constitutional Rights*. New Orleans: The Crusader Print, 1893.

von Phul, William. *Mechanical Equipment used in the Port of New Orleans*. New Orleans: n.p., 1916.

_____ *Physical Characteristics of Cotton Warehouses*. New Orleans: n.p., 1915.

RECORDS

Jelly Roll Morton: The Library of Congress Recordings (May–June 1938), Vol. 5, Riverside Records, N.Y., RLP 9005.

MAGAZINES

Get Busy. Official Bulletin of the New Orleans Progressive Union. 1906–1907.

The Crisis. 1910–1916.

Industrial Union Bulletin. 1907.

Machinists Monthly Journal. 1907–1908. (Washington, D.C.)

Studies in Socialism. (Girard, Ka.), 1907.

NEWSPAPERS

NEW ORLEANS

Crusader. July 19, 1890. Schomburg Center, New York.

Item. October–November 1907. New Orleans Public Library, New Orleans.

Morning Star. 1908–1909. Notre Dame Seminary, New Orleans.

Daily News. June–November 1907. Louisiana Historical Center, New Orleans.

Daily Picayune. 1901–1908. Columbia University, New York.

Republican Courier. 1899, 1900 — 3 issues. Schomburg Center, New York.

Republican Liberator. Official Organ, Screwmen's Benevolent Association No. 1, and the Longshoremen's Benevolent Association No. 21, September 9, 1905, January 4, 1908. Howard-Tilton Library, Tulane University, New Orleans.

Southwestern Christian Advocate. 1906–1908. New York Public Library, New York.

Southern Republican. 1899, 1900. Schomburg Center, New York.

Daily States. October–November 1907. New Orleans Public Library, New Orleans.

Times-Democrat. October–November 1907. New Orleans Public Library, New Orleans.

Union Advocate. Central Organ of the New Orleans Central Trades and Labor Council. 1903–1904. Wisconsin State Historical Society, Madison.

United Labor Journal. Official Organ of the Louisiana Label League. 1905–1911, scattered issues. Howard-Tilton Library, Tulane University, New Orleans.

NATIONAL NEWSPAPERS

Appeal to Reason. (Girard, Ka.) 1907–1908. Tamiment Institute, New York University, New York.

Brauer-Zeitung. 1907–1908 (Cincinnati.) New York Public Library, New York.

Cleveland Citizen. Organ of the United Trades and Labor Council of Cuyahoga Country. 1907. Tamiment Institute, New York University.

Galveston City-Times. 1905–1908, scattered issues. Rosenberg Memorial Library, Galveston.

Indianapolis Freeman. 1907. Schomburg Center, New York.

Labor World. January–July 1907. (Columbus, Oh.) Wisconsin State Historical Society, Madison.

New York Age. 1907. Schomburg Center, New York.

Daily People. 1907. (New York.) New York Public Library.

St. Louis Labor. 1907. Tamiment Institute, New York University.

Savannah Tribune. 1907–1908. Schomburg Center, New York.

Social Democratic Herald. 1907. (Milwaukee.) Tamiment Institute, New York University.

The Worker. 1907. (New York.) New York Public Library, New York.

II. Secondary Materials

A. Articles

Commons, John R. "Types of American Trade Unions: The Longshoremen of the Great Lakes," *Quarterly Journal of Economics*, 20, No. 1 (November 1905), 59–85.

Cunningham, George E. "The Italians: A Hindrance to White Solidarity in Louisiana, 1890–1898." *Journal of Negro History*, L, No. 1 (January 1965), 22–36.

Dethloff, Henry G. and Jones, Robert R. "Race Relations in Louisiana, 1877–1898." *Louisiana History*, IX, No. 4 (Fall 1968). 301–323.

Fink, Leon. "Irrespective of Party, Class or Social Standing, The Knights of Labor and Opposition Politics in Richmond." *Labor History*, 19, No. 3 (Summer 1978), 325–349.

Kaplan, Michael. "A Century of Struggle on the New Orleans Docks." *Class Struggle*, Winter 1976, No. 3, 325–349.

Kessler, Sidney. "The Organization of Negroes into the Knights of Labor." *Journal of Negro History*, XXXVII, No. 3 (July 1952), 248–276.

Mandel, Bernard. "Samuel Gompers and the Negro Workers, 1886–1914." *Journal of Negro History*, XL, No. 3 (July 1952), 248–276.

McLaurin, Melton A. "The Racial Policies of the Knights of Labor and the Organization of Southern Black Workers." *Labor History*, 17, No. 14 (Fall 1976), 568–585.

McWhiney, Grady. "Louisiana Socialists in the Early Twentieth Century: A Study of Rustic Radicalism." *Journal of Southern History*, 20, No. 3 (August 1954), 315–336.

Reed, Germaine A. "Race Legislation in Louisiana, 1864–1920." *Louisiana History*, VI, No. 4 (Fall 1965), 379–392.

Shugg, Roger W. "The New Orleans General Strike of 1892." *Louisiana Historical Quarterly*, 21 (April 1938), 547–560.

Wells, Dave and Stodder, Jim. "A Short History of New Orleans Dockworkers." *Radical America*, 10, No. 1 (January–February 1976).

Worthman, Paul B. "Black Workers and Labor Unions in Birmingham, Alabama, 1897–1904." *Labor History*, 10, No. 3 (Summer 1969), 375–407.

B. Books

Ameringer, Oscar. *If You Don't Weaken*. New York: Henry Holt & Co., 1940. [reissued by University of Oklahoma Press, Norman, 1983.]

Aptheker, Herbert. *Afro-American History*. New York: Citadel, 1971.

———— *A Documentary History of the Negro People in the United States*. Secaucus, N.J.: Citadel, 1951.

———— *The Unfolding Drama*. New York: International Publishers, 1979.

Barnes, Charles B. *The Longshoremen*. New York: Russell Sage Foundation, 1915.

Berlin, Ira. *Slaves Without Masters*. New York: Random House, 1974.

Blassingame, John W. *Black New Orleans: 1860–1880*. Chicago: University of Chicago Press, 1973.

The Book of New Orleans and the Industrial South. New Orleans: Ferry-Hanley Advertising Co., 1919.

Bridger, Herbert H. and Watts, Oswald. *The Stowage of Cargo*. London: Imray, Laurie, Norie & Wilson, 1927.

Brissenden, Paul F. *The IWW*. New York: Russell and Russell (1919), 1957.

Brody, David. *Workers in Industrial America.* New York: Oxford University Press, 1980.

Brooks, Thomas R. *Toil and Trouble.* New York: Dial, 1964.

Brown, David H. *A History of Who's Who in Louisiana Politics in 1916.* Baton Rouge: Louisiana Chronicle Democrat, 1916.

Brown, Warren. *A Checklist of Negro Newspapers in the United States.* Lincoln University Journalism Series No. 2, Jefferson City, Mo.: Lincoln University, 1946.

Buerkle, Jack W. and Barker, Danny. *Bourbon Street Black.* New York: Oxford University Press, 1973.

Carter, Hodding, ed. *The Past as Prelude.* New Orleans: Pelican Publishing House, 1968.

Casdorph, Paul D. *Republicans, Negroes, and Progressives in the South, 1912-1926.* University: University of Alabama Press, 1981.

Caskey, Willie Melvin. *Secession and Restoration of Louisiana.* Baton Rouge: Louisiana State University Press, 1938.

Charters, Samuel. *Jazz: New Orleans 1885-1963.* New York: Oak Publications, 1963.

Chase, John. *Frenchman, Desire, Good Children.* New York: Macmillan, 1979.

Christian, Marcus. *Negro Ironworkers in Louisiana, 1718-1900.* Gretna, La.: Pelican Publishing Company, 1972.

Commons, John R. and Associates. *History of Labour in the United States, Vol. II.* New York: Macmillan, 1921.

Conlin, Joseph Robert. *Bread and Roses Too: Studies of the Wobblies.* Westport, Ct.: Greenwood, 1969.

Cornish, Dudley Taylor. *The Sable Arm.* New York: Norton, 1966.

Cox, Oliver C. *Caste, Class & Race.* New York: Monthly Review Press, 1959.

Dean, William M. *Martin R. Behrman Administration Biography.* New Orleans: John J. Weihing Printing Co., 1917.

DeCaux, Len. *Labor Radical.* Boston: Beacon, 1970.

Degler, Carl. *The Other South.* New York: Harper and Row, 1971.

Desdunes, Rudolph Lucien. *Our People and Our History.* Baton Rouge: Louisiana State University Press (1911), 1973.

Dubofsky, Melvyn. *We Shall Be All: A History of the IWW.* Chicago: Quadrangle, 1969.

Du Bois, W. E. Burghardt, ed. *Economic Cooperation Among Negro Americans.* Atlanta University Publications No. 12. Atlanta: Atlanta University Press, 1907.

_____ *The Negro Artisan.* Atlanta University Publications No. 7. Atlanta University Press, 1902.

_____ *Some Efforts of American Negroes For Their Own Social Betterment.* Atlanta University Publications, No. 3. Atlanta: Atlanta University Press, 1898.

Dulles, Foster Rhea. *Labor in America.* New York: Crowell, 1949.

Finn, Father John. *New Orleans Irish: Arrivals-Departures.* Kenner, La.: Pirogue Press, 1983.

Fischer, Roger A. *The Segregation Struggle in Louisiana, 1862-1877.* Champaign-Urbana: University of Illinois Press, 1974.

Foner, Philip S. *American Socialism and Black Americans: From the Age of Jackson to World War II.* Westport, Ct.: Greenwood, 1977.

_____ *History of the Labor Movement in the United States, Vol. 2,* New York: International Publishers, 1955.

_____ *Vol. 3,* New York: International Publishers, 1964.

_____ *Vol. 4,* New York: International Publishers, 1965.

_____ *Organized Labor and the Black Worker.* New York: International Publishers, 1982.

_____ and Lewis, Ronald L., ed. *The Black Worker,* Vol. 4. Philadelphia: Temple University Press, 1979.

_____ *Vol. 5,* Philadelphia: Temple University Press, 1980.

Friedman, Lawrence J. *The White Savage: Racial Fantasies in the Post-Bellum South.* Englewood Cliffs, N.J.: Prentice-Hall, 1970.

Gambino, Richard. *Vendetta.* Garden City: Doubleday, 1977.

Ginger, Ray. *The Bending Cross.* New Brunswick, N.J.: Rutgers University Press, 1949.

Goodwyn, Lawrence. *The Populist Moment.* New York: Oxford, 1978.

Gossett, Thomas F. *Race: The History of an Idea in America.* New York: Schocken, 1969.

Gutman, Herbert. *Work, Culture and Society in Industrializing America.* New York: Knopf, 1976.

Green, James R. *Grass-Roots Socialism.* Baton Rouge: Louisiana State University Press, 1978.

Haas, Edward F., ed. *Louisiana's Legal Heritage*. Pensacola: Perdido Bay Press, 1983.

Hair, William Ivey. *Bourbonism and Agrarian Protest*. Baton Rouge: Louisiana State University Press, 1969.

_____ *Carnival of Fury*. Baton Rouge: Louisiana State University Press, 1976.

Harlan, Louis R. *Booker T. Washington: The Wizard of Tuskegee, 1901-1915*. New York: Oxford, 1983.

_____ and Smock, Raymond W., ed. *The Booker T. Washington Papers*, Vol. 6 (1977), Vol. 7 (1977), Vol. 8 (1979), Vol. 9 (1980). Urbana: University of Illinois Press.

Haws, Robert, ed. *The Age of Segregation: Race Relations in the South, 1890-1945*. Jackson: University Press of Mississippi, 1978.

Hentoff, Nat and Shapiro, Nat, ed. *Hear Me Talkin' To Ya*. New York: Rinehart, 1955.

Hillcoat, Charles H. *Notes on the Stowage of Ships*. New York: Colonial Publishing Company (1904), 1919.

History and Manual of the Colored Knights of Pythias. Nashville: National Baptist Publishing Board, 1917.

Hoetink, H. *The Two Variants in Caribbean Race Relations*. London: Oxford University Press, 1967.

Howard, Perry H. *Political Tendencies in Louisiana*. Baton Rouge: Louisiana State University Press, 1971.

Huber, Leonard V. *Louisiana: A Pictorial History*. New York: Scribners, 1975.

Jackson, Joy J. *New Orleans in the Gilded Age*. Baton Rouge: Louisiana State University Press, 1969.

Johnston, James Hugo. *Race Relations in Virginia and Miscegenation in the South, 1776-1860*. Amherst: University of Massachusetts Press, 1970.

Jordan, Winthrop. *White Over Black*. Baltimore: Penguin, 1968.

Kemp, John R. ed. *Martin Behrman of New Orleans: Memoirs of a City Boss*. Baton Rouge: Louisiana State University Press, 1977.

King, Grace. *New Orleans: The Place and the People*. New York: Macmillan, 1895.

Kornbluh, Joyce L., ed. *Rebel Voices*. Ann Arbor: University of Michigan Press, 1968.

Kousser, J. Morgan. *The Shaping of Southern Politics*. New Haven, Ct.: Yale University Press, 1974.

Kousser, J. Morgan and MacPherson, James M., ed. *Region, Race, and Reconstruction*. New York: Oxford University Press, 1982.

Larrowe, Charles P. *Shape-Up and Hiring Hall*. Berkeley: University of California Press, 1955.

Leavitt, Mel. *A Short History of New Orleans*. San Francisco: Lexiko, 1982.

Lewis, Pierce F. *New Orleans: The Making of an Urban Landscape*. Cambridge, Mass.: Ballinger, 1976.

Logan, Rayford, W. *The Betrayal of the Negro*. New York: Macmillan, 1967.

Lorwin, Louis L. *The American Federation of Labor*. Washington, D. C.: The Brookings Institution, 1933.

Louisiana Chamber of Commerce and Industry. *The City of New Orleans*. New Orleans: Geo. W. Englehardt, 1894.

Lomax, Alan. *Mister Jelly Roll*. New York: Duell, Sloan and Pearce, 1950.

Louisiana Newspapers. Baton Rouge: Louisiana State University Press, 1965.

Lynd, Alice and Lynd, Staughton, ed. *Rank and File*. Boston: Beacon Press, 1974.

Macdonald, Robert R., Kemp, John R., and Haas, Edward F., ed. *Louisiana's Black Heritage*. New Orleans: Louisiana State Museum, 1979.

MacElwee, Roy and Taylor, Theodore R. *Wharf Management*. New York: Appleton, 1921.

McLaurin, Melton A. *The Knights of Labor in the South*. Westport, Ct.: Greenwood, 1978.

MacLeod, Duncan J. *Slavery, Race and the American Revolution*. London: Cambridge, 1974.

Mandel, Berhard. *Samuel Gompers*. Yellow Springs, Oh.: The Antioch Press, 1963.

Marquis, Donald M. *In Search of Buddy Bolden*. New York: Da Capo Press, 1980.

Marshall F. Ray. *Labor in the South*. Cambridge, Mass.: Harvard University Press, 1957.

_____ *The Negro and Organized Labor*. New York: John Wiley and Sons, 1965.

Martinez, Raymond J. *The Story of the Riverfront at New Orleans*. New Orleans: Pelican Press, 1948.

_____ same title, New Orleans: Industries Publishing Agency, 1955.

_____ and Holmes, Jack D. L. *New Orleans: Facts and Legends*. New Orleans: Hope Publications, n.d.

Meier, August. *Negro Thought in America, 1880-1915*. Ann Arbor: University of Michigan Press, 1964.

Millis, Harry A. and Montgomery, Royal E. *Organized Labor*. New York: McGraw Hill, 1945.

Montgomery, David. *Workers' Control in America*. New York: Cambridge, 1979.

Morgan, Edmund S. *American Slavery, American Freedom*. New York: Norton, 1975.

Morris, James O. *Conflict Within the AFL*. Ithaca, N.Y.: Cornell University Press, 1958.

Morrison, Andrew. *New Orleans and the New South*. New Orleans: Metropolitan Publishing Co., 1888.

Mugnier, George Francois. *Louisiana Images, 1880-1920*. Baton Rouge: Louisiana State University Press, 1975.

Myers, Gustavus. *History of the Great American Fortunes*. New York: Random House, 1936.

Nau, John F. *The German People of New Orleans, 1850-1900*. Leiden: E. J. Brill, 1958.

Newton, Francis. *The Jazz Scene*. New York: Monthly Review Press, 1960.

Niehaus, Earl F. *The Irish in New Orleans, 1800-1860*. Baton Rouge: Louisiana State University Press, 1965.

Nolen, Claude F. *The Negro's Image in the South*. Lexington: University of Kentucky Press, 1967.

Norhrup, Herbert. *Organized Labor and the Negro*. New York: Harper, 1944.

Perkins, A. E., ed. *Who's Who in Colored Louisiana*. Baton Rouge: Douglas Loan and Company, Inc., 1930.

The Progressive Union. *New Orleans: The Crescent City*. New Orleans: Graham Press, 1903.

Quarles, Benjamin. *The Negro in the Civil War*. Boston: Little-Brown, 1953.

Rabinowitz, Howard N. *Race Relations in the Urban South: 1865–1890*. New York: Oxford University Press, 1978.

Reich, Michael. *Racial Inequality*. Princeton, N.J.: Princeton University Press, 1981.

Roberts, Walter Adolphe. *Lake Ponchartrain*. Indianapolis, Ind.: Bobbs-Merrill, 1946.

Reynolds, George M. *Machine Politics in New Orleans: 1897–1926*. New York: Columbia University Press, 1930.

Rochester, Anna. *Rulers of America*. New York: International Publishers, 1936.

Rousseve, Charles B. *The Negro in Louisiana*. New Orleans: Xavier University Press, 1937.

Rubin, Lester. *The Negro in the Longshore Industry*. Philadelphia: Industrial Relations Unit, The Wharton School, University of Pennsylvania, 1974.

Schluter, Hermann. *The Brewing Industry and the Brewery Workers' Movement in America*. New York: Burt Franklin (1910), 1970.

Shugg, Roger W. *Origins of Class Struggle in Louisiana*. Baton Rouge: Louisiana State University Press, 1939.

Somers, Dale A. *The Rise of Sports in New Orleans*. Baton Rouge: Louisiana State University Press, 1972.

Spero, Sterling D. and Harris, Abram L. *The Black Worker*. New York: Atheneum, 1974.

Taft, Philip. *The AF of L in the Time of Gompers*. New York: Harper, 1957.

Tannebaum, Frank. *Slave and Citizen*. New York: Random House, 1946.

Taylor, Joe Gray. *Negro Slavery in Louisiana*. Baton Rouge: Louisiana Historical Association, 1963.

Turner, Frederick. *Remembering Song*. New York: Viking, 1982.

Ulriksson, Vidkun. *The Telegraphers*. Washington, D.C.: Public Affairs Press, 1953.

Vincent, Charles. *Black Legislators in Louisiana During Reconstruction*. Baton Rouge: Louisiana State University Press, 1976.

Wade, Richard C. *Slavery in the Cities: The South, 1820–1860*. New York: Oxford University Press, 1964.

Watts, Oswald. *Ship Stability and Trim Made Easy*. London: Crosby, Lockwood and Son, 1926.

Wesley, Charles. *Negro Labor in the United States*. New York: Vanguard, 1927.

White, Walter. *Rope and Fagot.* New York: Knopf, 1929.

Who's Who in Louisiana. Chicago: Larkin, Roosevelt and Larkin, Ltd., 1947.

Who's Who in Louisiana and Mississippi. New Orleans: Times-Picayune, 1918.

Wilds, John. *Afternoon Story: A Century of the New Orleans States-Item.* Baton Rouge: Louisiana State University Press, 1976.

Willets, Gideon, et. al. *Workers of the Nation, Vol. I and II.* New York: Collier and Son, 1903.

Williams, Martin. *Jazz Masters of New Orleans.* New York: Macmillan, 1967.

Wolman, Leo, *Ebb and Flow in Trade Unionism.* New York: National Bureau of Economic Research, 1936.

Wood, Peter H. *Black Majority.* New York: Norton, 1975.

Woodward, C. Vann. Origins of the New South. Baton Rouge: Louisiana State University Press, 1971.

_____ *The Strange Career of Jim Crow.* New York: Oxford University Press, 1966.

C. Dissertations and Unpublished Manuscripts

Bennetts, David Paul. *Black and White Workers: New Orleans, 1880–1900.* Doctoral dissertation. Urbana: University of Illinois, 1972.

Hall, Covington. *Labor Struggles in the Deep South.* Manuscript in Howard-Tilton Library, Tulane University, New Orleans, n.d.

Kearns, David Taylor. *The Social Mobility of New Orleans Laborers, 1870–1900.* Doctoral dissertation. New Orleans: Tulane, 1977.

Kelley, James Wilson. *Labor Problems of the Longshoremen in the United States.* Doctoral dissertation. Boston: Boston University, 1941.

Miller, Carroll George. *A Study of the New Orleans Longshoremen's Unions from 1850 to 1962.* Master's thesis. Baton Rouge: Louisiana State University, 1962.

Ortique, Charles Frederick. *A Study of the Longshore Industry in New Orleans with Emphasis on Negro Longshoremen.* Master's thesis. Urbana: University of Illinois, 1956.

Pearce, Arthur Raymond. *The Rise and Decline of Labor in New Orleans.* Master's thesis. New Orleans: Tulane University, 1938.

Index